CORRUPTION

Anthropology, Culture and Society

Series Editors:
Professor Thomas Hylland Eriksen, University of Oslo
Dr Jon P. Mitchell, University of Sussex

RECENT TITLES

Land, Law and Environment:
Mythical Land, Legal Boundaries
Edited by ALLEN ABRAMSON AND
DIMITRIOS THEODOSSOPOULOS

The Trouble with Community:
Anthropological Reflections on
Movement, Identity and Collectivity
VERED AMIT AND NIGEL RAPPORT

Anthropology and the Will to Meaning:
A Postcolonial Critique
VASSOS ARGYROU

Risk Revisited
Edited by PAT CAPLAN

Macedonia:
The Politics of Identity and Difference
Edited by JANE K. COWAN

Ethnicity and Nationalism:
Anthropological Perspectives
THOMAS HYLLAND ERIKSEN

Globalisation:
Studies in Anthropology
THOMAS HYLLAND ERIKSEN

A History of Anthropology
THOMAS HYLLAND ERIKSEN AND
FINN SIVERT NIELSEN

Small Places, Large Issues:
An Introduction to Social
and Cultural Anthropology
THOMAS HYLLAND ERIKSEN

What is Anthropology?
THOMAS HYLLAND ERIKSEN

Anthropology, Development and
the Post-modern Challenge
KATY GARDNER AND DAVID LEWIS

Power and its Disguises:
Anthropological Perspectives on Power
JOHN GLEDHILL

Control and Subversion:
Gender Relations in Tajikistan
COLETTE HARRIS

Youth and the State in Hungary:
Capitalism, Communism and Class
LÁSZLÓ KÜRTI

Locating Cultural Creativity
Edited by JOHN LIEP

Cord of Blood:
Possession and the Making of Voodoo
NADIA LOVELL

Cultivating Development:
An Ethnography of Aid Policy and Practice
DAVID MOSSE

Ethnography and Prostitution in Peru
LORRAINE NENCEL

Witchcraft, Power and Politics:
Exploring the Occult in
the South African Lowveld
ISAK A. NIEHAUS with ELIAZAAR MOHLALA
AND KALLY SHOKANE

Power Community and the State:
The Political Anthropology
of Organisation in Mexico
MONIQUE NUIJTEN

Social Mobility in Kerala:
Modernity and Identity in Conflict
FILIPPO OSELLA AND CAROLINE OSELLA

Negotiating Local Knowledge:
Power and Identity in Development
Edited by
JOHAN POTTIER, ALAN BICKER
AND PAUL SILLITOE

Class, Nation and Identity:
The Anthropology of Political Movements
JEFF PRATT

Ethnic Distinctions. Local Meanings:
Negotiating Cultural Identities in China
MARY RACK

The Cultural Politics of Markets:
Economic Liberalization and
Social Change in Nepal
KATHERINE NEILSON RANKIN

Bearing Witness:
Women and the Truth and Reconciliation
Commission in South Africa
FIONA C. ROSS

Landscape Memory and History:
Anthropological Perspectives
Edited by
PAMELA J. STEWART
AND ANDREW STRATHERN

Race, Nation and Culture:
An Anthropological Perspective
PETER WADE

CORRUPTION

Anthropological Perspectives

Edited by
DIETER HALLER AND CRIS SHORE

Pluto Press
LONDON • ANN ARBOR, MI

First published 2005 by Pluto Press
345 Archway Road, London N6 5AA
and 839 Greene Street,
Ann Arbor MI 48106, USA

www.plutobooks.com

British Library Cataloguing in Publication Data
A catalogue record for this book is available from the British Library

ISBN 0 7453 2158 5 hardback
ISBN 0 7453 2157 7 paperback

Library of Congress Cataloging in Publication Data applied for

10   9   8   7   6   5   4   3   2   1

Designed and produced for Pluto Press by
Chase Publishing Services Ltd, Fortescue, Sidmouth EX10 9QG, England
Typeset from disk by Stanford DTP Services, Northampton, England
Printed and bound in the European Union by
Antony Rowe, Chippenham and Eastbourne, England

CONTENTS

1   Introduction – Sharp Practice: Anthropology and the
    Study of Corruption   1
    Cris Shore and Dieter Haller

Part I   Corruption in 'Transitional' Societies?

2   The Sack of Two Cities: Organized Crime and Political
    Corruption in Youngstown and Palermo   29
    Jane Schneider and Peter Schneider

3   Bribes, Gifts and Unofficial Payments: Rethinking
    Corruption in Post-Soviet Russian Health Care   47
    Michele Rivkin-Fish

4   Corruption as a Transitional Phenomenon: Understanding
    Endemic Corruption in Postcommunist States   65
    David W. Lovell

5   Corruption, Property Restitution and Romanianness   83
    Filippo M. Zerilli

**Part II   Institutionalized Corruption and Institutions of
            Anti-corruption**

6   Integrity Warriors: Global Morality and the
    Anti-corruption Movement in the Balkans   103
    Steven Sampson

7   Culture and Corruption in the EU: Reflections on Fraud,
    Nepotism and Cronyism in the European Commission   131
    Cris Shore

8. Corruption in Corporate America: Enron – Before and
    After   156
    Carol MacLennan

Part III   Narratives and Practices of Everyday Corruption

9   Narrating the State of Corruption   173
    Akhil Gupta

10 Where the Jeeps Come From: Narratives of Corruption
    in the Alentejo (Southern Portugal)   194
    Dorle Dracklé

11 Citizens Despite the State: Everyday Corruption and
    Local Politics in El Alto, Bolivia   212
    Sian Lazar

12 Afterword – Anthropology and Corruption: The State of
    the Art   229
    Dorothy Louise Zinn

Contributors   243
Index   247

1 INTRODUCTION – SHARP PRACTICE: ANTHROPOLOGY AND THE STUDY OF CORRUPTION[1]

Cris Shore and Dieter Haller

The context for this book was set by several incidents, foremost among which were the dramatic fraud and corruption scandals that rocked corporate America at the end of 2001 following the collapse of the US energy corporation Enron. Some authors have predicted that in years to come the Enron scandal, not the terrorist attacks of 11 September, will be seen as the greater turning point in US society[2] – an unlikely claim, but one that invites us to ask what deeper lessons are to be learned from an analysis of what happened.[3] Enron's demise was precipitated by revelations about its complex financial manoeuvres designed to hide debt and conceal its various offshore and off-balance sheet partnerships. These were created in order to give a false impression of the company's profitability and make millionaires of its senior managers. Its success in both of these aims was exemplary – at least in the short term. However, in December 2001 Enron filed the largest bankruptcy petition in the history of the United States. Three months later, Enron's accountants Arthur Andersen were also indicted on criminal charges of obstruction of justice and 'knowingly, intentionally and corruptly' inducing employees to shred documents relating to Enron (Gledhill 2003). The sheer magnitude of these accountancy scandals was unprecedented, as was the fact that they occurred at the heart of the US financial system. Yet barely three months later, in June 2002, they were eclipsed by an even larger scandal when the global telecoms giant WorldCom was discovered to have inflated its profits by $3.8 billion – a figure later revised upwards to a staggering $7 billion.[4]

What is significant about these events from an anthropological perspective is that they remind us that Europeans and Americans cannot assume that grand corruption is something that belongs primarily to the non-Western 'Other' or to public-sector officials in defective state bureaucracies: corruption (both massive and systemic), we should not be surprised to learn, can also be found in the very heart of the regulated world capitalist system. The Enron and WorldCom affairs also provided a fitting backdrop to the international panel on 'corruption' that met in August 2002 at the 7th European Association of Social Anthropologists' conference in Copenhagen.[5] Significantly, we met in a nation-state ranked the 'second least corrupt country in the world' according to Transparency International's (TI) 'Corruption Perception Index'. To borrow a phrase from Shakespeare, all would seem to be remarkably well in the Kingdom of Denmark. But what exactly do indices like 'second least corrupt' or 'most corrupt' country mean in this context, and how should we interpret such measurements or the moral claims they produce? Is corruption something that can be quantified and rated in such an abstract and disembodied manner, and how accurately do measures of people's 'perceptions' reflect the 'reality' or complexity of how corruption is practised or experienced? As these questions indicate, the aim of this book is to interrogate the *idea* of corruption as a category of thought and organizing principle, and to examine its political and cultural implications. The overarching question that frames our analysis is 'What contribution can anthropology make to understanding corruption in the world today?' As the contributors to this volume show, looking at corruption from an anthropological perspective necessarily draws our attention towards problems of meaning and representation, rather than the more conventional institutional approaches and theoretical model-building that seem to characterize so much of the corruption studies literature. To embark on such a project, however, we must first ask what exactly *is* corruption, and how useful is this term as an analytical concept? What are the conditions that encourage corrupt practices to flourish, and how are such behaviours manifested and interpreted in different contexts?

Part of the reason for opening up such arguably intractable questions is to counter the tendency among governments and policy-makers engaged in the anti-corruption movement to bring about a premature closure on the question of how to define 'corruption' as an analytical category. According to the World Bank, that whole debate is now effectively closed. 'Corruption', it confidently asserts, is 'the abuse of public office for private gain' (World Bank 2002) – and upon this definition now rests a whole raft of policies concerning transparency, liberalization and 'good governance'. But this definition reduces corruption simply to a problem of dishonest individuals or 'rotten apples' working in the public sector. It also reduces explanations for corruption to individual greed and personal venality so that our focus – to extend the metaphor – is on the individual apples rather than the barrel that contains them. But what if corruption is institutional and systemic? Is the Catholic Church corrupt, or Cardinal Law of Boston, who recently confessed to having turned a blind eye to reports of paedophilia within the clergy? Who is the corrupt party in the case of the Enron, Merck, Xerox and Andersen scandals? Is it the lowly official who shredded the incriminating documents, his line-manager who gave him the order, or the company executives who played fast and loose with the markets? And how do we measure 'abuse of public office' or 'private gain' (more on this later)? In France, prosecuting magistrates recently uncovered information indicating that successive presidents (from General de Gaulle onwards) used money from the state-owned oil company Elf-Aquitaine to bribe foreign leaders. President Mitterrand used these illegal funds to finance the election campaign of his German Christian Democrat ally, Chancellor Helmut Kohl. How do these activities square with the World Bank's definition of corruption, and what are the implications of this apparent 'lack of fit'?

THEORIZING CORRUPTION: SOCIAL SCIENCE PERSPECTIVES

Generally speaking, the social sciences have approached corruption from two broad perspectives: structural and interactional. Structural approaches, with their moral and evolutionary overtones, are more commonly found in development studies as well as popular media representations. These add 'corruption' to the list of those negative characteristics that are typically applied to the 'Other', such as underdevelopment, poverty, ignorance, repression of women, fundamentalism, fanaticism and irrationality. Naturally, these 'Others' are located outside modern, civilized, Western-style democracies, and they are intrinsically caught in the webs of 'their' culture. Corruption here is seen as endemic to some societies (i.e. 'non-Western' or, equally Eurocentric, 'transitional' or 'developing' societies), and not (or less) to others.

This stereotype inevitably recalls colonial discourse about the 'primitiveness' of 'savage society'. But equally, it reflects more recent writings of those who, like Edward Banfield (1958), saw backwardness and underdevelopment as a product of the 'moral' basis of certain societies. Even in the 1970s corruption was commonly perceived as a social pathology symptomatic of Third World instability and lack of 'social discipline'. On the other hand, many scholars of that period rejected this, arguing instead that corruption has a positive function in development because it 'fills the gap' left by partial bureaucratization and the incomplete penetration of the state. According to this logic, corruption eases the transition to modernity and is therefore, theoretically speaking, associated with the 'early phase of state formation' (Blok 1988: 228). It was also assumed that corruption would disappear with increasing state penetration and the advance of more 'rational' formal organizations. As Stephen

Sampson wryly observes in his critique of Bayley (1966), Scott and other supporters of this type of argument: 'corruption presumably encourages capital formation and entrepreneurship, diminishes red tape, mitigates ethnic or class conflicts, integrates pariah groups into society, and gives more people a stake in the system' (Sampson 1983: 72).

A second structural approach, prevalent in the field of International Relations (IR), is directed more towards analysing the system of formal rules and institutions. Its aim is to determine how and why certain actors – particularly elites – are able to act for personal gain. IR scholars examine various factors, such as how ruling elites are composed, what sorts of competition exist among them, and how accountable they are. The result, as Postero (2000) observes, 'is a set of correlations between certain factors and corruption, which form the basis for prescriptions against corruption'. Transparency International, whose 'index' attempts to quantify corruption across countries on an annual basis, also uses this approach. These measures are then used to promote 'modern' notions of governance, efficiency, accountability and transparency – which are seen as prerequisites for promoting international free trade. While advocates of this approach claim that the concept of 'good governance' is based on neutral, objective and a-cultural values, critics argue that it reinforces the hegemonic values of the West as universal – precisely by defining them as 'above' the realm of politics and culture. As has been noted elsewhere, this is a familiar tactic of normative power and part of the art of modern liberal government (see Foucault 1991).

In contrast to structural approaches, 'interactional' approaches focus on the behaviour of actors in particular public-office settings. Here corruption is defined as behaviour that deviates from the formal duties of a public role in favour of private or personal gain. Alternatively, corrupt behaviour is that which 'harms the public-interest' (Friedrich 1966; Heidenheimer 1989a, 1989b). This might include a corrupt civil servant who uses his office as a private business (see Van Klaveren 1989), or who creates an informal 'black market' for official favours and 'rents', for example, by helping certain clients to cut through the 'red tape' of bureaucracy in order to obtain the necessary permit or licence.

While these contrasting approaches may offer some useful insights, most are based on questionable assumptions and none are adequate for understanding the complexity of the relationships involved. For example, 'misuse of public office' begs the question of how we define 'public' or 'private gain' – or even '*mis*-use'? What happens when politicians (such as Italy's premier, Silvio Berlusconi) change the law so that their previously 'illegal' practices of book-keeping are reclassified as legal? Furthermore, laws are notoriously ambiguous and open to contestation – a quality to which a whole professional class, that of lawyers, owes its existence. The definition of 'the public interest' (and who speaks for the public) is equally vague and contested – and precisely the terrain over which democratic politics are fought.

The problem with both structural and interactional models is that they assume these variables to be fixed and unproblematic, whereas these categories are not at all bounded or clear-cut. Take, for example, the public/private dualism. Most definitions of corruption rest on the separation between the state or its agents and the rest of society. As salaried public officials, politicians, bureaucrats and judges are expected to draw a sharp distinction between their personal interests and the public resources they administer. In the conventional political science approach, as in neoliberal ideology and in TI initiatives, it is the violation of this public/private distinction by individuals that fundamentally defines corrupt behaviour. Corruption scandals are thus viewed as a measure of how well a society distinguishes between public and private spheres (Rose-Ackerman 1996: 366). However, anthropologists have long recognized that this public–private dichotomy is often an arbitrary and inherently ambiguous cultural category. As Gupta's analysis of state officials in northern India illustrates, Western assumptions about the rational activity of office-holders simply do not translate. The distinction between an official's role as public servant and private citizen is collapsed not only at the site of their activity, but also in their styles of operation. 'One has a better chance of finding them [the officials]' says Gupta (1995: 384) 'at the roadside tea stalls and in their homes than in their offices.' As one contemporary Indian scholar explains, 'the greatest weakness of our polity [is that] we enshrined in the constitution a value system which was never internalised, and which was external to the Indian ethos' (Gill 1998: 230, cited in Parry 2000: 51).

The same argument could be made for many other countries. In post-Soviet Russia, for example, the growth of what Wedel (2001) calls 'flex organisations' (ambiguous organizations that can shift between public agencies and private NGOs), challenges the conventional tidy separation of state and private sector enterprises. But equally, closer analysis of the Enron affair reveals the extent to which a culture of clientelism, extortion and contempt for ordinary society and its rules characterized company practices in which favour-giving and complicity between senior Enron executives and officials in Wall Street and Washington were commonplace. As Schneider and Schneider (2003) point out, comparisons between corporate scandals and organized crime 'raise the question whether organisational crime, extortion and illegal trafficking are not full-fledged elements of the workings of capitalism, as such'.

While public and private realms may be codified by rules in most Western democracies, there are invariably 'grey zones' between these domains. Officials will always have discretion and room for manoeuvre – they could not fulfil their duties otherwise. But this discretion allows for flexibility and particularism in the way clients are treated, which opens up the possibility for favouritism and cronyism and blurs any categorical public/private distinctions. For example, when German Minister Hans Eichel was accused in 2001 of using the ministerial jet to attend a 'private' party political rally in his constituency, he defended himself arguing that as minister with 24-hours a day duties, such public–private distinctions were inapplicable. Similarly, when former German Chancellor Helmut Kohl disclosed in 2000 that he had used secret funds to finance his Christian Democratic (CDU) party in the former GDR he insisted (drawing on the strategically useful IMF definition) that this was not 'corruption' as he had not made any private or personal gain. Does this mean that 'private gain' can only ever be defined in pecuniary terms, or that other factors – power, prestige, authority and symbolic capital – are to be discounted?

WHY AN ANTHROPOLOGY OF CORRUPTION?

Few anthropologists go into the field with the aim of studying corruption per se.[6] In most cases, our interest in the subject arises because it matters to our informants and because of the prevalence of 'corruption talk' in the areas where we conduct fieldwork. As anthropologists working in contemporary India have observed, stories about corruption are told more often than almost any other genre of folklore, and as a topic of daily *chah*-shop conversation corruption beats even the state of the crops (Parry 2000; see also Wade 1982). Or as Sian Lazar (this volume) noted doing her fieldwork in Bolivia, 'people just talked about corruption non-stop: corruption was how they made sense of politics and the state'. This is no less true of parts of Europe as it is for Latin America, as Jon Mitchell's recent ethnography of Malta demonstrates (Mitchell 2002).

At one level then, corruption merits closer anthropological attention simply because of its inexplicable pervasiveness and the curious fascination that people, in almost every part of the world, seem to have with stories of corruption. In this sense corruption represents both an ethnographic enigma and a 'social fact' in the classical Durkheimian sense. Or perhaps what makes corruption such an interesting object of study is not so much the 'reality' of its existence as the fact that it is widely *believed* to exist, the complex narratives that enfold it, and the new relationships and objects of study that those narratives create. Visvanathan and Sethi (1998) give a vivid illustration of this in their analysis of the seeming pervasiveness of corruption in India, and the invasive logic of bribery that permeates all dealings with the state and its officials. Even the mundane act of paying a water bill or getting one's electricity supply reconnected apparently draws the would-be customer into a labyrinth of illicit transactions with touts, middlemen and officials that are 'more elaborate than the mating rituals of animals and as stylised as an initiation ritual' (1998: 2). The point that Visvanathan and Sethi stress is that we should not see corruption in the narrow English sense of the word – with all its restrictive, provincial and puritan connotations – but rather as something more subtle, layered and complex, like 'a conversation, a ritual' (1998: 3).[7] In this respect, corruption is a form of exchange: a polysemous and multi-stranded relationship and part of the way in which individuals connect with the state. Dorothy Zinn makes a similar point reflecting on the 'poetics of clientelism' as part of the key to understanding the system of '*raccomandazione*' that underlies corruption in modern Italy (Zinn 2001). We need to grasp both the politics *and* the poetics of corruption to gain the measure of its cultural complexity. Seen in this light bribery and '*raccomandazione*' become something far richer and more complex than simply the 'abuse' of public office. As Visvanathan and Sethi suggest, the bribe might be considered as the first act of citizenship; the tie that binds political subjects to the state whilst making the state visible to its citizens. However, to acknowledge the complexity of bribery is not to condone it or minimize its consequences. Corruption may be defended in some quarters as a 'weapon of the weak', but typically its effects are inflated contracts, distorted development priorities, increased exploitation and inequality and heightened uncertainty. Corruption is also particularly undermining for democracy and the rule of law (Della Porta and Mény 1997; Rose-Ackerman 1996), although paradoxically the rule of law and legal-rational bureaucracy are what give rise to the concept of corruption in the first place.

Yet for all its apparent ubiquity and importance, anthropologists have contributed relatively little to debates about corruption. Why is this? Nancy Postero (2000) has suggested three main reasons. First, because anthropologists are reluctant to criticize their informants, and to highlight immorality or rule-breaking may feel like a betrayal of trust and confidence (which is itself one of the main moral arguments against corruption); second, because investigating corruption could jeopardize one's research, and 'one doesn't want to risk being shut out of the information loop' (Postero 2000: 1); and third, because people tend to keep these things secret, especially from outsiders. In short, being an observer – or participant-observer in the proper anthropological sense – is not always easy or possible where corruption is involved.

Given these ethical and methodological objections, what justification can there be for an 'anthropology of corruption'? And what can anthropology contribute to understanding corruption given the vast literature that already exists on the subject in other disciplines, particularly economics, politics and international relations? Ernest Gellner once wrote with regard to patronage that 'we may as well admit that the subject appeals to our political voyeurism. We like to observe a political relationship which we suspect of being illicit' (Gellner 1977: 1). No doubt corruption has similar appeal, as it too is an illicit type of political relationship and behaviour, but we believe there are more substantive arguments for an 'anthropology of corruption'. Four of these are particularly salient.

First, corruption raises issues of major conceptual and epistemological significance. If anthropology is concerned with understanding the rules and norms that govern social conduct, then a good way of exploring these codes is to examine instances where they are violated, how people react to such transgressions, and the strategies and tactics that actors use to negotiate between different norms and rules. We may also discover that there are rules (albeit informal and pragmatic) and cultural codes that govern the way corruption itself should, or does, take place (more on this later) – a point exemplified by Arlacchi's study of the Italian mafia, for example (Arlacchi 1986). A focus on corruption draws our attention to the ambiguous realm of activities that occur 'inside' and 'outside' the law (see Harris 1996), and invites us to reflect critically not only on wider questions of morality, ethics and accountability, but also on our own assumptions about the morality of corruption or whether it is a unitary phenomenon cross-culturally. Studying corruption and its cultural manifestations also provides an optic for examining larger and more complex social and political issues, including conceptions of citizenship, styles of governance and constructions of the state as an imagined entity (see Gupta 1995). The study of corruption might also offer a way of probing other, more philosophical and symbolic domains, such as ideas about 'personhood' or rules governing reciprocity and exchange (for example, what makes a 'good leader' in different cultural contexts, or how to distinguish between gift-giving and bribery).

Second is the issue of how to define a concept as slippery and protean as 'corruption'.[8] Contrary to the claim of the World Bank, this debate is far from closed and most anthropologists would agree that the Bank's definition is problematic and far too restrictive. How we define our objects of study has implications not only for the methods we use to study them, but also for the kinds of research question we ask, or fail to ask. Definitions (like theories) provide alternative 'ways of seeing', but they also entail ways of 'not seeing'.

What anthropology can bring to the study of corruption is not only a focus on the language by which (and through which) ideas about corruption are articulated, but also on the broader cultural contexts in which corruption and discourses of corruption take place; an approach to the study of corruption that is sensitive to the politics of corruption but goes beyond the study of political institutions or politics per se.

Third, corruption presents us with a major theoretical challenge. How can we theorize a phenomenon so polysemous and diffuse? Is the concept of 'corruption' translatable across cultures in a way that allows for meaningful comparison? After all, what is classified as nepotism and cronyism in Scandinavia, may well be regarded as a moral duty to help one's friends and family in parts of Asia and Africa – or indeed, among sections of France's *classe politique* (Mény 1997; Parry 2000). We might do well to recall the debates over patronage in the 1970s. Like patronage, corruption seems to thrive under almost any kind of political regime (Gellner 1977): as David Lovell (this volume) sums it up, 'wherever opportunities for illicit gain exist, and wherever institutions have monopolies over resources and individuals have discretion'. The old assumption that corruption is primarily a product of over-regulated states and the absence of the free market has been shattered by the many scandals that followed the post-1980s privatization bonanza. If anything, deregulation and globalization appear to have enlarged the scope and opportunities for corruption, not only by enlarging the rewards of fraud and chicanery, but by eroding public ethics, reducing the state's legitimate interest, and diluting the general interest through the pursuit of profit and the defence of selfish private interests (Mény 1996; Rose-Ackerman 1996). The increasing dependency of political parties on private donors and corporations for their core funding has also enlarged those opportunities.

To sum up, and to borrow a phrase from Lévi-Strauss, corruption is 'good to think with': we may not be able to unravel the paradoxes surrounding it, but we can learn a great deal about the world by interrogating the idea of corruption and exploring its many different manifestations. Indeed, we would go further than this. Corruption is not only conceptually useful for anthropology; we believe anthropology has much to offer to debates on corruption. In particular, it can help us to understand what corruption *means* in different parts of the world and how it is embedded in everyday life; why intolerance to corruption is greater in some places than others; how it becomes institutionalized and reproduced; and the distinctions people make between what American political scientist A.J. Heidenheimer (1989a) termed 'white' corruption, 'grey' corruption and 'black' corruption – distinctions that go a long way towards explaining why everyday forms of corruption become accepted and institutionalized. As both Sampson and MacLennan show (this volume), anthropology can also provide a useful critique of the burgeoning 'anti-corruption' literature and the concept of 'good governance' that currently drives World Bank and IMF policies.

Finally, an anthropology of corruption is timely simply because the problem of corruption has become such a prevalent aspect of the post-Cold War political agenda. It is now recognized to be not only a problem endemic to supposedly 'backward' Third World or developing countries (including Russia, the Indian subcontinent, Latin America and most of Africa), but one increasingly prevalent in the very heartlands of advanced capitalist democracy, as was demonstrated by the collapse of Enron, Arthur Andersen, the Bank of Commerce and Credit International and Maxwell Communications plc. Indeed, since the 1990s there have been a growing number of high-profile corruption scandals involving major international organizations, including UNESCO, UEFA, the United Nations, the International Olympic Committee and the European Commission.[9] There has also been a dramatic rise in the number of scandals involving the illegal funding of parties, from the '*tangentopoli*' scandals in Italy, to cases of sleaze among the political classes in Spain, Belgium and France. Outside of war, corruption poses probably the greatest single threat to democracy, and sleaze scandals have brought down governments in a host of countries, including Japan, Argentina, Germany, the Sudan and Great Britain. We have also seen an equally dramatic rise in the number of anti-corruption initiatives and movements across the globe, spearheaded by the US government and NGOs such as Transparency International.

But is corruption really on the increase, or is it simply our perceptions that have altered? Might it not just be that since the end of the Cold War some countries have become more aware – and more intolerant – of the kind of corrupt practices that previously went unchecked? If corruption really has increased, what are the reasons that might account for this? And what is the link between the advance of neoliberalism and the discourse of anti-corruption? Even if, as some might argue, explaining this 'corruption eruption' is a task best left to other disciplines, it is nonetheless important for us to understand the way corruption is understood and interpreted, and its effects on the peoples we study. Thus a further critical reason for an anthropology of corruption is anthropology's reflexive understanding of social science itself as a social phenomenon. Focusing on the narratives and discourses of corruption might also help us to explore the way in which key concepts like 'fraud', 'transparency' and 'good governance' interconnect and become embedded in the discourse of policy and practice.

STUDYING CORRUPTION: CONCEPTUAL, METHODOLOGICAL AND ETHICAL PROBLEMS

Challenging received wisdom and questioning conventional categories are therefore the first steps towards an anthropology of political corruption. But, rather than building models against which local discourses and practices can be measured, anthropologists would do better to deliver theoretical or empirically based contributions that consider the cultural and social dimension of corruption and the way it is experienced by, and its effects upon, those we study. However, to do this we must first resolve certain conceptual, methodological and ethical problems anthropologists have to deal with when facing corruption.

Much academic research on corruption either implicitly or explicitly sees corruption as a sign of social instability and decay, an idea reinforced by the frequent 'disease' and 'cancer' metaphors used to describe corruption. This idea is critiqued by anthropologist Thomas Hauschild (2000). Using Germany as a case study, Hauschild rejects the conventional stereotype that links crime and corruption with weak state structures by exploring the web of relationships of personal trust, patronage, loyalty, gift-giving and public silence revealed in the 'Bimbes and Bimbos' scandal surrounding Helmut Kohl and the nefarious financial dealings of the German Christian Democrat Party.[10] Following Eric Wolf's seminal article on 'Kinship, Friendship, and Patron–Client Relations in Complex Societies' (Wolf 1977), Hauschild sees corruption not as endemic only to so-called weak states, but equally to all stable and hegemonic political structures where external controls are absent.[11] Rather than being incompatible with stable bureaucratic structures, informal personal networks may actually be complementary and necessary arrangements in maintaining stability. This was also what Shore's ethnographic study of the European Commission found (Shore 2000). However, in the case of the European Union, this informal web of personal networks that had developed alongside in the EU's formal administrative system – a 'parallel system of administration' that was previously hailed as the secret underlying the EU's dynamism and efficiency (Middlemas 1995) – was also found to be the source of fraud and cronyism within the Commission.

Corruption as a 'Hidden', 'Occult' and 'Immoral' Phenomenon

It is often assumed that corruption takes place only in hidden, occult and unofficial settings, clandestinely, and with the knowledge of the immediate exchange-partners only. The notion of corruption as something hidden is linked intrinsically to the concept of 'transparency', which 'is a major watchword – if not *the* major watchword – for policymakers, politicians, and other proponents of "modernity" at this *début de siècle*' (Sanders 2003: 149). Beginning with this desire to know what is hidden being not only of the political sphere, but of the economic sphere as well, Sanders states that 'transparency is both a process and an outcome – it is modernity's moral compulsion as well as its characteristic feature, at once its motor and its message' (2003: 149). People want to know what is going on – and modernity gives us that right to know. Yet modernity has also provided the officials in government and economic dealings the right to conceal what it is that they are doing. But what is termed as 'transparency' in the guidelines of good governance and neoliberal thinking, is often perceived as unpredictable and confusing from the perspective of the less privileged, the marginalized and excluded.

According to West and Sanders (2003), this has given rise to a vast range of expressions of the popular suspicions of power – including accusations of conspiracy theories and sorcery (cf. Sedlenieks 2002) – which try to make sense of the opaqueness of decision-making in an increasingly globalized context. The impression that corruption is on the rise worldwide may yet be another expression of this attempt to make sense of what Giddens (echoing Edmund Leach) calls our modern 'runaway world' (Giddens 2000).

On the other hand, it may well be that the concept of corruption as something necessarily hidden and occult reflects the ethnocentric, puritan, rationalist bias in the Anglophone social sciences. Ethnographic studies show that what is termed 'corruption' from an outsider's (or 'etic') perspective, is often linked to a code of values and behaviour that is widely known and accepted from an insider's (or 'emic') perspective; people know how the system of favours works and how to work it – even if they are reluctant to admit this publicly. Like patronage and clientelism, corruption may not be legal, but it nonetheless has its own morality, at least in the eyes of the local public. Covert funding of political parties, small bribes and kickbacks for the granting of contracts and licences, and the informal economy of small favours and services are often 'open secrets' (see Herzfeld 1992; Mitchell 2002; Pardo 2000; Shore 1989). As Gore Vidal (1999) wrote of the US, the public 'know that political offices are bought by those who can pay and denied to all the rest, that politicians are better identified with their corporate ancestry than voting base'.

In the British crown colony of Gibraltar corruption was constantly discussed in public, but it only became a heated issue during the electoral campaign for the House of Assembly 1996, when socialist Chief Minister Joe Bossano was openly accused by the conservative opposition of cronyism, nepotism and favouritism (Haller 2000). One conservative party campaign leaflet even displayed a diagram showing the extent of Bossano's involvement in recently privatized companies – and confirmed what local gossip had consistently highlighted: that the chief minister and his seven ministers were the primary shareholder and beneficiaries of these privatized enterprises. Here, it is important to focus on the meaning of 'openness' and 'public': it is not that people simply talk about corruption – what matters is the manner in which it is discussed, and the venues where such talk takes place. Electoral campaigns are exceptional situations where issues known to everybody and normally given little weight may suddenly become charged with importance and subjects for the exercise of subversive knowledge (Haller 2000).

Despite the perception that corruption is everywhere and increasing, most people are well aware that there are degrees (or shades) of corruption. For example, writing about Yaroslavl in Russia, Nancy Ries comments:

most people concurred that the moral waters are murkier the higher one looks. The more money a person has (or the more money that circulates around a person), the more corrupt he or she must be. Government officials and the new business class are seen as being the most corrupt of all, as being utterly disinterested in what happens to 'the people' as long as their pockets are full and their dachas protected by high walls. (Ries 2002)

Those who know distinguish between 'correct' (i.e. acceptable) and 'incorrect' corruption. In rural Mexico, for example, Lomnitz (1995: 41) reports that corruption is accepted if 'some of the benefits of this appropriation spill over to the rest of the population' – that is, by patrons who demonstrate generosity and solidarity with their people and who finance local fiestas.

Methodological Concerns

The study of corruption inevitably poses major challenges to field research and participant observation. One primary difficulty may be funding. Researchers must first convince funding organizations to provide money for 'gifts', and even if granted, the sum of money will only allow gift-giving on a very small scale. A research programme aimed explicitly at exploring corruption may also result in a refusal to be granted a research permit in many states.

A second problem, mentioned earlier, concerns the issue of trust and research ethics. How can trust be established if the anthropologist asks questions about illegal or immoral practices? Who would admit to bribe-giving or bribe-taking? How can stories about other participants in bribing be confirmed? Researching corruption and other aspects viewed as immoral and/or illegal may also be counterproductive, for one risks betraying the confidence of the informants with whom one has lived and probably developed strong emotional ties. Observing corrupt acts (as opposed to recording what people say about them) is a further problem. The advantage of anthropological fieldwork lies in the noting and discovery of informal connections, which can usually only be recognized through long-term participant-observation and intimate knowledge of actors in the field. This privileged empirical perspective, however, is unlikely to stretch into the realm of the illegal or immoral. As with the study of sexuality, people may be extremely loquacious when discussing the actions of others, but guarded or obtuse when discussing their own behaviour. Like sexuality, therefore, most anthropological work on corruption deals with second-order data; the perceived effects of corruption and what people *say* about it (i.e. narratives and representations), rather than direct observations. One strategy used by Werner (2000) in Kazakhstan was to ask hypothetical questions, and only when people brought up the subject of corruption. Since bribe-giving was morally acceptable and legally less criminalized than bribe-taking in Kazakhstan, she only asked about situations where informants had given bribes.

In this respect, and as the chapters in this volume illustrate, anthropology is perhaps better placed to deal not so much with corruption per se as with allegations of corruption and their effects. There are important parallels here with the anthropological study of witchcraft. Like witchcraft allegations, accusations of corruption also mirror structural cleavages and tensions in society and are often used by politicians to undermine the credibility of opponents in the competitive game of political reputation management. Observation is also problematic in another way. Participant-observation may offer little insight into corruption that is 'translocal'. According to Gupta, local and lower-level corruption is just the most visible part of a system of corruption and bribing which resembles a pyramid:

Politicians raise funds through senior bureaucrats for electoral purposes, senior bureaucrats squeeze this money from their subordinates as well as directly from projects that they oversee, and subordinates follow suit. (Gupta 1995: 384)

Access to data is thus a further methodological problem, not only because corruption often takes place in closed settings, but because, through networks of loyalty, kinship, friendship or interest, local and national cases are often connected to transnational politics and economic structures that are beyond the access of the local fieldworker. Corruption often depends on the existence of far away 'enclaves of intransparency', such as offshore companies in the Cayman Islands, Bermuda, the Isle of Man, Gibraltar and elsewhere. These provide a space where legal and illegal money float into one another. For example, via Gibraltar, Vladimir Gusinski, owner of the Russian multi-media enterprise Media-Most, evaded taxes and vast credit payments to Gazprom, Russia's largest gas producer.[12] The question of whether corruption is increasing globally is undoubtedly linked to the question of whether the infrastructure enabling grand-scale corruption is expanding, stagnating or decreasing.

The proposal of Marcus (1995), Fog Olwig and Hastrup (1997), Welz (1998) and others to no longer observe phenomena exclusively at a single place but rather to conduct 'multi-sited' ethnography is certainly sensible in principle, but its practical implementation often fails due to the obvious constraints (institutional, temporal, financial) such projects entail. More pragmatically, Gupta advocates an approach that combines fieldwork and 'being there' with the analysis of newspapers and other media – for one cannot understand the state by focusing on the local level only, but rather through its links to the wider context of society. As Gupta notes, 'the state' is an entity constructed not only through the practice of interaction between locals and bureaucrats, but also through discourses of corruption – and newspapers are particularly important to the way corruption narratives are reproduced. But what does that mean methodologically? Shall we add another 'there' (i.e. media agencies) to our local 'there'? Or is it sufficient to focus on the local perception of media representations of corruption, and how this representation shapes our informants' understanding of 'the state'? Whatever our focus is, Gupta's stance that the local should not be treated as an unproblematic and coherent spatial unit is essential to research in translocal transactions. Rather we should 'pay attention to the "multiply mediated" contexts through which the state comes to be constructed' (1995: 377) through corruption, i.e. taking into account narratives about other places such as 'the capital', 'the government', 'the transnational enterprises' or 'the banks', which of course are mediated through media.

Research on Corruption as an Ethical Question

Research ethics are intimately linked to the question of why corruption is rarely discussed openly within anthropology. One reason is that people under study are often poor and marginalized anyway, and that anthropologists do not want to add to the problems of 'their' people. Our research on corruption can put them in serious jeopardy. Another reason is that we may see corruption among our informants as a subversive form of revenge and empowerment, and we 'do not want to throw stones at the protagonists of potential liberation' (Postero 2000). Third, anthropologists may themselves benefit from and take part in 'corruptive' behaviour; many will have invited officials to dinner, given presents, sworn never to write about the exchange of gifts or disclose the source of their sensitive information (promising instead just to keep it 'in mind'). Our failure to write about bribery arises not only from a reluctance to betray our informants, but also perhaps because it might cast a pall on our own behaviour; because it would be considered embarrassing, immoral or illegal amongst our colleagues, or for the sake of own personal or professional ethics. And finally, a more threatening aspect is the fact that research on corruption might put researchers themselves in danger. Haller (2000), working in Gibraltar, was probably not the only anthropologist to be warned off delving too deeply into corruption and the links between politics, finance and drug smuggling. For example, after being told about local smuggling and low-level bribery ('everybody knows that anyway') by one local informant, it immediately became apparent that asking about larger-scale deals, or specific names was off limits. 'This is something you don't want to know', his informant informed him gravely. The implied threat was backed up with stories about individuals killed in shootings between rival 'mafia groups' in 'other' Mediterranean ports, where certain people from 'around here' had been implicated. Although these stories were vague and indirect and relatively mild by comparison with threats some colleagues may have encountered, they were effective in stemming any further questions Haller might have wished to ask in researching small-scale corruption in Gibraltar.

TOWARDS AN ANTHROPOLOGY OF CORRUPTION?

As we have tried to illustrate, anthropological perspectives can make an important contribution to *understanding* corruption and its different meanings. In this final section we outline some further avenues of investigation for the discipline.

Both the IMF and Transparency International have tended to present – in the vein of their anti-corruptionist discourse – a definition of corruption that is a-cultural and universal. Unsurprisingly (to anthropologists, at least) these have been in conflict with local practices and categories, especially where gifts are distinguished from bribes. In Marcel Mauss's classical text on gift exchange (1989 [1925]), the obligation to repay intrinsic to gift-giving is basic to all forms of social structure. Contrary to this view, the IMF's anti-corruption leadership distinguishes gifts from bribes by drawing the line exactly at the moment of reciprocity: whereas bribes always imply the obligation to reciprocity, gifts do not. The anti-corruptionist agenda is in conflict here with the fulfilment of local needs, for in many cultures, gifts and bribes establish social bonds that help secure informal networks for people (like the Kazakh) 'with few economic resources, insufficient state welfare benefits, and/or limited access to goods and services' (Werner 2000: 12). Often, there are several – and sometimes contradictory – standards coexisting at the same time. Werner offers a sample of such standards to distinguish gifts from bribes, such as 'content of exchange' (cash/no cash), 'employment status of recipient' (official/irrelevant), 'motive for exchange' (to return a gift/to get something done quickly and avoid hassle), 'cultural definition of exchange' (traditional/immoral), 'transparency of exchange' (transparent/discreet), and 'legal definition of exchange' (legal/illegal). In the Kazakh case, the line between gift and bribe cannot be drawn properly. The notion of gift is an imported category, whilst Kazakhs have different terms for different occasions of gift-giving, some of them overlap with what Westerners call bribes. The important point is that these overlapping practices are not perceived to be immoral. Hence, a key task for anthropology – if it is to go beyond disembodied theorizing – is to explore the way people classify behaviours as appropriate/inappropriate, moral/immoral and legal/illegal in the specific cultures we study, and analyse these in the context of local standards and practices. It is also necessary to distinguish corruption – as it is defined by local actors themselves as well as by legal norms – from activities such as lobbyism, sponsorship, nepotism, patronage, clientelism, gift-giving and networking (such as the Chinese *guanxi*) to which it may appear to be linked. As Della Porta and Mény (1997: 133) observe, while clientelism and political corruption may be considered as related (and sometimes even indistinguishable) phenomena, there are good reasons for considering the two concepts as separate as there are considerable differences in the medium of barter (i.e. 'protection' and favours on the one hand, and money on the other – cf. Weingrod 1968).

However, siding with our informants' perspectives often runs the risk of romanticizing local standards of exchange. We should not lose sight of the fact that transactions of bribery and corruption always take place in power relationships that invariably stratify, marginalize and exclude. As Dougherty (2000) reminds us:

Those who have the power to grant access to resources, to give contracts, reduce taxes, help put someone else in a position of power, turn a blind eye on illegal activities etc., are one part of this equation. Those who have something valuable to give in exchange are another part of the equation. Often the poorest sector of the population, who has little monetary or social capital with which to negotiate deals, are unable to partake and benefit from these informal systems of exchange and gift giving.

A second field of investigation is the productivity of corruption, or what discourses and practices of corruption actually 'produce'. Following Foucault's notion of 'productivity', Gupta (1995) has argued that corruption discourses and practices help to create different kinds of actor: whereas the abstract notion of 'the state' itself is created and made tangible through the practices of client–bureaucrat interaction, which in the Indian case almost always implies some form of bribery, the media discourse of newspapers creates 'the public' with rights and 'the politicians' with responsibilities. However, corruption narratives produce other phenomena besides 'the state'. In the case of Postero (2000), these include, on the one hand, a form of conflict over land ownership between the two actors implicated in the corruption accusations, but on the other, silence, impotence and powerlessness among those unable to participate in the transaction. In the case of Giglioli (1996), it includes a powerful dichotomy between the 'good public' and 'bad politicians'.

Third, anthropology has always benefited from reflecting critically on the relationship between its own research focuses and the wider socio-political context in which these develop as relevant. Reflecting on the links between scientific epistemology and society highlights hegemonic perspectives and the blind spots they produce. This has been done quite successfully with other hegemonic notions such as 'Orientalism' (Said 1978), 'male bias' (Lamphere 1996; Slocum 1975), 'heteronormativity' (Haller 2001), and imperial nostalgia (Rosaldo 1989).[13] In the case of the 'corruption' and 'anti-corruption', what anthropology highlights above are the links between these terms and the current neoliberal IMF discourse of 'deregulation', 'privatization' and 'good governance'. Neoliberalism has set the frame for analytical models of corruption, particularly in its restrictive World Bank definition of corruption as the abuse of 'public' office. Stripped to its basics, the neoliberal thesis holds that since corruption is primarily a pathology of the public sector, the solution lies in reducing public spending and a rolling back the frontiers of the state. Shrinking the public sector, so the argument goes, reduces the scope for public officials to engage in malfeasance. It also subjects public officials to the regulatory disciplines of the market, to cost-consciousness, and to entrepreneurial business ethics. To focus on corporate crimes and corruption within the private sector is simply not on the current agenda of the US government or the IMF.

Anthropology is well placed to take up this challenge and shed light on non-regulated and informal forms of private-sector exchange, and turn its critical gaze towards the frame that sustains the 'blind spot' that exists regarding corruption in the private sector. At the same time, the motives and actions of certain Western governments and international organizations might also merit closer anthropological attention. Why, we might ask, was it only in 1998 that the head of the World Bank launched the crusade against the 'cancer of corruption'? And why was it only in 1999 that the OECD Convention on Combating the Bribery of Foreign Public Officials in International

Business Transactions – an act designed to make the bribery of foreign public officials in order to obtain business advantage illegal – came into force?[14] In fact, it is still common practice for American arms manufacturers to use 'offsets' (effectively legal bribes or sweeteners) to secure contract deals.[15] Why has this anti-corruption discourse arisen now, in the form that it has? Is this, as Lovell suggests (this volume), a response to the social and economic upheavals that followed the end of the Cold War – the so-called 'Third Wave' of democratization? Is it instead a belated reaction to the consequences of neoliberalism, the post-1980s consumer boom, and the new opportunities for self-enrichment that have swept away the old moral restraints? Or is anti-corruption (like 'good governance' and 'accountability') the new stick to beat non-Western governments into compliance with the economic and political agenda of the United States and the dictates of global capitalism? Steven Sampson (this volume) is unequivocal: the anti-corruption agenda is not a reaction to the neoliberal agenda: it *is* the neoliberal agenda. However, and as the chapters in this volume suggest, macro-political structures are not the only context for understanding contemporary forms of corruption.

SCOPE OF THIS BOOK

The aim of this book is to offer a tentative vision of what an anthropology of political corruption might look like. To do this we need studies that provide rich ethnographical detail (or 'thick descriptions') of the way corruption is manifested and reproduced in everyday life. The chapters in this volume address this using examples from three continents: Asia, the Americas – particularly the United States – and Europe. While some of the 'usual suspects' feature prominently (notably Italy, Africa and the former Soviet bloc countries), we also analyse corruption in less researched and less conspicuous settings, including New York, Washington and Brussels. The chapters that follow fall into three sections. Part I, 'Corruption in "Transitional" Societies?', examines the phenomena of *blat*, crony capitalism and organized crime in what some scholars have called 'transitional societies'. The question mark in the part title indicates our scepticism about the utility of the term 'transitional' as an analytical category (insofar as all societies are in a state change and 'transitional' suggests a progressive movement between fixed states such as 'underdeveloped/developed, post-communist/free market, etc., that are themselves problematic categories). Despite that caveat, what unites these chapters is their shared concern with the analysis of corruption in contexts of rapid economic change and social upheaval.

Chapter 2 by Jane and Peter Schneider is a comparative study of political corruption in two cities: Youngstown, USA, and Palermo in Sicily. Central to the analysis of the contemporary mafia is the complex web of relations (an *intreccio* in Italian) between political institutions and organized crime, the former providing cover and protection for the activities of the latter. The chapter highlights some striking parallels in the way organized crime has developed in these two cities, particularly when viewed from an historical and political economy perspective. In Chapter 3, Michele Rivkin-Fish also investigates social relations and illicit practices in a fast-changing urban setting, in this case the exchanges between patients and doctors in a St Petersburg maternity hospital. Her study tries to understand why patients continue to offer unofficial gifts and payments to providers, despite the introduction of official payments for elective medical services.

David Lovell (Chapter 4) also deals with post-Soviet states, but from a political and historical perspective that speaks directly to debates about corruption as a 'transitional' phenomenon. As Lovell argues, endemic corruption is perhaps best explained as a response that officials adopt when confronted with the conflicting demands of traditional obligations and loyalties on the one hand, and legal-rational forms of rule on the other. The final chapter of this section (Filippo Zerilli) provides a rich ethnographic account of the multiple meanings of corruption in post-communist Romania through an analysis of recent legal cases involving the restitution of property confiscated under communism. These stories – and the deprecatory stereotypes and jokes Romanians make about their national identity – provide a lens for exploring the symbolic associations that corruption holds for ordinary Romanians today.

Part II, 'Institutionalized Corruption and Institutions of Anti-corruption', explores actors, institutions and countries that are supposedly at the forefront of the anti-corruption movement and the struggle for good governance. This shift of focus 'upwards' towards the rich and powerful societies of the northern hemisphere provides a springboard for critiquing the view that endemic corruption is essentially a problem of 'developing' and 'underdeveloped' societies. It also raises interesting questions about the connection between post-1980s neoliberalism and the rise of corruption as a major theme in international relations. In Chapter 6, Steven Sampson provides a clear analysis of this relationship in his study of Transparency International, one the most influential international NGOs operating today. As Sampson demonstrates, TI's transformation of the fight against corruption into a fully fledged global ideology and practice of 'anti-corruptionism', together with its new discourse of 'global accountability', have promoted a powerful (albeit illusory) vision of a unified moral and global 'community'.

Cris Shore (Chapter 7) also explores the inner world of one of the major political actors in the anti-corruption crusade: the European Union (EU) and its civil service. The European Commission frequently claims to represent a new 'European' model of administration, one that embodies Europe's supranational ethos and higher political ideals. Drawing on fieldwork among EU staff shortly before the resignation of the Santer Commission in 1999 (following a damning Parliamentary report into allegations of fraud, mismanagement and cronyism), Shore interrogates these assumptions. He also asks 'how successful has the EU been in its attempts to reform itself since 1999'?

Carol MacLennan (Chapter 8) also investigates a context where corruption has become pervasive and institutionalized: corporate America. Her study challenges the assumption that corporate corruption is a recent phenomenon resulting from post-1980 economic changes. Like Peter and Jane Schneider, she suggests that corruption is far more systemic than previously imagined, and that its pervasiveness is linked to the same market-driven values and practices that sustain contemporary capitalism. Assessing the work of C. Wright Mills, William Domhoff and Laura Nader, she concludes that class and kinship networks remain decisive factors of analysis for understanding how corruption operates.

Part III, 'Narratives and Practices of Everyday Corruption', returns to the third major theme of this book, corruption as a type of narrative and symbolic system. What these chapters show is how corruption typically functions as an idiom through which people try to make sense of the political world they inhabit. In this respect, discourses of corruption (like accusations of sleaze or witchcraft) are not only powerful tools for constructing social facts, they also provide a lens for exploring disputes, contested meanings and the structure of social relations. In Chapter 9, Akhil Gupta, taking rural India as a case study, shows how narratives of corruption not only create conflicting statements about 'proper' and 'improper' moral behaviour, but also enable rural citizens and bureaucrats to *imagine* the state. Indeed, in India, corruption narratives play a fundamental role in the very constitution of the state and what it can and should do for its citizens. As Gupta shows, it is not enough that anti-corruption policy calls for 'transparency' and institutional reform; what is needed is practical (and ideological) work to change those dominant narratives themselves.

In Chapter 10, Dorle Dracklé uses narratives of corruption to examine Portugal's relationship with the EU. Her study explores how people in one of Europe's most peripheral regions interpret the relationships that local elites have created in order to enhance their access to EU funds. These relationships are played out in stories about the virtual economy, the acquisition of luxury consumer goods bought with EU money, and in the various tales of suicide by farmers who were unable to repay their EU grants. Chapter 11 by Sian Lazar also concerns a peripheral region, this time in Bolivia, a country reputedly wracked by endemic corruption. The focus of Lazar's study is on how ordinary Bolivians perceive and define corruption. As she argues, corruption and its necessary counterpart, public works (*obras*), are both crucial discursive elements in the way that Bolivian citizens articulate their expectations of their leaders. The interaction between perceptions of corruption and the delivery of *obras* enables Bolivians to imagine themselves as a collective entity, as residents of a particular neighbourhood, and beyond this, as 'the Bolivian people'. Leaders are thus held to account pre-emptively through rumour and gossip. In this way, Bolivians establish a sense of the public good and, hopefully, an obligation on the part of their leaders to serve that good. Concluding the volume, Dorothy Louise Zinn's erudite and thoughtful afterword links current ideas about the anthropology of corruption to earlier anthropological debates about patronage and clientelism. Reflecting on some of the unifying themes of the volume (including its omissions and commissions), her chapter concludes with a call for us to recuperate *class* and *gender* as key analytical categories in any future project for an anthropology of corruption.

NOTES

1. This chapter has undergone numerous revisions since it was first presented to colleagues at Goldsmiths College and at the University of Copenhagen. We would like to acknowledge the contribution of all those who participated in those lively research seminars on the anthropology of corruption. We would particularly like to thank Dr Mark Busse for critical comments on the penultimate draft.
2. See Paul Krugman, *New York Times* (29 January 2002) cited in Aiyer (2003: 141).
3. For anthropological perspectives on the Enron scandal and its significance, see the contributions to *Social Analysis* 47 (3) by Gledhill, Aiyer, Schneider and Schneider, and Shore.
4. <http://news.bbc.co.uk/l/hi/business/2182201.stm>.
5. We wish to thank the EASA Executive and organisers of the 7th EASA conference for providing the forum for that meeting. Five of the chapters in this volume (Sampson; Lovell, Rivkin-Fish, Zerilli, Schneider and Schneider) were first presented as papers at that panel. The other chapters were either commissioned for this volume or presented at two further international workshops on anthropology and corruption organized by the editors: the first at the 2001 'Sozialanthropologie Europas' Conference in Göttingen, the second at Goldsmiths in May 2002. We are grateful to all of those who participated in these three conferences.

6. Notable exceptions include Anton Blok's study of the Sicilian Mafia (1988) and Gerald Mars' study of 'cheats at work' (1984).
7. As Visvanathan and Sethi (1998: 6) eloquently put it: 'The bribe is not a pathology. It is the fundamental transaction of the Indian state', and: 'The English word corruption sounds too provincial, too puritan, too restricted, too knee-jerk. It has the sense of arid prose that cannot capture the labyrinthine quality of this world. It is like comparing an election survey with a Dantesque view of hell. There are layers to be unravelled' (1998: 3).
8. See Johnston (1996) for a more comprehensive discussion of definitions.
9. See Shore (2000) for an anthropological examination of corruption in the European Commission.
10. In Helmut Kohl's Palatine dialect, 'Bimbes' is a colloquial for 'money'. In German, by contrast, 'Bimbos' is slang for 'Blacks', i.e. synonymous with 'Niggers'. The use of this polemic slogan is directed against the German anthropological tradition of researching the exotic only by neglecting the familiar.
11. Cf. Rose-Ackerman (1996) for a similar argument.
12. El presidente ruso justifica el arresto del editor Gusinski, <http://www.elmundo.org/2000/06/15/europa/15N0060.html>.
13. We might add to this list the categories of 'whiteness' (Dyer 1997), 'Westernness' (Ouroussoff 1993) and 'policy' (Shore and Wright 1997).
14. See the UK's Department of Trade and Industry website, <www2.dti.gov.uk/ewt/bribery.htm>.
15. Wayne (2003). See also <www.d-n-i.net/fcs/comments/c474.htm>.

REFERENCES

Arlacchi, P. (1986) *Mafia Business: The Mafia Ethic and the Spirit of Capitalism* (London: Verso).

Aiyer, A. (2003) Lights Out, *Social Analysis* (Forum: The Enron Scandal), Vol. 47, No. 3: 141–6.

Banfield, E. (1958) *The Moral Basis of a Backward Society* (Glencoe, IL: Free Press).

Bayley, D.H. (1966) The Effects of Corruption in a Developing Nation, *Western Political Quarterly*, Vol. 19: 719–32.

Blok, A. (1988) *The Mafia of a Sicilian Village, 1860–1960: A Study of Violent Peasant Entrepreneurs* (Prospect Heights, IL: Waveland Press).

Della Porta, D. and Y. Mény (eds) (1997) *Democracy and Corruption in Europe* (London: Cassell).

Dougherty, E. (2000) The Hegemony of Corruption. Paper delivered at 2000 AAA meeting, San Francisco.

Dyer, R. (1997) *White* (London and New York: Routledge).

Fog Olwig, K. and K. Hastrup (eds) (1997) *Siting Culture – The Shifting Anthropological Object* (London: Routledge & Kegan Paul).

Foucault, M. (1991) 'Governability', in G. Burchell et al. (eds) *The Foucault Effect: Studies in Governmentality* (London: Harvester Wheatsheaf).

Friedrich, C.J. (1966) Political Pathology, *Political Quarterly*, Vol. 37: 70–85.

Gellner, E. (1977) Patrons and Clients, in E. Gellner and J. Waterbury (eds) *Patrons and Clients*, pp. 1–6 (London: Duckworth).

Giddens, A. (2000) *Runaway World* (London: Routledge).

Giglioli, P.P. (1996) Political Corruption and the Media: The Tangentopoli Affair, *International Social Science Journal*, Vol. 149: 381–94.

Gledhill, J. (2003) Old Economy, New Economy; Old Corruption, New Corruption, *Social Analysis* (Forum: The Enron Scandal), Vol. 47, No. 3: 130–5.

Gupta, A. (1995) Blurred Boundaries: The Discourse of Corruption, the Culture of Politics, and the imagined State, *American Ethnologist*, Vol. 22, No. 2: 375–402.

Haller, D. (2000) *Gelebte Grenze Gibraltar – Transnationalismus, Lokalität und Identität in kulturanthropologischer Perspektive* (Wiesbaden: Deutscher Universitätsverlag).

—— (2001) Die Entdeckung des Selbstverständlichen: Heteronormativität im Blick. *Kea*, Vol. 14: 1–28.

Harris, O. (ed.) 1996 *Inside and Outside the Law: Anthropological Studies of Authority and Ambiguity,* (London: Routledge).

Hauschild, T. (2000) Ein müder Heller für die CDU! Ethnologen erforschen den Parteienskandal – Eine kleine Anthropologie des 'Bimbes', *Die Zeit* Nr. 6/2000.

Heidenheimer, A. (1989a) Perspectives on the Perception of Corruption, in A. Heidenheimer, M. Johnston and V. LeVine (eds) *Political Corruption: A Handbook* (New Brunswick, NJ: Transaction).

—— (1989b) Terms, Concepts, and Definitions: An Introduction, in A. Heidenheimer, M. Johnston and V. LeVine (eds) *Political Corruption: A Handbook* (New Brunswick, NJ: Transaction).

Herzfeld, M. (1992) *The Social Production of Indifference: Exploring the Symbolic Roots of Western Bureaucracy* (Oxford: Berg).

Johnston, M. (1996) The Search for Definition: The Vitality of Politics and the Issue of Corruption, *International Social Science Journal*, Vol. 149: 321–37.

Lamphere, L. (1996) Gender, in D. Levinson and M. Ember (eds) *Encyclopedia of Cultural Anthropology*, Vol. 2, pp. 488–93 (New York: Henry Holt & Co.).

Lomnitz, C. (1995) Ritual, Rumor and Corruption in the Constitution of Polity in Mexico, *Journal of Latin American Anthropology*, Vol. I, No. 1: 20–4.

Marcus, G. (1995) Ethnography in/of the World System: The Emergence of Multi-sited Ethnography, *Annual Review of Anthropology*, Vol. 24: 95–117.

Mars, G. (1984) *Cheats at Work: An Anthropology of Workplace Crime* (London: George Allen & Unwin).

Mauss, M. (1989 [1925]) Die Gabe, in M. Mauss, *Soziologie und Anthropologie 2*, pp. 11–148 (Frankfurt/Main: Fischer Taschenbuch Verlag).

Mény, Yves (1997) France: The End of the Republican Ethic?, in D. Della Porta and Y. Mény (eds) *Democracy and Corruption in Europe* (London: Cassell).

Middlemas, K. (1995) *Orchestrating Europe: The Informal Politics of European Union 1973–1995* (London: Fontana).

Mitchell, J. (2002) *Ambivalent Europeans: Ritual, Memory and the Public Sphere in Malta* (London: Routledge).

Ouroussoff, A. (1993) Illusions of Rationality: False Premises of the Liberal Tradition, *Man*, Vol. 28, No. 2: 281–98.

Pardo, I. (2000) *The Morals of Legitimacy* (Oxford and New York: Berghahn Books).

Parry, J. (2000) The 'Crisis of Corruption' and 'the Idea of India': A Worm's Eye View, in Italo Pardo (ed.) *The Morals of Legitimacy*, pp. 27–55 (New York and Oxford: Berghahn Books).

Postero, N. (2000) A Case Study of Land Loss and Leadership in a Guaraní Village. Paper delivered at 2000 AAA meeting, San Francisco.

Ries, N. (2002) 'Honest' Bandits and 'Warped People' – Russian Narratives about Money, Corruption and Moral Decay, in C. Greenhouse, K. Warren and E. Mertz (eds) *Ethnography in Unstable Places*, pp. 276–315 (Durham, NC and London: Duke University Press).

Rosaldo, R. (1989) *Culture and Truth: The Remaking of Social Analysis* (Boston, MA: Beacon Press).

Rose-Ackerman, S. (1996) Democracy and 'Grand' Corruption, *International Social Science Journal*, Vol. 149: 365–81.

Said, E. (1978) *Orientalism* (London: Routledge & Kegan Paul).

Sampson, S. (1983) Bureaucracy and Corruption as Anthropological Problems: A Case Study from Romania, *Folk*, Vol. 25: 63–96.

Sanders, T. (2003) Invisible Hands and Visible Goods: Revealed and Concealed Economies in Millennial Tanzania, in H.G. West and T. Sanders (eds) *Transparency and Conspiracy – Ethnographies of Suspicion in the New World Order*, pp. 148–75 (Durham, NC and London: Duke University Press).

Schneider, J. and P. Schneider (2003) Power Projects: Comparing Corporate Scandal and Organized Crime, *Social Analysis*, Vol. 47, No. 3: 136–40.

Sedlenieks, K. (2002) Latvian–Azande Parallel – Corruption as Witchcraft for Latvia during the Transition. Paper presented at the Fourth Nordic Conference on the Anthropology of Post-Socialism, April 2002. Available online <http://www.anthrobase.com/txt/S/Sedlenieks_K_01.htm>. Accessed 18 Nov. 2004.

Shore, C. (1989) Patronage and Bureaucracy in Complex Societies: Social Rules and Social Relations in an Italian University, *Journal of the Anthropology Society of Oxford*, Vol. 29, No. 1: 56–73.

—— (2000) *Building Europe. The Cultural Politics of European Integration* (London: Routledge).

—— (2003) Corruption Scandals in America and Europe: Enron and EU Fraud in Comparative Perspective, *Social Analysis*, Vol. 47, No. 3: 147–53.

Shore, C. and S. Wright (eds) (1997) *Anthropology of Policy: Critical Perspectives on Governance and Power* (London/New York: Routledge).

Slocum, S. (1975) Woman the Gatherer: Male Bias in Anthropology, in R. Reiter (ed.) *Toward the Anthropology of Women*, pp. 36–50 (New York: Monthly Review Press).

Van Klaveren, J. (1989) The Concept of Corruption, in A. Heidenheimer, M. Johnston and V. LeVine (eds) *Political Corruption: A Handbook* (New Brunswick, NJ: Transaction).

Vidal, G. (1999) A Corrupt System: The People Who Own the Country Shouldn't Run It, in J. Cohen and J. Rogers (eds) *Money and Politics: Financing Our Elections Democratically* (Boston, MA: Beacon Press).

Visvanathan, S. and H. Sethi (1998) By Way of a Beginning, in S. Visvanathan and H. Sethi (eds) *Foul Play: Chronicles of Corruption 1947–97* (New Delhi: Banyan Books).

Wade, R. (1982) The System of Administrative and Political Corruption: Canal Irrigation in South India, *Journal of Development Studies*, Vol. 18, No. 3: 287–328.

Wayne, L. (2003) Foreigners Exact Trade-offs from US Contractors, *New York Times* (Money and Business), 16 February.

Wedel, J. (2001) *Collision and Collusion: The Strange Case of Western Aid to Eastern Europe* (New York: Palgrave).

Weingrod, A. (1968) Patrons, Patronage and Political Parties, *Comparative Studies in Society and History*, Vol. 10: 376–400.

Welz, G. (1998) Moving Targets – Feldforschung unter Mobilitätsdruck, in *Zeitschrift für Volkskunde* II. Halbjahresband: 177–95.

Werner, C. (2000) Gifts, Bribes, and Development in Post-Soviet Kazakhstan, *Human Organization*, Vol. 59, No. 1: 11–22.

West, H.G. and T. Sanders (eds) (2003) *Transparency and Conspiracy – Ethnographies of Suspicion in the New World Order* (Durham, NC and London: Duke University Press)

Wolf, E. (1977) Kinship, Friendship, and Patron–Client Relations in Complex Societies, in S.W. Schmidt, J.C. Scott, C. Landé and L. Guasti (eds) *Friends, Followers and Factions – A Reader in Political Clientelism*, pp. 167–79 (Berkeley: University of California Press).

World Bank (2002) The New Anticorruption Home Page, <www.WorldBank-homepage.htm>.

Zinn, D. (2001) *La Raccomandazzione: Clientelismo vecchio e nouvo* (Roma: Donzelli).

PART I

Corruption in 'Transitional' Societies?

2 THE SACK OF TWO CITIES: ORGANIZED CRIME AND POLITICAL CORRUPTION IN YOUNGSTOWN AND PALERMO

Jane Schneider and Peter Schneider

The Piazza Marina of Palermo was the centre of elegance for the aristocratic and upper bourgeois classes in eighteenth- and early nineteenth-century Palermo, but after the unification of Italy in 1860 a northward expansion of the city privileged new piazzas and boulevards as the places to be seen. By the end of the Second World War it was a place to avoid, Allied bombers having destroyed many of its waterfront palazzi. In the last decade, however, several historic buildings surrounding the Piazza have been restored, its garden cleaned and replanted. Children play there, contributing to the sense of rejuvenation, as do its trendy outdoor restaurants. Palermo's large historic centre, formerly neglected, and a shabby symbol of degradation and decay, sprang to life in the 1990s with many such projects for recuperation. The refurbished Teatro Massimo, the third largest opera house in Europe, reopened in 1997 after 23 years of silence. In December 2000, it hosted the opening ceremony of the United Nations Convention against Transnational Organized Crime, during which distinguished speakers praised what they called the 'Palermo Renaissance'. The city that was once the 'capital of the mafia' now offered itself to the world as the 'capital of the antimafia', its people having suppressed, according to official rhetoric, a 'crime-friendly culture' of indifference and cynicism in favour of a 'law-abiding culture' of civic pride.

We attended the United Nations Convention and, rather to our amazement, met there a delegation of 20 citizens from Youngstown, Ohio, invited by the mayor of Palermo under the auspices of a Washington-based NGO called the National Strategy Information Center, which supports educational and other projects dedicated to 'legality' and 'transparency'. Thus we learned of the depth of these citizens' despair over the decay of Youngstown, which they attribute in part to an unhealthy synergy between organized crime and political corruption. We have since spent a few days in Youngstown, renewing acquaintances and developing a bibliography of local history. Although there are vast historical and social differences between Youngstown and Palermo, not to mention between the American and Sicilian mafias, there are also some intriguing parallels and these are the subject of this chapter.

CRIME AND CORRUPTION: AMBIGUOUS CONCEPTS

'Crime' is an intrinsically ambivalent term, referring on the one hand to acts committed or omitted in violation of laws forbidding or commanding them – acts that lead to punishment upon conviction – and, on the other hand, to unjust, senseless or injurious acts that offend morality. Laws only imperfectly interdict crimes in the second, morally offensive sense; it is widely recognized that many 'criminal acts' go unpunished. By the same token, states regularly prosecute and convict persons for acts that, although illegal, are, from the perspective of at least some segments of society, entirely moral.

'Corruption' also sits awkwardly astride the domains of rule and morality. Dictionary definitions emphasize depravity, dishonesty, perversion, evoking the idea of something whole and good becoming tainted or rotten. In application, this whole and good thing is usually a public office or bureaucracy engaged in the administration of public resources according to established laws and rules. For many, misappropriating public resources for private ends or betraying public confidence lie at the heart of corruption (Ledeneva 1998: 42–3). Johansen (2002) provides a more inclusive formulation, proposing that corruption has to do with the interpenetration of value-normative subsystems as, for example, when rules of kinship/friendship are applied to public service or corporate administration.

Anthropologists, generally sensitive to conditions of inequality and uneven development in the world, have long recognized that in all of the world's societies, the holders of wealth and power are less likely to be punished for crimes or exposed for corruption than are members of less privileged groups. Not only do such persons command extraordinary resources for defending themselves when their acts violate the law; surrounded with an aura of respectability, they also have a stronger purchase on creating the laws and setting the rules in the first place. Conversely, subaltern groups are more likely to bear the brunt of labelling processes – of moral and legal movements that redefine their everyday practices, not to mention their resistance, as corrupt or criminal. And yet, even for marginal or stigmatized groups, the reality of crime and corruption is more than their social constructions; it is a matter of the interaction between social action and social perception. There may well be prejudicial elements in any given accusation; issues of culpability will always be contested. But to exonerate criminal and corrupt activity among groups that are vulnerable, have stigmatized histories or otherwise garner our sympathy, is to underestimate the possibly devastating consequences of this activity even for these very groups.

MAFIA FORMATION AND POLITICAL CORRUPTION

Antecedents of the mafia lie in the period 1815–60 when the Neapolitan Bourbons, then rulers of Sicily, attempted to abolish feudalism, create a land market and enclose common holdings, diverting their use from (collective) pasture to (private) cultivation. The immature state, however, was unable to control the actions of rapacious landlords and rural thugs, or respond effectively to the demands of peasant uprisings. State repression notwithstanding, bandits still roamed the countryside and landowners either remained vulnerable to theft and kidnapping or employed thieves and kidnappers for protection (Riall 1998: 163–78).

Mafiosi arose from the interstices of this situation – among an incipient entrepreneurial class of carters, muleteers, itinerant merchants, bandits and herders. Both gentry and noble landowners recruited such persons as estate guards, rentiers and administrators. Serving as private avengers and judges, such henchmen in turn claimed to restore order – a function that included disciplining rebellious peasants. Although they abandoned the bandit practice that the elites most feared, kidnapping, they themselves became a source of disorder through their racketeering (Lupo 1993; Pezzino 1995).

A succession of governing regimes in Italy looked the other way as mafia 'families' proliferated, especially along the 'bandit corridor' that extended through Sicily's western mountains, and in the rich commercial orchard district surrounding Palermo (Lupo 1990, 1993; Pezzino 1995). This tolerant stance was for a while reversed by Mussolini, whose specially appointed Prefect for Palermo initiated a crackdown. But after the Allied invasion of the island the occupying military government turned to influential landowners for advice, and mafiosi connected to these elites were appointed to local government positions. Under the subsequent Italian Republic, the mafia, now restored, protected the landed elite from the re-emergent problems of banditry and peasant protest, intimidating and even murdering left-wing peasant leaders, for the most part with impunity (Lupo 1997; Mangiameli 1994; Santino 1997).

In 1950, a land reform was enacted, but by this time mafiosi had something new to offer: electoral support for the national-level Christian Democratic Party. Referred to as 'that wicked deal'

(Renda 1987: 201–2), this arrangement meant that the Communist Party, the principal backer of the peasant struggle, would remain excluded from participation in governing alliances, both regional and national (Ginsborg 1990: 100–1, 146–52; Lupo 1997: 28; McCarthy 1995: 44). Estimates are that, between friends and kin, each mafioso could muster at least 40 to 50 votes, adding up to 75,000 to 100,000 'friendly' votes in the province of Palermo alone (Calderone, in Arlacchi 1993: 182–4). The quid pro quo for these votes was the mafia's relative immunity from prosecution or long jail terms and the tacit permission to penetrate several new domains: the administration of the land reform, urban produce markets, new house construction and public works, in particular. The state's failure to prevent the Sicilian mafia from taking over the global traffic in heroin in the 1970s was perhaps the most consequential outcome of the 'wicked deal' (Rossetti 1994: 183–5).

Antecedents of the American mafia are of course quite different, but the similarities are nevertheless worthy of attention. After the Civil War, immigrants from southern and eastern Europe poured into the cities of the north-east and Midwest, supplying extremely exploitable labour to the burgeoning industries and construction crews for the expanding nation. Inevitably, associations of tough guys formed within the new communities, intervening in the settlement of disputes and regulating access to jobs, other economic opportunities and housing in the territories they controlled. By the 1890s, some of the immigrant groups, most famously Sicilians and Neapolitans, included members of organized criminal formations that had already developed in the old world. The spontaneous gangs both complemented and competed with the more organized criminal fraternities.

All of these formations came into their own in the context of extreme labour strife during and after the First World War. A pivotal aspect of the repression of this strife was legislation interdicting the so-called vices – drinking, gambling and prostitution – practices that allegedly made the labouring classes dangerous. Of these measures, the National Alcohol Prohibition (Volstead) Act of 1919 stands out. Part of the background of the Act was a temperance movement dating to the 1830s. Starting off with an estimated 1.5 million proselytizing followers, it had been reinvigorated as a moral crusade against alcohol around the turn of the century (Goode and Nachman 1994). The movement rested on a broad base of evangelical churches, in turn the foundation of the Women's Christian Temperance Union (WCTU); in 1903 it spawned a special interest association, the Anti-saloon League, which defined as hideously criminal the manufacture, transport, sale and consumption of all alcohol. Members of the league backed prohibition candidates in state and national legislative races, as did the WCTU. Their energetic lobbying effort, petition drives, approach to churches, corporations and unions, and printing of 100 million pamphlets in 1909 were, clearly, the direct impetus for the Act.

More broadly, the Alcohol Prohibition Act expressed the exploding tensions of social class in America, inflected, as always, by ethnicity and race. One congressman, the democrat Richmond Pearson Hobson, thundered that 'liquor will actually make a brute out of a Negro, causing him to commit unnatural crimes' (quoted in Goode and Nachman 1994: 15). Before 1900, the temperance movement was humanitarian in tone, aimed at helping the poor and treating alcoholics. After 1900, however, pity for drinkers ended, replaced by self-righteous wrath, indignation and demands for coercive reform. Drinkers were no longer to be saved but punished. The WCTU declared temperance a 'patriotic duty'; the liquor traffic, they said, was 'un-American' (Goode and Nachman 1994). The more it intensified, the more the moral crusade underlying Prohibition pitted the lifestyle of sober small-town native-born WASP Americans – white-collar workers and farmers – against immigrants who were urban, Catholic, and working class. Youngstown, the heart of the American steel industry, illustrates this point extremely well (Linkon and Russo 2002: 26).

Between 1900 and the First World War, Youngstown grew from 45,000 to 132,000 residents, about a quarter of whom were foreign-born. More than half of the city's steel workers were in this category, the earliest having come from Germany, Wales and Ireland, followed by waves from Italy, Czechoslovakia, Hungary, Lithuania, Poland and the Ukraine. Predominantly male and unmarried, they lived in crowded and jerry-built structures near the mills, within walking distance of their long and arduous shifts. Small taverns, nestled along roads near the factory gates, beckoned the tired men on their way home; here they could socialize, drink and bet on numbers in a game called 'bug' or, for higher stakes, fast-roll dice in the famed Greek-Turkish game of 'barbut' (Callen 1984). In 1916, knowing that wartime orders were flowing in, these workers struck for higher pay. The mill owners brought in strike-breakers, many of them blacks from the South. This provocation led to some violence, but local histories also emphasize another source of tension: the strikers were 'sometimes drunk', so much so that the owners feared to close the saloons, lest the mood become 'uglier' (Galida 1976: 10). One account of the workers' takeover of the mill offices at Campbell Works of Youngstown Sheet and Tube, where they set fire to the records, describes them 'breaking into nearby saloons [where they] drank whatever they found, and once filled with drink, the attempt was to burn everything in sight' (1976: 10). Prohibition, coming just three years later, was clearly seen to be a measure of labour discipline (and encouraging to capitalist consumption, too; what men did not spend on drink, women would have to buy things for their families and homes).

Prohibition, together with anti-gambling legislation, constituted an explosive opportunity for organized crime in Youngstown, which was allowed to control the forbidden practices, under terms that were favorable to local politicians. The Sicilian and Neapolitan crime families, in particular, scaled up and flourished, undoubtedly because of the technologies and organizational know-how at their command. As they did so, they became, in a way, mediators of the class relations of American capitalism – not unlike the way mafiosi in Sicily mediated the development of agrarian capitalism. In the United States, too, this mediation evolved into a political role as municipal governments became more 'democratic'.

The democratization of Youngstown began in the 1930s, during the Roosevelt administration. Labour unions gained increased legitimacy and legal standing in this period while companies became more involved in the amelioration of workers' lives. Like many other firms of that period, the steel barons indulged in 'welfare capitalism' in an attempt to mitigate the growing power of the unions (Linkon and Russo 2002). Thus Campbell and other mill owners built (small and racially segregated) row houses for their employees; invested in land development companies which also built houses billed for 'desirable families'; and expressed a new-found paternalism through the sponsorship of amusement parks, sports teams and company stores. Constituting the core of the Republican establishment of the city, they also watched with relative calm as the Democratic Party took over City Hall by appealing to an increasingly enfranchised immigrant working class.

Because its history had landed it in the position of mediating class relations, the American mafia, like the mafia in Sicily, was in a position to deliver working-class votes not only to the Democrats, but to particular candidates among them. Indeed, from the 1920s on, a dialectic unfolded in United States industrial cities between corrupt political 'machines', well-oiled by organized crime figures rounding up immigrant workers' votes, and middle class, often nativist movements for reform. Significantly, the industry owners and managers tolerated the political machines as an alternative to the threatening labour militancy exemplified by Youngstown's steel strike in 1916. We believe this is why, as in Sicily, until the 1980s, American organized crime enjoyed a surprising degree of immunity from prosecution.

THE SACK OF TWO CITIES: MODERNISM IN THE 1960s

Palermo was damaged by its rush into modernism after the Second World War. Sadly distorted because unregulated and undercapitalized, and further warped by the aggressive involvement of mafiosi in real estate speculation and construction, the modernist transformation of the 1950s through the mid-1980s is now referred to as the *scempio* or 'sack' of the city. The years 1957 to 1963 were the high point in private construction, followed in the 1970s and 1980s by a greater emphasis on public works (Chubb 1982: 132, 150–1). Overall, the rhythm reflected the rapid urbanization of Sicily after the Second World War, as a land reform and resultant mechanization of agriculture created a massive peasant exodus, and as rural landlords – owners of vast *latifundia* – moved their investments into urban real estate. In the same period, an expanding national welfare state made cities attractive as a locus of public employment. Palermo, which in 1946 became the capital of the newly autonomous Region of Sicily, grew from a population of 503,000 in 1951 to 709,000 in 1981, an increase of 41 percent. Although an urban plan, mandated by the Regional Government, was developed in 1962, it did not deter the unregulated building projects of large and small investors who hoped to profit from the resulting demand for housing.

Uniquely unhappy events further distorted the postwar construction boom. Bombed by the Allied forces in 1943, the city's historic centre was then abandoned by the authorities. More severely damaged than any other southern Italian city, 70,000 rooms were lost, leaving nearly 150,000 people condemned to live in crowded slums, shantytowns and even caves (Chubb 1982: 129). Opulent palazzi were severely affected, so much so that their noble owners, rattled by the pending land reform, abandoned them to roof leaks and water damage. Vandals removed architectural embellishments from their empty carcasses – statues, columns, fountains, even the plumbing. Bombing raids also affected popular neighborhoods of the historic centre where precarious buildings, at risk of collapse, were either demolished or stabilized by a dense crisscrossing of long wooden beams. Meanwhile, vibrant informal uses of space proliferated. Immigrants from Africa and Asia moved into the condemned buildings; cloisters and courtyards were turned into parking lots, depots for construction materials and stolen goods, or artisans' noisy workshops; and empty quarters of all kinds lent themselves to prostitution and the retail sale of drugs.

More serious than the destruction was the political decision to turn away from restoration in favour of building a 'new Palermo', at first concentrated at the northern end, beyond an Art Nouveau neighbourhood of nineteenth-century expansion, then in other peripheral zones to the west and south. Here the built environment spread over and, in irregular patches, obliterated orchards, villas and hamlets. Aristocratic landowners were, apparently, as eager to sell their orchards as to sell their *latifundia* and this fact accelerated the cementification of what was formerly green. At the same time, the automobile, multiplying in tandem with the suburban population, turned once-sleepy village streets into quagmires of congestion.

Nor was this the worst of the 'sack' or *scempio*. The thinking of the time was that if the buildings in the historic centre continued to succumb to neglect and disasters, so be it: eventually they could be leveled to create space for a thoroughly modern, New York-inspired downtown. City investments in outlying public housing and infrastructure, including a multiple-lane ring-road, enticed private housing developers to the outskirts – often in advance of the promised lines for gas and water, electricity and transportation and the provisioning of services like schools (Chubb 1982: 151–6). In 1968, an earthquake in the Belice Valley south of Palermo shook the old centre again. Subsequent decisions replicated the established pattern: the city would cover more orchards with tracts of public housing and relocate city-centre residents rather than attempt to repair their compromised buildings. Numbering 125,000 in 1951, the population of the historic centre fell to fewer than 40,000 over the next 30 years (Cole 1997: 30). Hence peripheral Palermo's vast expanses of multi-storey condominium and rental slabs, laid out in block after monotonous block, distinguished from their eastern European equivalents mainly by the profusion of cacti and geraniums that overflow the balconies. Today the slabs seem shabby, both for their flaking and chipped cement surfaces and because a heavy reliance on iron rods and railings for support and decoration has produced, over the years, the stains of spreading rust.

Some blame the *scempio* partly on 'the times', recollecting from personal experience how attractive modernism had seemed. Given Palermo's pattern of postwar growth, a large proportion of the consumers of new housing were formerly rural people encouraged by the land reform, or by work stints in northern Europe, to dream of escaping from 'backwardness' – to imagine becoming, in their terms, *evoluto* or modern. Easy credit, commingled with migrants' remittances, facilitated their project. For employees of the Regional Government, low-cost loans were a standard benefit (Chubb 1982: 129). In such an atmosphere, even native Palermitans got the idea that anything old was unworthy, unless perhaps it was *really* old, with the patina of antiquity. When, in 1960, Palermo's one and only 'skyscraper' was completed, these modernists raced with excitement to see its crowning red light go on for the very first time. In retrospect, they confess, Prague would have been a better model than New York.

But blaming what happened on the power of style – on the desire to be modern – only takes us so far. Narratives of the construction boom are far more likely to point to the corrupt *intreccio* or 'tangle' between political, economic and mafia interests. Christian Democratic politicians owed their success in local and regional elections to votes that were mobilized by mafiosi, particularly those who had their roots in the zones of urban expansion. Formerly agriculturalists, mafiosi in these zones flooded into activities associated with construction – hauling materials, pouring cement, speculating on land, building apartments for family, friends and profit. Their role and the role of the politicians in the mutilation of Palermo in its postwar development cannot be overstated.

The construction industry and the industries supplying construction materials together account for a greatly disproportionate share of the Palermo economy – 33 percent of the industrial work force in the 1970s compared with 10 percent in Milan. Made up of myriad firms employing between 25 and 30 workers or less, this sector also provided the city's 'major source of wealth', the more so as national government moneys became available for public housing (Chubb 1982: 131). As late as 1999, a glossy brochure put out by City Hall to attract investment capital indicated that 48.2 percent of the 14,201 firms registered with the Palermo Chamber of Commerce were in the construction sector, more than all other forms of manufacturing activity combined.

Also to the point is the almost predictable 'organic permeability' of this industry to organized crime. Consisting of numerous branches (commercial, highway, industrial, pipelines, housing, monuments); divided between public works and private projects; and employing a broad mix of skilled and unskilled workers, it is perhaps best characterized as an economic sector rather than an industry as such (Kelly 1999: 76–7).

In this sector, heavily capitalized construction firms – American, Italian, Saudi Arabian, German, Japanese, to name a few – bid on contracts the world over. By the same token, construction components are increasingly modular; transportable from place to place (see Linder 1994). And yet, by its very nature, the building business is grounded – dependent for profit and promise on local contractors and subcontractors, on local materials, and on the local and regional administration of laws governing transportation, public housing, zoning, contract bidding, taxation, credit and finance. This, plus the dependence of the industry on local labour, or labour that has immigrated into the area, constitutes a rich terrain for mediating clientelist relationships – for industry representatives and friends to deliver the votes of construction workers and suppliers to compliant municipal and regional politicians, in turn prepared to look the other way when the 'maze of regulations' is violated. In many places, the story of the expansion of organized crime in recent decades, and of the very recent attempts to suppress it, is also a story of municipal authorities transforming the built environment.

YOUNGSTOWN, TOO?

Youngstown (with a population of 168,000 at the end of the Second World War) is a case in point. Not a victim of wartime bombing, or of earthquakes, its suffering was clearly not on the scale of Palermo's. And Youngstown's postwar suburban development was propelled by the laying down of single family homes, replete with front and back yards, rather than high-rise apartment buildings. Many urbanists would argue, however, that American-style suburbanization was from the outset hugely distorted by the influence of the manufacturing, real estate and automobile lobbies on public policy (see Hayden 1997). Growing Cold War hysteria, crystallized by Senator McCarthy, also had its impact on postwar urban growth. The National Association of Real Estate Boards (which dated to the 1920s), together with ideologically anti-communist developers like Leavitt, encouraged the production of prefabricated houses in factories with non-union labour to the disadvantage of unions in the construction trades. (McCarthy, himself, attacked public housing as communist; see Hayden 1997). At the same time, the rapidly increasing production of low-cost houses articulated with a rising demand. Parallel to the peasants who left the rural towns for Palermo (and abroad) in the 1950s and 1960s, at the first opportunity American workers fled the shadows of the noisy and polluting factories for the clean air and quiet of the suburbs.

The impetus for the peasant migrants was the land reform and the introduction of mechanical harvesters and threshers into agriculture. For industrial workers in America, it was the automobile. The Fordist foundation of these transformations is critical in both cases. Cheap, accessible machinery enabled the lower classes of society to move ahead. In both cases, too, they moved along roads that were the creation of government policy and investment. Palermo's ring-road, mentioned above, was matched, in Youngstown, by highway construction coupled with urban renewal projects that, in the 1960s, displaced immense tracts of downtown housing with public buildings and expressways designed for rapid access to the suburbs. The resulting resettlement increased the racial, ethnic and class segregation of the local residents at the same time as it initiated a decline in the population and tax base of the city proper (Linkon and Russo 2002: 26, 43–5).

In Youngstown, as in many other American cities and in Palermo, housing was built, often speculatively, ahead of infrastructure like sewage treatment facilities. It was built in a hurry, many corners cut, in a monotonous, cookie-cutter architecture that would not encourage reinvestment. Most important, it was built with the expectation that government, local as well as national, would absorb a great deal of the cost. As Palermo's postwar history also suggests, a city like Youngstown with a well-established organized crime tradition was likely to witness mafiosi penetrating and manipulating the resulting boom to their advantage. Their strategic role in the political machinery of local government put them in touch with officials responsible for licensing, zoning and public works. Real estate and construction entrepreneurs were eager to befriend them. And because they had, to the ready, capital accumulated from racketeering – although the highly lucrative bootleg liquor business ended with the repeal of Prohibition in 1933, gambling operations already netted some $8 million annually by the 1940s (Callen 1984) – they were quick to invest, themselves, in these incredible growth sectors. They were, thereby, among the important players in the transformation of the built environment, for better or for worse.

Assessing the 'for worse' part of this equation, it would be misleading to focus only on the architectural tragedy of the 'sack': the neglect and decay of historic structures, and the over-investment in unworkable and aesthetically compromised suburbs, are features of urbanism throughout the world, whether organized crime is involved or not. Yet the presence of an organized crime tradition exaggerated these tendencies, almost to the exclusion of other, countervailing possibilities, exposing cities like Youngstown and Palermo to their violence in a particularly acute way. In addition, another kind of violence, against people, marred the development process. Not only Palermo, but Youngstown as well, produced rates of murder and attacks on property through gasoline bombs and other forms of arson (sometimes staged to appear to cover a burglary) that was off the charts in the late 1950s and early 1960s, as rival mafia factions warred for territorial control of gambling and extortion, and for a foothold in the vast new construction linked to urban/suburban expansion (Callen 1984; Linkon and Russo 2002).

THE LONG 1980s

During what we for convenience call the 'long 1980s' (roughly 1978 to 1992), Palermo became a major hub in the global heroin trade. Clandestine refineries were situated in the region (Pezzino 1995: 300–1), and over the next few years, 4–5 tons of pure heroin were produced each year in Sicily, worth $600 million in annual profits and meeting roughly 30 percent of United States demand (Paoli 1997: 317–18).

Already in the 1960s mafiosi had confronted one another violently over the control of urban territory; but now conflict intensified.

Contestations for new urban opportunities and drugs led to the insurgence, between 1979 and 1983, of a particularly aggressive group of mafiosi known as the Corleonesi (because they were originally from the interior town of Corleone). Feeling excluded from Palermo's postwar real estate and construction boom, which mafia *cosche* (sing. *cosca*, the tightly bound head of an artichoke, i.e. a group) in the city's environs had pounced on, and apprehensive about being disrespected as junior partners in drug deals, also initially dominated by the Palermo 'families', they launched a series of kidnappings for ransom, committed without the approval of the Palermo groups and against the mafia's own rules. Not only were the targets of these kidnappings rich men, several were construction impresarios closely allied to the Palermo bosses.

The Corleonesi assassinated a succession of these bosses during their *scalata* or rise to power and, more audaciously, 15 police officers, magistrates and public officials. They organized the savage bombings that killed two of the most important anti-mafia prosecutors, Giovanni Falcone and Paolo Borsellino, in 1992. Two bomb blasts intended to destroy artistic monuments, one in Rome and the other in Florence, are attributed to them, as are bombings in Milan. The anti-mafia movement and police–judicial repression of the 1980s and 1990s developed in response to the Corleonese aggression (see Arlacchi 1994; Brusca in Lodato 1999; Calderone in Arlacchi 1993; Lupo 1993; Paoli 2000; Pezzino 1995; Santino 1989; Stille 1995).

The golden age of narco-trafficking did not last long for Sicilian mafiosi. Both the anti-mafia operations of the mid-1980s, the growing popularity and availability of Andean cocaine, and the global trend toward processing drugs closer to their point of production, relegated them to a minor and less lucrative role. Nevertheless, the moment of accumulation enabled the Corleonesi to capitalize several new construction firms, broaching their postwar ambition of directing the construction sector of the Palermo, and regional, economy. More seriously, according to DIA (Direzione Italiana Antimafia) evidence, public works became a privileged locus for reinvesting drug profits, the goal being 'complete control and the substantial internal conditioning of the entrepreneurial world' in this sector (DIA, quoted in Paoli 1997: 319).

In the past, each mafia *cosca* had been free to impose kickbacks on contractors working within its territory, but now the Corleonesi sought exclusive claims over these relations regardless of place, engaging Angelo Siino, a wealthy businessman, as coordinator. Siino (described in the press as the mafia's 'Minister of Public Works') articulated the bosses with local coalitions of businessmen, politicians and public officials whose hands were on the system of parcelling out bids at auction. Classically, the *cosca* of the territory where the work was being done received 2–3 percent and was permitted to determine the subcontractors, the suppliers and the temporary workforce – if necessary backing its requests with letters of extortion or menacing fires. By 'piloting' which companies would win the contracts, in what order, and under what terms, Siino spread the rewards as even-handedly as possible, enhancing the mafia's reputation for 'taking care of its people' (Paoli 1997: 320–1).

Youngstown also had a 'long 1980s', although for different reasons and with different consequences. For this Midwestern steel town, the crisis decade was launched between 1977 and 1979 by the steel mill closings, ordered in spite of a protracted labour and citizens' struggle to keep them open. Mill owners claimed the necessity to disinvest on the grounds that rising labour costs made American steel ever less competitive with German and Japanese manufacturers. While union leaders railed against the owners' failure to invest a portion of their substantial profits in order to upgrade their mills with postwar technology, thousands of jobs were lost and thousands of citizens emigrated, not only to the suburbs, but also to more distant places. Every decade after 1960, the census registered a drop of more than 15 percent for Youngstown. Only 82,000 people lived there in 2000 – half the immediate postwar population of 168,000 (Linkon and Russo 2002: 26). The population of Mahoning County, home to other, smaller steel towns, declined from 300,000 to 260,000. What had once been the heart of the economy of the region ceased beating (Bruno 1999; Lynd 1982).

In the 1960s, the warring factions of the Youngstown mafia – basically two grand coalitions, one oriented toward Pittsburgh and New York, the other towards Cleveland, Chicago and New Orleans – reached a truce which lasted until 1977. During this brief respite, neither faction had the mayor or the police chief or the captain of the vice squad in its pocket. But shortly after the truce was broken in 1977, the Pittsburgh-oriented faction got a newly elected mayor to install the police chief of its choice and to let the Democratic majority on the city council know of their 'definite interest in who was appointed city finance director' (Lynd 1982: 11). Meanwhile, the car of a councilman, parked in front of his house, was firebombed as a warning that he desist from responding to constituent complaints about prostitution in his ward. In the Democratic primary for mayor in 1980, a reform candidate withdrew, intimidated by demands that he negotiate the naming of the police chief, and by the vice squad's continued tolerance for illegal activities including drug sales. The winner of the primary and then of the election bent to the demands. A grand jury concluded that 'crime of the stature [with] which we are presently confronted could not have developed without the total indifference, acquiescence or direct permissive assistance of some politicians and law enforcement officials ...' (quoted in Callen 1984: 6).

A similar pattern of corruption pervaded the county level, where both factions not only worked to secure the tenure of friendly sheriffs and prosecutors, but also bribed them handsomely to guarantee the continued operation of illegal gambling and prostitution. It was, indeed, the exposure of egregious payoffs of $163,000 from the Cleveland group and $60,000 from the Pittsburgh group to Sheriff James A. Traficant in 1982 that galvanized the founding of the reform-minded Youngstown Citizens' League (Callen 1984: 15).

Complaining Youngstown citizens found the regional office of the FBI too busy or uninterested to hear them out. Their most corrupt police chief was, in fact, a former FBI official, adding to their sense of 'isolation and helplessness, not knowing whom to turn to for help or whom to trust' (Callen 1984: 32). Even the Youngstown fire chief, Charles O'Nesti, was implicated. In 1984, County Sheriff Traficant, his receipt of bribes notwithstanding, was elected to the United States House of Representatives, only to be indicted (in 2001) and convicted (in 2002) in Federal Court on ten counts involving racketeering and other violations. O'Nesti, who later served as Representative Traficant's chief of staff, was an associate (bag man) of confessed mafioso Lenine 'Lenny' Strollo.

Youngstown's interwoven organized crime and political corruption was solidly in place as the city confronted the exodus of the steel industry. A telling set of municipal and regional decisions, influenced by this nexus, pointed toward more building as a way to staunch decline. Even before the hulks of the old mills sat rusting (one has been dismantled), two local developers, both alleged to be descendants of racketeering families, the De Bartolos and the Cafaros, had built shopping malls beyond the older suburbs, in opposite directions from the city centre, with a minor league ballpark strategically located near one of them. (Both families became major mall developers on a national scale.) Youngstown has also hosted the construction of an immense storage facility for one of America's big box chains and hopes to court more facilities of this kind. Perhaps most egregiously – but not uniquely, this being a 'development strategy' pursued by many dying communities in America – local construction workers found employment putting up three prisons, where many former steelworkers hoped to find work (Linkon and Russo 2002: 227–37).

The 'long 1980s' crisis of disinvestment produced in Youngstown, as in all of America's rust belt, conditions of community break-up and the replacement of decent industrial careers with demoralizing, low-wage and part-time jobs, or simply no jobs at all. All of the paternalistic amenities of the past – museums, theatres, the amusement park – are suffering. The amusement park, indeed, has been closed. Coming on top of the dislocations of the postwar decades, and exacerbated by racial tensions, a terrain was created for the expansion of a narcotics economy. Despite the local presence of organized crime groups, however, the city came nowhere near Palermo's status as the world centre of heroin trafficking. Drugs procured through the mafias of much larger and more important centres – Cleveland, Pittsburgh, Chicago, New York – were locally distributed, not trans-shipped; local traffickers were relative small potatoes. The collapse of the truce between factions in 1977 led to eight gangland murders and two disappearances, but for most of the 'long 1980s', Youngstown escaped the internecine struggles to control narcotics that so bloodied Palermo's streets and image. The most serious drug-related incident was the attempted murder, in 2000, of county prosecutor-elect Paul Gains, allegedly because organized crime leaders feared that he would not be so tolerant of drug trafficking as his predecessor.

Nevertheless, Youngstown continued to suffer violence to its built environment. Through the 1990s, and indeed up to the present, local political leaders seem to believe that whatever the future may bring, the livelihoods of all, rich and poor, hinge upon continued speculative building. If one owns, or can acquire, property on which something is planned to happen, so much the better. Many are suspicious that their leaders, and certain leading organized crime figures, have personally benefited from the zoning, licensing and contracting decisions – and the locational decisions for government offices – of the last two decades. Why else, it is asked, would they be found in attendance at the 'Cafaro Roundtable' – a regular gathering of business and political elites at Anthony's on the River, a downtown restaurant, from which the press and public are excluded?

In the 1960s, an elder of the Cafaro family began the Roundtable as a weekly opportunity for friends and business associates to socialize; subsequently his son, Anthony, turned it into a monthly event, inviting a wider range of guests. Late in the summer of 2001, a member of the Citizens' League – which had long been concerned with bringing Youngstown's 'culture of deal-making' to public attention – positioned himself near the meeting place with binoculars. As their press release of 20 August explained:

The practice of secretive, brokered politics, in which a few wealthy, powerful individuals control stables of politicians and public officials, is part of a culture and value system where the line between lawfulness and illegality has been dangerously blurred, if not obliterated altogether.

The result is a 'shadow government', fraught with the 'appearance of impropriety, and the potential for undue influence and conflicts of interest', where the 'recipients or potential recipients of government contracts and money … leases and other financial dealings with the local government' find a home. It matters, their communiqué continued, that J.J. Cafaro, Anthony's brother, has been convicted on federal charges of attempting to bribe Traficant, and that he, too, is a host (Citizens' League 2001).

The observer was spotted by the mayor who was one of the invited guests. His objections and the publicity surrounding the incident provoked a wider than usual attendance at the September meeting. As reported by the *Youngstown Vindicator* (the not-very-critical local newspaper, on 9 September 2001), the guest list included the chief operating officer of the Cleveland Browns football team, there because 'Anthony [is] a great guy'; the archbishop of the Youngstown diocese, who came 'to lend support to the family and find out what all the hoopla is about'; and a Republican Party county chair who 'believes the community is lucky to have Tony Cafaro. He's very public-minded, public-spirited.'

In Youngstown, as in Palermo, speculative building has been accompanied by speculative destruction of the built environment. Historic buildings – the city has a substantial heritage of Victorian homes and elaborately decorated downtown buildings dating to its past as a steel barons' centre – are particularly vulnerable. Most dramatic was a rash of polyfunctional arsons in the central city, about two a day during much of the 1980s (Linkon and Russo 2002: 51). Houses that were not marketable after the exodus could be burned so that their owners might at least collect insurance compensation. Houses or commercial buildings that were scheduled for demolition because they were abandoned, unsightly or dangerous, were burned to facilitate the job of the demolition firms that had contracted the work. Anticipating the fire, hired scarfers removed copper fixtures and other valuable elements from the target house. Arsonists then hung a plastic sack filled with gasoline from the ceiling on the ground floor, set a number of small fires and left. The massive detonation of the gasoline bag would rapidly and effectively destroy the structure (not without putting firemen at grave risk if they had entered the burning building before the explosion occurred). Ultimately, the designated demolition firm carted off the debris without having to suffer the expense of conforming to local building codes and rules for environmental safety (Linkon and Russo 2002: 222–7).

As Linkon and Russo point out:

while no clear evidence exists to link Youngstown's arson epidemic to the mob, many firefighters and community members believed that arson, and the demolition and insurance fraud that often came after a house was burned down, involved collusion between members of the fire department, organized crime, and public officials. (2002: 225)

The fire chief during the period of peak arson activity was the above-noted Charles O'Nesti. To the regret of activist citizens, a number of landmark houses went up in smoke.

CONCLUSION

This brings us back to the delegation attending the United Nations Convention on Transnational Organized Crime in Palermo. Inheritors, in part, of the Ecumenical Coalition of labour and church leaders mobilized to fight the closing of the mills in the 1970s, they also represented the Youngstown Citizens' League, an organization with 200 members which had become more active since the shooting of Paul Gains. Indeed, the League took the courageous step of exposing the Cafaro Roundtable, as we have seen. Much like the anti-mafia movement in Palermo, these citizens are responding to a synergy between organized crime and political corruption which damages urban life even beyond the damage that results from the great swings of capitalism – the cycles of unplanned hyper-investment and abrupt disinvestment, the roller-coaster of boom and bust. As citizens of both movements emphasize, the crime and corruption nexus weakens a city's possibility for responding intelligently to these swings. And it introduces another element: the violent menace to people and patrimony alike.

REFERENCES

Arlacchi, P. (1993) *Men of Dishonor: Inside the Sicilian Mafia* (New York: William Morrow).

—— (1994) *Addio Cosa Nostra: La Vita di Tommaso Buscetta* (Milan: Rizzoli).

Brancato, F. (1977) Dall'Unità ai Fasci dei Lavoratori, in R. Romeo (ed.) *Storia della Sicilia*, Vol. 8, pp. 85–173 (Palermo: Società Editrice Storia di Napoli e della Sicilia).

Bruno, R. (1999) *Steelworker Alley: How Class Works in Youngstown* (Ithaca, NY: Cornell University Press).

Callen, J.B. (1984) Statement before the US Senate Permanent Subcommittee on Investigations, Hearings on Profile of Organized Crime: Great Lakes Region, unpublished document, 26 January.

Citizens' League (2001) Citizens' League of Greater Youngstown Calls for an End to the Participation of Public Officials in the 'Cafaro Roundtable', unpublished document, 20 August.

Chubb, J. (1982) *Patronage, Power, and Poverty in Southern Italy: A Tale of Two Cities* (Cambridge, MA: MIT Press).

Cole, J. (1997) *The New Racism in Europe: A Sicilian Ethnography* (Cambridge: Cambridge University Press).

Galida, F. (1976) *Fascinating History of the City of Campbell* (State College, PA: Josten's American Yearbook Co.).

Ginsborg, P. (1990) *A History of Contemporary Italy: Society and Politics, 1943–1988* (London: Penguin Books).

Goode, E. and B.Y. Nachman (1994) *Moral Panics: The Social Construction of Deviance* (Malden, MA: Blackwell).

Hayden, D. (1997) *The Power of Place: Urban Landscape as Public History* (Cambridge, MA: MIT Press, original 1995).

Johansen, B. (2002) La Corruption: un délit contre l'ordre social, *Annales: Histoire, Sciences Sociales*, No. 6 (nov–déc): 1561–89.

Kelly, R.J. (1999) *The Upperworld and the Underworld: Case Studies of Racketeering and Business Infiltrations in the United States* (New York: Kluwer Academic/ Plenum Publishers).

Ledeneva, A.V. (1998) *Russia's Economy of Favors: Blat, Networking and Informal Exchange* (Cambridge: Cambridge University Press).

Linder, M. (1994) *Projecting Capitalism: A History of the Internationalization of the Construction Industry* (Westport, CT: Greenwood Press).

Linkon, S.L. and J. Russo (2002) *Steeltown USA: Work and Memory in Youngstown* (Lawrence, KA: University Press of Kansas).

Lodato, S. (1999) *'Ho Ucciso Giovanni Falcone': La Confessione di Giovanni Brusca* (Milano: Mondadori).

Lupo, S. (1990) Tra Banca e Politica: Il Delitto Notarbartolo, *Meridiana; Rivista di Storia e Scienze Sociali*, Vol. 7–8: 119–56.

—— (1993) *Storia della Mafia; dalle Origini ai Giorni Nostri* (Rome: Donzelli Editore).

—— (1997) The Allies and the Mafia, *Journal of Modern Italian Studies*, Vol. 2: 21–33.

Lynd, S. (1982) *The Fight against Shutdowns: Youngstown's Steel Mill Closings* (San Pedro, CA: Singlejack Books).

Mangiameli, R. (1994) Saggio Introduttivo, in Foreign Office (ed.) *Sicily Zone Handbook 1943*, pp. V–LXXXIV (Caltanissetta-Roma: Salvatore Sciascia Editore).

McCarthy, P. (1995) *The Crisis of the Italian State: From the Origins of the Cold War to the Fall of Berlusconi and Beyond* (New York: St Martins Press).

Paoli, L. (1997) The Pledge to Secrecy: Culture, Structure and Action of Mafia Associations. PhD Dissertation, European University Institute, Florence.

—— (2000) *Fratelli di Mafia: Cosa Nostra e 'Ndrangheta*. (Bologna: Il Mulino).

Pezzino, P. (ed.) (1995) *Mafia: Industria della Violenza. Scritti e Documenti Inediti Sulla Mafia dalle Origini ai Giorni Nostri* (Florence: La Nuova Italia).

Renda, F. (1987) *Storia della Sicilia dal 1860 al 1970.* 2nd edn, Vol. I (Palermo: Sellerio Editore).

Riall, L. (1998) *Sicily and the Unification of Italy: Liberal Policy and Local Power, 1859–1866* (Oxford: Clarendon Press).

Rossetti, C. (1994) *L'Attacco allo Stato di Diritto: Le Associazioni Segrete e la Costituzione* (Napoli: Liguori Editore).

Santino, U. (1997) *La Democrazia Bloccata: La Strage di Portella della Ginestra e L'emarginazione delle Sinistre* (Soveria Mannelli, Italy: Rubbettino Editore).

Schneider, J. and P. Schneider (1999) Is Transparency Possible? The Political-economic and Epistemological Implications of Cold War Conspiracies and Subterfuge in Italy, in J.McC. Heyman (ed.) *States and Illegal Practices*, pp. 169–99 (Oxford/New York: Berg).

Smart, A. (1999) States and Illegal Practices: An Overview, in J.McC. Heyman (ed.) *States and Illegal Practices*, pp. 1–24 (Oxford/New York: Berg).

Stille, A. (1995) *Excellent Cadavers: the Mafia and the Death of the First Italian Republic* (New York: Vintage Books).

3   BRIBES, GIFTS AND UNOFFICIAL PAYMENTS: RETHINKING CORRUPTION IN POST-SOVIET RUSSIAN HEALTH CARE

Michele Rivkin-Fish

During fieldwork in St Petersburg in the summer of 1998, I asked a friend of mine named Valya about her strategies for accessing competent, reliable health care.[1] Valya was 30 years old and spending considerable time and effort undergoing gynaecological procedures in the hopes of eventually becoming pregnant. Socially and economically, she occupied an interesting place in the emerging fabric of post-Soviet Russian society: she had been raised in modest conditions in a provincial town four hours from Leningrad, with parents who were both engineers, and had completed two degrees of higher education. In 1994, when I first met her, she and her husband had just started what soon became a highly successful business in the import sector. Having grown up with no special privileges besides those obtained through cultural forms of capital associated with higher education, by the late 1990s, Valya had access to money, and quite a bit of it. So my questions regarding her strategies of accessing health care immediately opened our discussion to issues of how the social changes of the last decade, in particular, market reforms, were being inscribed in her daily life, and how she was interpreting and improvising with these forces in seeking health care. The first thing Valya explained was that her treatment in a well-respected clinic was arranged by her long-term friend, Nina, who had recently begun practising medicine. Some of the procedures Valya needed were being undertaken by Nina herself, while other, more complicated ones were being referred to one of Nina's more experienced colleagues, Vladimir Sergeevich. I then asked Valya if she was paying for the treatments, and if so, how. She explained that Nina had arranged an agreement with Vladimir Sergeevich for Valya to pay him $150 and a few bottles of vodka. The payment would go to Vladimir Sergeevich personally and would not go through the hospital administration. I then asked Valya a question that turned out to raise a set of issues that provided many insights into the ways money was coming to inform ideological changes in the aftermath of the socialist era. 'How did you feel about making these payments for health care? Do you think it's right for doctors to take money for services?' My questions alluded to the fact that paying physicians for medical care had been illegal during the Soviet period; a doctor who demanded money was viewed as engaging in the worst form of corruption imaginable – selfishly withholding humanitarian assistance unless he was compensated by personal, material gain. This entailed a betrayal not only of Soviet laws, but of the Hippocratic oath and its universal ethics of professional and human morality. Yet when I asked Valya if she considered it appropriate to pay her doctor, she answered immediately and without ambivalence: 'Oh, definitely,' she asserted. 'We have to get over that Soviet nonsense that people should work for free. I feel that I *should* pay, I have the money, and so it's right that I pay for their professionalism and time.'

With this comment, Valya made the use of money significant symbolically. She defined paying for health care as a moral action that conveyed recognition and respect for the professional's attention and expertise. Moreover, she equated a personal obligation to pay for services with the process of transcending Soviet-era values and modes of interrelating. Yet when Nina suggested that Valya pay Vladimir Sergeevich '$150 and a few bottles of vodka', Valya sent the informal payment to the doctor through her friend as an intermediary. Nonetheless, both Valya and Nina considered this informal presentation distinct from earlier, Soviet-style informal exchanges: no longer an illicit act of 'bribery', it was now considered a 'payment', a proper and ethical compensation for a patient to offer. In Valya's understanding, paying for health care raised her integrity as a recipient of care, for by paying money, she was paying respect – both to her doctor and to herself. Acquiring new ways of relating to money and relating to people, she implied, are central developments for the creation of a post-socialist society.

Still, the unofficial way in which Valya accessed and paid for her services suggests that the ethics of such health care relations and payments are rather paradoxical: why was it necessary to go through an acquaintance, if official channels of accessing special levels of care were being established; why did Valya not wish to pay through official channels, at a cashier, where her payment would be direct and where she would get a receipt, and, most interestingly, why was it not ethically problematic to pay the doctor personally? In this chapter, I begin by exploring why familiar strategies such as mobilizing acquaintance relations are being combined with new practices, such as paying for services unofficially. I then examine how patients and providers distinguish these monetary exchanges from earlier, illicit exchanges considered to be 'bribes'. A new category has emerged to describe this relationship between a doctor and patient – *lichnyi vrach* – a personal doctor. The concept of *lichnyi vrach* implies that a personal agreement has superseded the official, institutional framework of state health care, that the doctor and patient share a degree of trust, and that the patient most likely pays the doctor personally and monetarily (unless he or she is a very close friend). I claim that such unofficial relations and payments should not be dismissed summarily as the incorrigible persistence of Russian 'corruption', as proof of the inability of Russians to comply with the disciplines of private enterprise and the democratic 'rule of law'. Rather, these unofficial practices make sense as *ethical* forms of interaction within the broader context of institutional changes taking place in the post-Soviet era. As patients seek out informal relations such as the *lichnyi vrach*, they strive to obtain competent and professional treatment and also demonstrate their respect and gratitude for providers' time and effort. The official framework of fee-for-service health care, however, is perceived to reflect the continuing injustice of Russian bureaucratic institutions – the 'genuine' source of corruption, where only higher-ups, not the ordinary person or provider, will benefit. Where official channels of payment are viewed as ethically problematic and unjust, patients often view unofficial payments directly to their provider as constituting important, *moral* forms of exchange.

INSTITUTIONAL CONSTRAINTS, PERSONALIZED SOLUTIONS: A PATIENT'S PERSPECTIVE

Universal, free health care was a hallmark of the Soviet welfare system, but most women I met felt that the quality of care afforded by that system was severely compromised. Long queues and the need for a rapid rate of patient turnover meant that care was inconvenient and harried, and gave the clinic a factory-like atmosphere. Doctors were widely viewed as having neither the time nor energy to pay close attention to patients' concerns. Women described the care available through official channels as an experience of being on a 'conveyor', given standardized diagnoses and prescriptions rather than being closely examined and understood individually, and often being vulnerable to providers' 'indifference'. Speaking of the dental care provided to her children at schools, one woman explained that 'It's traumatic and they don't give good service at all – they must work so quickly, and they don't care about you.' Not incidentally, this woman was, herself, an obstetrician who worked for the state health system. As a consequence of these inadequacies, women with acquaintances in health care tried hard to arrange care through personal channels. This is not to say that patients asked their friends for recommendations of 'good doctors', in the way that Americans, for example, do. When American patients seek out the care of a recommended physician, they generally do so through formal channels, by calling the office and making an appointment. By contrast, Russians who counted physicians among their personal friends asked these doctors to treat them, their relatives, and other friends, as a personal favour. And patients without physician acquaintances sought out kin, neighbours, and acquaintances who did, with the same hopes in mind. Such a connection allowed people to bypass official channels of accessing health care where they would be just another anonymous patient.

From the late 1980s and early 1990s, the Russian state public health care system began to permit hospitals to charge for elective services such as abortions, and for non-medical aspects of care, such as private rooms for childbirth. In this way, the realm of health care reflected broader economic and social transformations in Russia at large. In 1991 price controls ended, inflation soared and, within a relatively short period of time, a massive influx of goods appeared in stores, albeit at prices very few Russians could afford. Basic medical needs, including pre-natal care and childbirth remained officially free, but clinics and hospitals now had the legal right to offer services with official price tags, too. Market reforms thus granted money a pragmatic importance it lacked during most of the Soviet era, when personal relationships were the most important currency for obtaining items in short supply or for ensuring bureaucratic efficiency. For women without acquaintances in health care, money opened up a new strategy for trying to access improved levels of care beyond the state system.

Yet fee-for-service payment was not established evenly throughout the health care system; not all services could be purchased, and not all providers were able to charge fees. I discuss these constraints further below. At present, it is important to recognize that even when money was given in exchange for services, it was not viewed as a perfect substitute for all other kinds of offerings, and did not entirely replace them. When I asked Valya why she gave the physician vodka in addition to the money, she explained that it was a gift, conveying a sense of gratitude and, I would add, obligation. In other words, the gift offered a way of diminishing the sense created by the exchange of money that the services he provided were indistinguishable from any other commodity exchange: the care and expertise he provided as a doctor were different and special, and she wanted to *thank* him, not only *pay* him for them. Thus, despite the emergence of market reforms and the growing importance of money in daily life, alternative forms of exchange, and informal modes of acknowledging and repaying debt, continue.

Additionally, while money had unquestionably become important in post-Soviet health care, many of those I interviewed stated that accessing paid forms of health care through official channels was not the most effective way of ensuring competent health care – and nor was it the most ethical way of conveying the payments. The best tactic, people said, was to continue the familiar strategy of accessing health care through personal acquaintances, while paying these acquaintances unofficially for their work. Again, the use of money did not simply substitute for the use of personal relations; a universal currency did not make the perceived need for acquaintances obsolete. Instead, money became integrated into pre-existing patterns of accessing health care through *un*official channels of personal relations. The establishment of official payments at a *kassa* (cashier) was considered a new and improved option over the socialist requirement that all health care would be free and equal – which was taken to mean it would be equally impoverished and equally bureaucratized for everyone. But services paid for officially and through official channels of payment would not necessarily surpass the level of care one could expect from acquaintances.

In discussing this preference for paying physicians unofficially even when official administrative procedures for collecting fees had been established, Russians explained that official payments would most likely be consumed by hospital administrators, with the actual caregiver receiving at best only a small portion of the payment. It was common knowledge that physicians' salaries remained very low, hovering at about $100 per month, while the costs of living a post-Soviet life had skyrocketed. And money was not merely a pragmatic necessity, either: having money had become an important marker of success and professional status. It was a symbolic means for conveying physicians' high standards, competence, and public recognition. But the newly established channels for payment would not, it seemed, fulfil such needs of the provider. They worked mainly to legitimate the exchange of money for health care in an abstract sense. The creation of official prices paved the way for the use of money to be symbolically transformed from a 'dirty' act that tainted the doctor's integrity, as it had been portrayed in Soviet times, to a 'normal', acceptable and even imperative kind of exchange. But because official channels of payment did not function effectively to provide the means for compensating the actual physicians who cared for a patient, Valya and others strove to ensure that the money would reach her doctor, and only her doctor, unofficially.

Day-to-day life thus involved both the struggle to fulfil one's needs satisfactorily and to maintain a sense of integrity, to 'do the right thing'. In seeking competent health care, Russians often expected to make payments. Paying unofficially could be considered ethical, morally clean and just, as long as it was given in an appropriate manner (see also Ledeneva 1998). Yet what was 'appropriate' had little to do with adhering to official institutional regulations or legal channels of payment. What had changed little since Soviet times was the view that institutions were still unaccountable to people's needs – either as workers or as recipients of services – and that fulfilling one's needs through the personal obligations of kinship and friendship continued to be an ethical means of action.

In this story of post-socialist change, my discussions with Valya offered insights into the perspective of the health care user. I find Valya's comment interesting because of the ways she connected a new ethics of payment with the transcendence of the Soviet era – through her everyday practices, she was enacting different values from those associated with the Soviet era, and making new distinctions. The need to make unofficial payments was no longer considered an illicit act, nor were professionals who accepted them regarded in a negative light as corrupt. It had been transformed into a positive act that represented her respect for the provider's efforts and expertise.[2] For Valya, what remained 'corrupt' and unethical was the overall system of health care, the new bureaucratic structures of compensation and, more generally, the laws, rules and procedures of the official, Russian state.[3]

To capture more fully the significance of the moral shifts that have emerged with new, unofficial forms of payment in health care, I turn now to the perspective of physicians. The changes that have occurred in their perspectives and practices reflect substantial reconsiderations of the obligations and rights of a professional, and of the boundaries between ethical exchange and exploitation.

INSTITUTIONAL CONSTRAINTS, PERSONAL RESPONSIBILITIES AND ENTITLEMENTS

It is important to recognize that physicians trained during the Soviet era, more than many educated groups in that regime, considered their professional occupation a calling. This view was inspired by a range of cultural discourses: romantic images in Chekhov stories that portrayed the doctor as a beneficent authority in the community; the legacy of generations of physicians in families; and by the seemingly non-political nature of the work: for those disaffected by Soviet ideology and its imperatives to incorporate political commitments in all aspects of one's life, medical expertise seemed to be a pure retreat to the objectivity of science and the humane work of relieving suffering. Physicians' sense of themselves as called to the healing profession is often forgotten in much of the scholarly literature on Russian health care, which has tended to describe the pervasive problem of 'bribery' (Cassileth et al. 1995). The notion of bribery in such accounts is used to characterize all informal activities as illicit, corrupting practices, and fails to capture the complex varieties of informal exchange that took place, or the discrete purposes they served. These accounts lead us to imagine that bribery is a clear-cut practice, undertaken directly and with no ambiguity; that health care providers have no ethical quandaries about violating their professional code of ethics and are motivated by economic interests alone – as if the quality of physicians' interaction with patients has nothing to do with the integrity of their professional identity.

My argument is not that no physician in Russia ever demanded a bribe, but that such acts were the exception rather than the rule. What was more common was the practice of *blat* – providing special services to patients with connections. Karina, a member of the housekeeping staff at the hospital where I did much of my fieldwork, described the following types of informal relations for accessing special care:

First, of course, is *svoi liudi* [one's own people]. That's not *blat* at all but my daughter, my close friend. They will be treated as one's own relative. Then you have *blatnyi doktorov* – acquaintances of acquaintances of the doctor. Midwives and other personnel won't feel any obligation to treat them specially. Then you have *blatnyi administratsii* – acquaintances of the hospital administrators. They will be given a degree of special treatment, everything will be done officiously and painstakingly, but there will be no warm, caring feelings. Then you have *blatnyi* for the maternity hospital itself – people who must be cared for well because they have the power to close the hospital down.

This typology and my fieldwork experiences indicate that most physicians undertook informal exchanges with patients not primarily for economic interests, but for social ones: informal exchanges were embedded in larger relational contexts, and thus served to communicate sentiments such as professional respect and dignity, or, on the other hand, suspicion and disdain. The privileges that physicians *wanted* to offer through informal relations were privileges that they perceived would enhance, rather than threaten, their professional legitimacy. As the free, state system unravelled further in the late 1990s, money became more acceptable in the eyes of providers. Many labelled it expected compensation for their informal services. Yet, even then, money was important for its symbolic no less than its material power.

I begin with ethnographic accounts of interactions I witnessed between providers and patients in 1994 and 1995, when monetary exchange was illegal and ethically taboo. What we see in these examples is that the issue of informal compensation was highly charged and emotionally fraught for providers, who interpreted

women's offerings as a sign of whether or not they were respected
and their work valued. The kinds of informal offerings women made
ranged from gifts of thanks to questions about cost, and tacitly
revealed patients' assumptions about providers' ethical integrity and
professional commitment. By 1998, however, the downturn of the
economy, together with the increasing prevalence of paid services
throughout the city, led to changes in providers' sensibilities of what
was right to do and receive; monetary fees were now viewed as the fair
compensation one should get for one's work; and informal channels
were often the *only* practical way to obtain it. Such reconsiderations
constituted profound changes in the moral character of money and
the ethics of provider–patient relations, yet they were not simply
shifts in values. They were reflections of the uneven kinds of
institutional reforms taking place in the official health care system,
and the continued injustices perceived to characterize them.

SONIA'S STORY: THE TRANSFORMATIVE POSSIBILITITES OF FRIENDSHIIP

As a service to the community, the maternity hospital where I
conducted fieldwork in 1994–5 instituted weekly opportunities for
pregnant women to meet with an obstetrician for a one-time pre-natal
consultation. Since this maternity hospital did not offer pre-natal
care, such a consultation was the only chance a woman would have to
get a sense of the hospital and learn first-hand about the procedures
for being admitted there for childbirth. Frequently, women learned
of the service through acquaintances of the staff themselves, for
there was no advertising or 'outreach' to neighborhood residents.
Nonetheless, word travelled fast, and twice a week in the afternoons,
the obstetricians met with prospective patients, usually in their third
trimesters of pregnancy. During one such consultation I attended
with the obstetrician Natalia Borisovna, we met Sonia, a 30-year-
old woman who was in her 36th week of pregnancy. A native of
Leningrad, Sonia had studied pharmacy and was familiar with the
medical field. Her circle of acquaintances included health providers
but did not consist of highly placed specialists or bureaucratic power
brokers. She and her husband lived in a one-room apartment in a
neighborhood not far from the maternity home.

Meeting in the outpatient section of the maternity home, Natalia
Borisovna greeted Sonia with a comfortable smile, almost as if meeting
an old friend. As they began reviewing her medical history, Natalia
Borisovna created a warm, trusting atmosphere by speaking to Sonia
gently, addressing her alternately with the affectionate diminutive
'Soniachka' and the even more familiar 'my child'. Her voice was firm
and caring, but unmistakably cautious, conveying a sincere interest

in Sonia's health and her pregnancy. In fact, Natalia Borisovna's concern for Sonia far surpassed the level of attention usually shown patients, and it became quickly evident to me that Sonia was in danger of serious complications. Natalia Borisovna noted that her blood pressure was inordinately high at 140, her haemoglobin was low, and the baby was in breach position. After asking Sonia how she felt, she measured her stomach and the foetal heart rate. Then she told her to take vitamin E and iron, and to stay in close contact over the next two weeks.

Listen, I'm asking you, Soniachka, if your head or your stomach hurts, please call and tell me, and come right over. We may need to admit you for observation. This is very important, we need to give you this baby. Be careful, don't run around now. Do you have any questions?

Sonia smiled in thanks and said, 'No, I understand. But I want to give you this, for your tea.' Sonia handed Natalia Borisovna a small white plastic bag with a store-bought waffle cake inside. Natalia Borisovna at first resisted the gesture, objecting graciously, 'No, what for? This isn't necessary.' Sonia insisted, pushing the bag into Natalia Borisovna's hands, 'Yes, yes, please, take it.'

After Sonia left, Natalia Borisovna and I walked together to her office on the third floor of the maternity hospital, and she told me about Sonia's medical history. Four years earlier, Sonia had given birth, but there had been a series of last-minute complications, including a breach delivery that was unexpected. The umbilical cord was twisted around the baby's neck, and it died a few minutes after being born. In the years since, Sonia had conceived twice more; the first time she had an abortion, and the second time she had a miscarriage at twelve weeks. The attending physician suspected the beginnings of a cancerous growth and she had been observed by an oncologist for some time since. Natalia Borisovna noted the serious character of Sonia's physical condition, and emphasized the need for her to rest and take the prescribed vitamins. Her sense of urgency, moreover, was heightened by the fact that Sonia was already 30 years old and did not yet have a child.

Natalia Borisovna had not been involved in Sonia's first birth or any of her reproductive health care since, so I wondered how Sonia had decided to come for a consultation at this maternity hospital now. Natalia Borisovna explained that she and Sonia share a mutual acquaintance, a former classmate of Natalia Borisovna's who is a dentist. This friend told Natalia Borisovna about Sonia, and the outpatient consultation was arranged. Given the close acquaintance link and Natalia Borisovna's sympathy for Sonia's case, they developed a comfortable relationship at once. Though the physician directed the conversation, she also listened attentively to her patient and met her story with an engaged concern. To express her commitment and sense of responsibility for seeing Sonia's pregnancy through to a successful outcome, Natalia Borisovna spoke to Sonia in the imagery of teamwork or collective endeavour, with herself as physician acting as 'captain': 'We must give you a baby...', 'We need to give you this baby.' Moreover, Natalia Borisovna drew on the concept of 'need' in a dual way; the baby was needed by Sonia and her husband, and Natalia Borisovna herself was needed to ensure the baby's life. Both her use of language and her nonverbal gestures signified a nurturing, warm, concerned feeling, conveying the explicit message that she was in charge and taking care of Sonia's needs.

In the course of the next two weeks, Sonia did admit herself to the maternity home for a few days' rest and observation. At that time, Natalia Borisovna got acquainted with Sonia's husband, Mitia, who worked as a hairdresser. Mitia offered to give Natalia Borisovna a cut and style, which she gladly accepted. The acquaintance chain started by Natalia Borisovna's and Sonia's mutual dentist friend had quickly grown into a relationship of its own, characterized by gift exchanges that expressed friendship as well as mutual obligation and reciprocity. The close acquaintance link that brought together Sonia and Natalia Borisovna inspired the doctor to care for Sonia as if she was a long-term friend or even relative. The waffle cake Sonia gave Natalia Borisovna after their first meeting, handed over directly and in the context of a mutually warm, friendly interaction, was perceived by both sides as a 'gift'. It was, moreover, followed by a series of gift exchanges between Sonia, Mitia and Natalia Borisovna, whose relationships continue to this day. The close acquaintance link enabled Sonia and Natalia Borisovna to transcend the official, bureaucratic framework of interaction that constrained most interactions between patients and providers – the so-called 'conveyor' – by mobilizing the ethically superior obligations of kinship.

LIUDMILA AND THE BRIBE: UNSPOKEN EXPECTATIONS WITH DISTANT ACQUAINTANCES

Another of this doctor's consultations in 1995 went drastically differently. Meeting Liudmila several months later in the same office where we had been with Sonia, Natalia Borisovna mumbled hello and in an official tone of voice that conveyed no prior acquaintanceship whatsoever, said 'Yes, what can I do for you?'

Liudmila handed Natalia Borisovna her the medical history and explained in a matter-of-fact tone: 'You told me you wanted to see me at this time, so I've come back.'

Natalia Borisovna measured the foetus with her hands, and asked how she was feeling, if she had any discomfort. Liudmila was in her

39th week of pregnancy, and the conversation focused on the process of admission to the maternity hospital, what Liudmila should bring with her, and what day to come.[4]

Natalia Borisovna listened to Liudmila's stomach with the wooden foetal heart stethoscope, and felt the outlines of her stomach, first on the left side, then on the right, and on top, silently distinguishing where the foetus's limbs were. 'I'm feeling here the size, he's pretty big, I'd say 3,500, 3,700 [grams], it's not small, definitely ready to be born [*vpolne rodivshiisia*].' They agreed that Liudmila would come the following Monday, and Natalia Borisovna said with restrained affection, 'OK my dear [*moia khoroshaia*], get dressed.'

Natalia Borisovna jotted down her notes down regarding Liudmila's history and then we all started walking out of the door and to the lobby.

Liudmila was clearly worried about the birth and anxious to ensure that she would have competent, attentive care. At one point she mentioned, 'My doctor at the pre-natal clinic's not very qualified.' Soon after she asked Natalia Borisovna, 'Are you always in the unit?'

Natalia Borisovna replied, 'Yes, I'm the head of the pre-natal unit, I'm here daily during the week except Saturday and Sunday, unless I come in briefly to do rounds. I also work two 24 hour shifts in the delivery room per month.'

Natalia Borisovna did not promise to come to the delivery, or to undertake any interventions to ensure that Liudmila would, in fact, go into labour during her shift.

We then reached the lobby where Liudmila's husband was waiting. He handed her two green plastic bags and Liudmila quickly handed them to Natalia Borisovna, mumbled a barely audible 'Thank you', and goodbye. Natalia Borisovna took the bags without responding, turned around and accompanied me back upstairs. I noticed a strained, awkward expression on Liudmila's face as she handed Natalia Borisovna these bags, and I was confused as to what had just happened. 'She passed you these bags in such a strange way, with such little ceremony that it was barely noticeable', I said, questioningly.

Natalia Borisovna didn't look in the bags. As we walked down the hall of the first floor, she didn't say anything at all, but only mumbled, 'I'll explain it to you.' As we walked up the stairs, Natalia Borisovna explained this encounter to me:

You see, I didn't want to reach out to her. I got a call from the former head of this unit who I know well, and she told me that her acquaintance would be coming by. She came for a consultation a while ago and I examined her. She asked me, 'How much do we need to pay you? We're financially well-off and just tell us how much it'll cost. We can afford anything.'

'She thought she'd pay you personally?' I asked.

Natalia Borisovna continued with a tone of disdain:

Me personally, the maternity hospital's administration, it made absolutely no difference to her. She just wanted to pay us money so that we'd guarantee that everything went all right. So I explained to her that we're a maternity hospital for poor women, we have no paid services, nothing is done for money, and you don't have to give me anything. I don't need anything. Well, I figured that they'd never come back, I thought I'd never see them again. And here, I guess despite it all she's decided to give birth here.

Natalia Borisovna and I walked into her office where her colleague Nina Sergeevna was sitting sewing the strap together on a worn-out sandal. Natalia Borisovna pulled out a hefty green box of chocolates wrapped in plastic with a copy of some piece of artwork on the front. Judging from the packaging, this was an expensive, imported box of chocolates. There was also a white, plastic bottle of liqueur with a palm tree on the label, a gold elastic band around the neck with another colorful label hanging down the front and the words 'Whiskey Cocktail' printed on it in English.

Natalia Borisovna frowned as she took out the items: 'Here you go, another bribe [*vziatka*]. I hate getting these things. You know, they think "Oh, we'll give them a damn box of chocolates and that'll guarantee everything."'

Nina Sergeevna looked up from sewing and asked, 'Oh, is this before or after [the patient gave birth]?'

With a look of disgust and frustration, Natalia Borisovna said only: 'Before.'

Nina Sergeevna continued sewing her sandal strap and empathized with her colleague: 'Oh I can't stand that either, it's terrible. No, no, I hate that.' Turning to me, she explained: 'You know, they always do this and it puts us in a very difficult position. I'm superstitious and I hate taking things beforehand.'

I sat there listening and looking at the two of them in wonder at the fact that they were complaining about it, but yet Natalia Borisovna had nonetheless accepted the bags.

Natalia Borisovna continued the explanation: 'You know why it's a problem – [they'll say to us] "Well I gave you [something], so you owe me – [*raz ia tebe dal, ty mne dolzhen*]."'

'Well, how would you feel if they didn't give you anything? Nothing at all?' I asked. Natalia Borisovna hastened to respond: 'It's all the same to us. I don't care. I don't need anything.'

Nina Sergeevna, however, was more candid about the complexity of her feelings. While not in favour of turning health care into a commodity given the widespread poverty, she did want to feel appreciated and respected:

You know what kills me? When afterwards, they don't say 'thank you', they just leave. No 'thank you', no 'goodbye', nothing. I've already gotten used to it, I don't let it bother me anymore. But you know, they could – ok, I know that not everyone can afford roses. I understand that. Three roses for some people is a really significant amount. But one rose, just one single rose, just a 'thank you' – is that too much to ask?

Natalia Borisovna then handed the box of chocolates and the bottle to Nina Sergeevna, who hid it away in the top of the closet, saying for my benefit, 'We won't touch this now. It's better not to take anything or do anything until after everything works out. Then you can celebrate, all we want [*radi boga*].'

Liudmila's case exemplified a typical miscommunication between patients and providers. Liudmila saw her strategy as attempting to receive good treatment within the corrupt framework of the state bureaucratic system. Despite the fact that she and Natalia Borisovna shared an acquaintance, someone who was able to arrange the initial consultation, Liudmila still expected that she would need to 'pay'. And at the first meeting, according to Natalia Borisovna, Liudmila explicitly offered 'to pay anything', whatever it would cost to be assured good care. Although Natalia Borisovna explained that no payments were necessary, at the second meeting, Liudmila nonetheless came prepared 'to pay' and handed Natalia Borisovna the bags, as if an unstated agreement had been established between them in the past that would govern all future interactions. Natalia Borisovna, however, resented the assumption that her medical expertise and care needed to be 'bought'. She felt deeply insulted at what she perceived was an affront to her integrity as a physician, and lost the desire to establish a close personal relationship with Liudmila. 'I didn't want to reach out to her', she said candidly to me. Nonetheless, by accepting the bags that Liudmila held out for her at the end of the second consultation, the physician unwittingly appeared to confirm that she had, indeed, expected such 'payment'.

Unravelling the distinctions between gifts of thanks and bribes required attention to the nuances of interpersonal behaviours and practices. Chocolate, alcohol, and flowers were not only typical gifts of thanks in Russia, but also frequently the assumed 'requirements' or 'payments' for services rendered or speeded up, in short, for the special access and privileges known as *blat*. Consequently, subtle distinctions in the way the objects were presented became signifiers for the kind of exchange being conducted. On the one hand, words of thanks or emotional warmth conveyed through a smile and gentle insistence helped frame the exchange as a 'gift', as when Sonia gave Natalia Borisovna the waffle cake. On the other hand, Liudmila's serious face, awkward glance and uncomfortable mutter reflected her own interpretation of the exchange as an illegal payment. Moreover, as Natalia Borisovna and Nina Sergeevna revealed in their discussion back in their office, the timing of the exchange also had significance. Offered *before* a woman gives birth, a box of chocolates appeared closer to a bribe; given afterwards, it was unmistakably a gift of thanks. Finally, Nina Sergeevna's comment, 'But one rose, just one single rose, just a thank you – is that too much to ask?' demonstrates that patients were not mistaken in assuming that many providers had some level of expectations for exchange. Physicians hoped that their efforts and services would be recognized and applauded; but most of all they wanted to feel that they were respected for their skills as honest professionals and not cynically 'paid off' by patients desperate to negotiate the corrupt demands of the state bureaucratic system.

Liudmila's acquaintance link to Natalia Borisovna was too 'distant' to transform the provider–patient relationship into the extension of their personal networks and thus did not have the power to mobilize the doctor's sense of personal (rather than professional) involvement and obligation. Moreover, Liudmila's direct question to Natalia Borisovna about paying for services 'disqualified' her from gaining the physician's sympathy and personal care. It amounted to a statement that she saw the physician as a corrupt, bribe-taking representative of 'our system', rather than as an expert endowed with legitimate authority whose professional integrity generated automatic respect. As a result, Liudmila's acquaintanceship appeared as a utilitarian strategy, intended to facilitate her ability to 'buy' the physician, rather than incorporate her into a moral bond of friendship and mutual obligation. Yet, as Sonia's story shows, Natalia Borisovna became motivated by personal concerns not merely because a patient had an acquaintance link, but because a patient sent by a close acquaintance was also more likely to grant the physician the symbolic authority and trust based on her stature as medical expert. In the context of an interaction based on mutual obligations, physicians were no longer viewed as authorities simply because they were empowered by the state; instead, they were seen through the lens of a charismatic ideology that attributed their healing power to individual knowledge and personal skill. When the bureaucratic framework of 'our system' could be superseded by the more ethical framework of a personal relationship marked by gifts of gratitude, the patient was more likely to approach the physician's dominance as legitimate – not as the capricious, dangerous power of an anonymous worker on the health care 'conveyor'. A bribe, by contrast, did not transform the provider into a trusted authority, did not convey the patient's respect and gratitude, and was not able to heal the wounds of mutual distrust.

POST-SOVIET HEALTH CARE: A SHIFTING SENSE OF SELF AND PROFESSIONAL STANDARDS

When fee-for-service care became possible in the early 1990s and grew increasingly prevalent throughout the decade, many doctors first responded with ambivalence. It was clearly a double-edged sword, for, on the one hand, increased revenues could translate into better equipment, less harried schedules, and increased economic stability for doctors. Yet there were also ethical concerns accompanying the acceptance of monetary payments. In 1994–95, physicians felt compelled to reassert the integrity of their professional commitments, claiming that what was available to be purchased was not their competence, but medically unimportant issues like a private room. Also, working in paid services was not the right of any physician in the hospital, but a privilege bestowed by hospital administrators on staff members of their choosing. All others would be paid their meagre salaries alone. In this context, paid services led to new forms of stratification and feelings of injustice among staff. The introduction of official forms of payment was thus not done in a way that repaired the sense shared by all physicians in the Soviet system that their work was undervalued. It extended pre-existing injustices of the official system to create new forms of inequalities, between hospital staff in particular.

By 1998, many physicians I knew felt less ambivalent about taking payments and even doing so informally. Several factors influenced these changes. Paid services had become very widespread throughout the health care system. The colloquial expression, 'We pretend to work, and they pretend to pay us', which had captured so perfectly the frustrations of work life under the Soviet era, no longer seemed the inevitable arrangement. In August of 1998, the rouble crashed, and the material situation in and outside hospitals worsened considerably. Maternity hospitals did not have sufficient amounts of essential medical supplies and doctors routinely had to tell women to purchase and bring their own antibiotics and sterile gloves to the birth. The hospital's hot water was often turned off. Hospital personnel were required to work after hours, trimming the bushes and picking up garbage in the hospital grounds. At the end of the summer in 1998, St Petersburg was hit by extensive floods. Hospital employees were called to bail water out of the maternity hospital's basement, which they did for a week straight, again with no compensation. The state was abdicating its role in 'pretending to pay', and doctors came to feel that they no longer had to continue 'working for free'. Nor was it a really possible to do so any longer, providers needed money for daily life needs. They viewed the failure of the state to provide the necessary resources for public health – to fulfil its basic obligations

– to be the foundation of 'corruption', and a reasonable justification for bypassing the laws to accept unofficial payments.

The hospital's chief doctor did not agree. She saw the establishment of distinct levels of comfort and care under the rubric of paid services to be unfair, both to poor patients and to hospital staff, for whom the introduction of such services would lead to unequal privileges. Providers, however, perceived the prohibition against earning money as deeply unfair, given that their colleagues in all other city hospitals had started doing so. 'Women who want to pay should have the opportunity to do so', Natalia Borisovna told me. My friend Karina, on the hospital's housekeeping staff, suggested that instituting such payments was the only way to improve the conditions of the hospital: 'Such money would help improve the standard of care for all women, even those who are too poor to pay', she explained. The chief doctor, however, did not budge.

In response, several doctors established an underground, informal system offering the services of a 'personal doctor' [*lichnyi vrach*], to trusted acquaintances of acquaintances. This business-type arrangement supplanted earlier *blat* exchanges of the type we saw with Sonia and Liudmila: now, the doctor gave the patient her beeper number, told her to call when labour began, and promised to attend the birth as the patient's own doctor. The compensation was monetary, and the price made known through the acquaintance. Still, this informal practice could be undertaken only by the more senior, respected doctors on staff, those who could garner the support of auxiliary personnel necessary to realize their promises to patients.

By 1998, the language of respect for expertise had been widely translated into idioms of monetary payment. If in 1995 doctors expressed resentment when Liudmila assumed that a payment would be expected, they now viewed the receipt of money for one's work as ethical, indeed, a necessary condition for not being exploited. Yet in the many cases where physicians were not authorized to accept money for services, they have felt forced to choose between two unsatisfying positions, both of which undermined their sense of respect and recognition in this new moral economy: on the one hand, they could accept money informally and acquire the feeling that their work was respected, but in doing so they would need to break the law, and risk being exposed as 'corrupt'. On the other hand, they could refuse to take payments, enjoy the safety of following the rules, but thereby exclude themselves from the possibility of receiving both symbolic status and material gain. When the legal framework itself seemed so unjust, deciding on the latter course felt deeply frustrating if not foolish.

In this new moral economy of a market society, providers and patients found it virtually impossible to both abide by the legal rules and experience a sense of personal and professional justice. Providers found themselves facing a new bind: many patients not only viewed payment of money as a sign of respect, but reified high prices as the charismatic proof of a physician's true medical competence, rather than as a reflection of her connections and privileges. Thus, if a provider did not name a price for her services, many patients took this as a sign that she had little of value to offer, rather than as a sign of her not being allowed to do so, her lack of the requisite connections or her commitment to alternative values – such as to the need for free health care. Providers, similarly, often told me that patients who pay have a 'higher culture', are those who truly care about their health. For both groups, the ethical use of money was unrelated to legal rules and restrictions, for the official sphere continued to be seen as an unjust bureaucratic machine, the ultimate locus of corruption. In such cases interpersonal relations were the primary site for fair exchange and ethical compensation.

In Russia's market society, both ordinary citizens and state employees find themselves increasingly vulnerable in an unregulated public sphere. Neither group has obtained greater legal protections. Market reforms have not resulted in increased transparency in the institutional operations of health care services; informal information and personal acquaintances continue to be critical resources for learning about what one is entitled to, for figuring out how different institutions do or do not provide those services, and even for getting the basics of care fulfilled. In contexts where ordinary people remain disenfranchised from formal decision making processes and public policies, their informal practices can be attempts to negotiate changing forms of entitlement, to forge mutually beneficial exchanges, and convey appreciation and respect in ethical ways.

NOTES

1. This study is based on 16 months of fieldwork conducted in maternity hospitals, women's outpatient clinics, and the homes of providers and patients in St. Petersburg, Russia, between 1994 and 2000. I conducted formal interviews and/or unstructured 'participant-conversations' with 76 Russian women and 71 providers. I met with 20 percent of these women at least twice, and usually numerous times, over the course of six years. To access women from the highest socio-economic classes who accessed paid services, I employed a Russian research assistant with extensive networks among these groups to conduct an additional nine interviews. All names used in this chapter are pseudonyms to protect informants' identities. The material presented here is further developed in my book, *Healing the Nation After Socialism: Women's Health and the Privatization of Agency in Russia*. I am grateful to the Andrew C. Mellon Foundation, Princeton University, the Council on Regional Studies at Princeton, the Peter B. Lewis Fund of the Center of International Studies at Princeton, the University of Kentucky

Summer Faculty Fellowship, and an IREX summer travel grant for funding this research.

2. In this sense, Valya's eagerness to pay for care because of what it said about *her* as a consumer was *not* overly common, but expressed her emerging class consciousness as someone who herself charged high fees for her time and expertise. Not all women saw the need to pay in this light: many with limited economic means viewed payments with pragmatic resignation. They agreed that doctors needed to earn money to survive, but described this obligation with understandably less enthusiasm.

3. In one of our conversations, Valya and her husband, Boris, emphasized that Russia had an enormous problem with corruption, and that it would not be right for me to offer a relativizing analysis of all behaviour to explain the practices of evading the law in Russia. They described bureaucrats who demand bribes in order to fulfil their responsibilities as utterly depraved. Yet they saw unofficial payment for health care as different, more akin to 'tips' that are 'voluntarily' given by patients. Flouting the law in Russia thus carried different moral valences depending on the context. It was pervasive because the law itself was unjust. And government leaders were the most thoroughly 'corrupt'. As Valya explained, 'the fish rots from the head'.

4. The maternity hospital system was organized such that patients could choose any hospital in the city to give birth at if they arrived with their own transportation. If they came by ambulance, as many needed to, they would be taken to whatever hospital was 'on duty' in their neighbourhood. Many women, moreover, preferred to be in the hospital before labour began, in part because the drawbridges over the Neva River in St Petersburg are raised every evening at 2 a.m. and travel is impossible until they close again at 6 a.m. If your preferred hospital was on the other side of a bridge from your home, you would end up going somewhere else.

REFERENCES

Cassileth, B.R., V.V. Vlassov and C.C. Chapman (1995) Health Care, Medical Practice, and Medical Ethics in Russia Today, *Journal of the American Medical Association*, Vol. 273, No. 20: 1569–73.

Ledeneva, A.V. (1998) *Russia's Economy of Favours: Blat, Networking and Informal Exchange* (Cambridge: Cambridge University Press).

4 CORRUPTION AS A TRANSITIONAL PHENOMENON: UNDERSTANDING ENDEMIC CORRUPTION IN POSTCOMMUNIST STATES

David W. Lovell

During the past decade, public sector corruption has become a prominent issue in national and international forums. It is increasingly discussed, legislated against and subject to international sanctions. It may even be increasing. The literature on corruption has expanded rapidly over the same period, as corruption has graduated from an issue in comparative politics to a central problem of political and economic development in democratizing states. The World Bank now has a major campaign against corruption, and NGOs – and especially Transparency International – have helped to bring the issue to the forefront of world attention. In 1996, the United Nations General Assembly adopted the UN Declaration against Corruption and Bribery in International Commercial Transactions. In 1999 and 2001, successive Global Forums on Fighting Corruption and Safeguarding Integrity were held in Washington, DC and The Hague. And there are substantial regional initiatives against corruption in Latin America, Africa and the Asia Pacific, the latter sponsored in part by the Asian Development Bank.

Established liberal democracies have well-publicized corruption allegations and investigations, often targeting senior politicians, bureaucrats and police. Significant corruption allegations have been made against former German Chancellor Helmut Kohl, and against French President Jacques Chirac. In Australia, to select some recent examples, a former federal parliamentarian was jailed for soliciting bribes from illegal immigrants to enable them to settle legally; and a number of elected local officials in the state of New South Wales were investigated by the Independent Commission Against Corruption for allegedly accepting bribes to facilitate construction work in their bailiwick. But while such cases reduce trust in politicians and other public officials, there remains a high level of confidence in the integrity of the state administration itself. The Australian public sector, like those of most established liberal democracies, is widely perceived as relatively uncorrupt (Grabosky and Larmour 2000). There are corruption scandals to be sure; but there are also anti-corruption institutions, public inquiries, investigative media, and a generalized intolerance of corrupt officials that threatens them with public exposure, disgrace and prosecution.

Yet in some countries, corruption seems to be rampant, anti-corruption measures are ineffective and many citizens are resigned to coping with corruption in their daily lives. The charge of rampant corruption has been levelled against the region of Southeast Asia (Backman 1999), with the notable exception of Singapore. Even senior politicians in many Southeast Asian countries identify corruption as a major problem, though their motives are often mixed, and may include political advantage. In July 2001 the then prime minister of Papua New Guinea, Sir Mekere Morauta, publicly described both his own party and his government as systematically corrupt (Forbes 2001). These corrupt elements, he suggested, were attempting to block the privatization of state assets (which would reduce their opportunities for exploiting public resources). Malaysia's then deputy premier, Abdullah Ahmad Badawi, was reported as conceding to a conference of the ruling United Malays National Organization in June 2001 that it was perceived as a corrupt organization (Lyall 2001). In many other parts of the world, corruption is at a level which does not simply discourage direct foreign investment, but brings the very legitimacy of states into question among their citizens. Close attention to the developments in some postcommunist states, for example, has revealed a rapid increase in corruption. Cohen (1995) argues that tens of thousands of businesses in Russia are controlled by organized crime. State officials are either powerless to act or are willing accomplices. The situation in Romania (Mungiu-Pippidi 1997) and Yugoslavia (Komlenovic 1997), among others, is similarly grim.

The point of this – rather blunt – distinction between the relatively uncorrupt and the rampantly corrupt, or between incidental and endemic corruption, is not to apportion praise or blame. 'Relatively uncorrupt' does not mean uncorrupt. Indeed, the relatively uncorrupt may be compounding the problem elsewhere. Thus Abramovici (2000) argues that corruption has become worse since decolonization in the 1960s: 'In simple terms the corrupted are public bodies in emerging countries, and the corrupters are companies based in rich countries.' The USA may have been one of the first to legislate against corruption, with its 1977 Foreign Corrupt Practices Act, but it still seems the preferred destination for 'laundered' funds. And many Western companies (sometimes even backed by their governments) corrupt foreign officials to gain an advantage over their competitors.

Rather, the distinction is meant to highlight the notion that there is a different dynamic of corruption occurring in the two situations. Any attempts to deal with corruption – to counteract its causes and address its effects – must take this difference into account.

This chapter makes a case for sustaining the distinction between incidental and endemic types of corruption, and explores endemic corruption through the experience of the postcommunist states, and particularly the former Soviet Union. It first discusses the usual (but generally unexamined) assumptions about public sector corruption, in terms of organizational mechanics and economic stimuli, and argues that these do not fit the range of non-Western social contexts within which much of the world's endemic corruption occurs. It goes on to examine the emergence of postcommunism, and its related endemic corruption, out of the communist governmental system. And it ends by arguing that postcommunism is a transitional experience, moving towards modernity, in ways similar to traditional societies confronted by the norms of individualist, legalistic, society. Dealing with endemic corruption requires a sensitivity to the social contexts which nurture it. Transforming corruption from an endemic to an incidental problem will require a major change in social, political and organizational culture that cannot simply be legislated into existence, nor imposed by international organizations, however well-meaning.

UNDERSTANDING CORRUPTION

The World Bank defines corruption as the abuse of public power for private benefit, and such a definition is widely accepted partly because it is relatively neutral as between different states, allowing cross-state comparisons. But while it is convenient, such a definition is too simple. In particular, it makes assumptions about the underlying norms of behaviour in public office – including the very distinction between public and private – that may not always be warranted. To understand corruption better, it is important to consider the social context within which it is constructed.

I shall confine my remarks here to corruption in the sphere of government, despite the recent extension of 'corruption' to cover the private sphere. Of course, abuses occur in the private sphere, as people take advantage of their positions to defraud their companies or shareholders for personal benefit. But the laws that identify and prohibit 'theft' from employers and customers tend to be clear and clearly understood, and direct self-interest on the part of all the actors in this sphere leads to a heightened scrutiny of transactions and a readiness to complain about irregularities. Irregularities or improprieties in the public sphere are more difficult to identify, both because of the mixed motives of public officials (for whom public office is usually a career, and thus in part a means of private gain), and because of the sometimes uncertain standards of public behaviour, and thus the difficulty of recognizing an abuse of the norms.

A legalistic account of the World Bank's definition identifies corruption as those acts performed by officials when departing from their legal obligations in exchange for personal advantages (LaPalombara 1994). This definition may be easy to operationalize, but it assumes the prevalence of the standards of rational-legal rule. Corruption on these terms is the use of public office in ways other than those sanctioned by rational-legal authority. And while Carl Friedrich agreed that corruption exists whenever 'a responsible functionary or office holder, is by monetary or other rewards … induced to take actions which favor whoever provides the reward and thereby damage the group or organization to which the functionary belongs, more specifically the government' (1972: 127–8), he nevertheless identified its core meaning as behaviour that deviates from a prevalent norm. The key issues, therefore, are not just determining whether a 'deviation' has occurred, but what is the norm.

The normative dimensions of corruption are most apparent when the term is used in its generic sense as 'deviation from a norm', and is applied to any phenomenon considered valuable. Passionate warnings about the corrupt society as diseased (Payne 1975) reveal the importance of norms, as do complaints about the corruption of many sporting codes because of the increasing importance of monetary incentives to their players and officials. The international Olympic movement, for example, has been beset with such criticisms for many years. The International Cricket Council even established an inquiry into the corruption of cricketers after revelations about the extent of bribery in the game. This is particularly significant, for cricket – though in many ways a peculiar game – was once a byword for decent behaviour and playing by the rules.

Some see public sector corruption as due to the rise of the career politician, who joins politics for personal gain. Others, economists in particular, see corruption as a product of the rise of state intervention, with more opportunities for bureaucrats and politicians to circumvent the rules and act arbitrarily in their own cause. Certainly, both these explanations have some purchase: they provide motive and opportunity. Another view explains corruption as a product of the exaltation of the market mechanism, and a blurring of the lines between public and private, and the primacy of greed (seemingly reinforced by the 'crony capitalism' involved in the growth and then the collapse of the Asian economic miracle in the mid to late 1990s). Corruption may also be driven by the rise of big donors to political parties, and a decline in membership by ordinary citizens. Longevity in power (a factor in non-democracies, but also in democracies where governments win many successive elections) may also contribute to corruption, with its disdain for accountability of the actions of public officers.

The 'structural temptation' to incidental corruption can be explained in a relatively straightforward way, despite the diversity of causes already identified. Corruption of this type occurs when government has a monopoly supply of a good, where there is discretion on the part of officials, and where there is relative secrecy. As Robert Klitgaard (1988) neatly put it, 'Monopoly + Discretion – Accountability = Corruption'. All of these conditions are met in a great deal of government business. Where the defences of hierarchical and other types of external surveillance, and the defences of a professional ethic, morality and other types of internal surveillance, are together insufficient, corruption will occur. Corruption of this type is ineradicable, though it may be greater or smaller in different states and in different components of those states, depending on opportunities and traditions.

Furthermore, there would seem to be greater opportunities for corruption the larger the public sphere (the more people it employs, or the wider the sphere of its interference and regulation of the private sphere, including the economy). But even if the opportunities exist, not all extensive states are extensively corrupt. Some of the least corrupt countries in the world – Canada, Denmark, Finland, the Netherlands and Sweden – have some of the largest public sectors, measured as shares of tax revenue or public spending in GDP. There is a genuine distinction between the *size* of government and its *quality*. Many developed states still have a significant problem with corruption, as the example of Italy shows. The United States, too, has its share of corruption (Dobel 1978; Rose-Ackerman 1999).

Much of the recent discussion about corruption, and the subsequent treaties and legislation, sees corruption as a type of mechanical problem, requiring some procedural fixes. Thus corruption is seen largely as the result of inadequate training, payment, professionalism and supervision of public officials. Evidence of growing corruption suggests merely that the fixes need to be more rigorously adopted and enforced. The corollary is that corruption can be limited, but never eradicated: the motivation of greed (let alone need) will always remain, opportunities to benefit from public office can never be entirely closed off, and corrupt transfers can generally be disguised. Corruption, therefore, is part of the price governments pay for having extensive administrations and complex laws.

Within this context Peter Eigen, founder of Transparency International, has put forward an elementary five-point anti-corruption programme (Eigen 1996: 162): commitment by leaders;

anti-corruption legislation and enforcement; review of government procedures; salary review of the government sector; and review of legal procedures and remedies to make them an effective deterrent. Keith Henderson, a senior adviser with the United States Agency for International Development (USAID) proposed an eight-point action plan 'aimed at (a) promoting more governmental accountability and transparent democratic processes; (b) increasing trade and investment and economic growth; (c) building capacity and public confidence in governmental institutions, and (d) developing public respect for rule of law societies' (Henderson 1998). His plan was adopted by USAID in December 1997 for East Central European and former Soviet Union states. And Robert Klitgaard has recently suggested some practical means for curing and preventing corruption in cities (Klitgaard et al. 2000).

Such approaches may be appropriate for countries where corruption is incidental, where the division between private and public is long-standing, and rational-legal norms of behaviour in the public sphere are established and accepted. But for much of the world, they seem inadequate, and destined to failure. For they assume that what we mean by 'corruption' is obvious and uncontentious. In many countries corruption is a much more complex problem connected with a transition from one political, cultural and organizational culture to another. The normative basis of 'corruption' in such countries is not clearly established, and public officials rely now on one and now on another understanding of their role. While procedural measures are not irrelevant in countering endemic corruption, there is a much more profound change in society and culture that needs to take place to address its roots.

The obvious objections to the usual understanding of corruption reveal that cultural contexts play an important role in the behaviour of public officials, and should play a larger role in our understanding of them. In the first place, the abuse of public power can be not solely (or even) for private benefit, but is sometimes for the benefit of one's class or party, or friends or kin. Officials may depart from the rules out of a sense of loyalty, and without any personal gain involved. In some societies, gift-giving is an important part of social relationships, including the giving of gifts to officials. Bribes should be distinguished from gifts; Tanzi (1998) explains that 'A bribe implies reciprocity while a gift should not.' The relationship is actually more complex and reciprocal, as Mauss revealed in his seminal study of gift-giving in pre-modern societies; such gift-giving can create and reinforce social relationships, including hierarchies (1970: 72). Such considerations led Heywood to argue that 'the meaning of political corruption might vary with the nature of the political system in question' (1997: 6).

LEGAL-RATIONALITY

Most discussions of political corruption seem to be based on the assumption that corruption is a deviation from the norm of the legal-rational form of authority, in the sense that was established by Max Weber. In Weber's model the relationships between officials and citizens are formalized and regulated, with officials serving the state; the office rather than the incumbent is the most important element of the administrative system; and personal relationships with clients of the administration are subordinate to the formal, professional elements. This model presumes a certain sort of society, relatively extensive and anonymous, with a reliance upon formal, legal mechanisms and upon the exchange of values for private benefit in a market economy. Individuals are the basic units, not families or estates. Such characteristics do not generally describe societies that have substantial traditional or kinship structures, nowadays often described as 'developing', nor all the societies that have emerged from communism.

Activities that are regarded as corrupt from an external perspective, whether because they offend Western norms, or even the legal code of the society in question, can nevertheless be functional. As Samuel Huntington (1968: 64) explained in his major study of changing societies:

> corruption provides immediate, specific, and concrete benefits to groups which might otherwise be thoroughly alienated from a society. Corruption might thus be functional to the maintenance of a political system in the way that reform is. Corruption itself may be a substitute for reform and both corruption and reform may be substitutes for revolution.

This is to see corruption as a pressure relief valve. It also fits with the Soviet experience, where a great deal of corrupt and illegal behaviour was undertaken with the tacit acceptance of the Communist Party:

> From an economic standpoint, the level of corruption that obtained in the Soviet system was no less a logical product of that system than were the queues of citizens seeking scarce food items. Given the nature of the Soviet system ... the creation of 'the corrupt society' was absolutely inevitable. (Clark 1993: 203)

This point is reinforced by an earlier study (Berliner 1957) of management methods in the USSR between 1938 and 1957; managers used the illegal methods of *blat* and *tolkachi* simply to make the system work.

In connection with the Soviet system, Clark offers a key insight:

> The law-based notion of official corruption, which may be defined as behavior of public officials aimed at the acquisition of forbidden or circumscribed benefits and made possible as a result of their official duties or position, can

exist only in those societies that have a relatively well-developed notion of public office. (1993: 8)

Corruption, in the generally used sense, assumes that the role of public official is clearly understood by both official and citizen. But this cannot be taken for granted. The code of behaviour, and the expectations, in transitional states – those where legal-rational forms of authority are not predominant – are not always the same as for those who criticize corruption (Nye 1970: 566–7). They tend to be characterized by different, and competing, sets of norms. Traditional forms of authority exist side by side with modern forms; councils of tribal elders alongside parliaments, for example. Often these types of authority coexist in one person, who may be a senior kin figure and also a senior politician or bureaucrat. The transitional period is a period of tension between these different codes, or standards. As Huntington put it: 'Corruption in a modernizing society is thus in part not so much the result of the deviance of behavior from accepted norms as it is the deviance of norms from the established pattern of behavior' (1968: 60).

Understood in this way, corruption is a problem not just for the reasons that it discourages investment and delegitimizes governments (which can become 'kleptocracies' (Andreski 1968)) but because it traps them in a vicious cycle. The weakness of developing, or transitional states in trying to build legitimate institutions – what Gunnar Myrdal (1970) has called 'soft states', characterized by corruption, racketeering, bribery, arbitrariness, political expediency and indiscipline – is due to the relative lack of power in the system, and the lack of countervailing powers. It has been noted of many developing countries that:

Coercion, force and authoritarian rule are all present in abundance, but power is a genuinely scarce commodity … There are few freely operating opposition political parties or independent judiciary systems. Most legislatures are or the rubber stamp variety. Interest groups are primitive and are mostly under the control of the government itself. Press freedom is rare … Laws are made or unmade and enforced or unenforced not according to some master guide, such as a constitution, but according to the whim of the administrator and the special access enjoyed by traditional elites. (Bertsch et al. 1991: 629–30)

LEGAL-RATIONALITY AND THE COMMUNIST SYSTEM

Soviet socialism was described in many different ways, and debates raged over 'totalitarian', 'vanguard party' and 'pluralist' models (Fortescue 1986) in an attempt to identify the key elements. It was particularly popular – whatever other description was used – to think of Soviet reality as 'bureaucratic'. It was a label that Lenin had used, and Trotsky (and those he inspired in some way, especially Bruno

Rizzi and James Burnham) had made popular. But this was not a professional bureaucracy of the type that Weber (1948: 196–204) described. The Soviet 'bureaucracy' was rather peculiar. Friedrich and Brzezinski (1965: 206) signalled this when they declared that the various political intrusions into administration by totalitarian systems meant that they 'are less rational and legal and hence less fully developed from a bureaucratic standpoint than, for example, the governmental services of some absolute monarchies in the eighteenth century'.

However Soviet reality was described, a rigid distinction between politics and administration, of the sort liberal democrats are accustomed to making, did not exist. The Weberian notion of bureaucracy and rational administration did not fit comfortably the Soviet political-administrative system (Pakulski 1986). It might be better to think of the Soviet administrative system as 'officialdom' rather than bureaucracy. Indeed, the whole function of government and its administration was different from merely setting the framework within which individuals and groups could pursue their own interests. Rather, the state set the tasks of individuals and groups. This embodied not formal rationality, but a substantive rationality where what is rational is whatever is appropriate to achieving the overall state goal. Harry Rigby, in identifying this problem, chose to call communist systems 'goal-rational systems' (1980: 19). Success in the Soviet bureaucracy was not measured in terms of compliance with rules, but in terms of achieving outcomes; the structure and function of the Soviet administrative staff were heavily influenced by this (Rigby 1976).

Schwartz adds that there was an informal administrative code in the USSR, based on the tension between 'party supremacy and system shoddiness – that demands and rewards risk taking for the good of the cause' (1979: 431). Informal networks and their functioning within the large-scale Soviet bureaucracy became an organizational ethos. The Soviet system threw up challenges that relied on these networks to survive. They became a *modus operandi*. Many needed goods and services were acquired by 'acquaintanceship and connections'; a related term for the informal system of exchange is *blat* (meaning 'pull', or 'influence'). Hedrick Smith (1976: 88) described this as follows:

In an economy of chronic shortages and carefully parceled out privileges, *blat* is an essential lubricant of life. The more rank and power one has, the more *blat* one normally has. But almost everyone can bestow the benefits of *blat* on someone else ... because each has access to things or services that are hard to get or that other people want or need.

The pressures on managers also led to the growth of a class of people who could procure materials: *tolkachi*, or 'pushers'. The plan was law, and thus the informal practices that most managers engaged in to fulfil the plan were illegal – but they tended to be regarded as 'technical' rather than 'real' crimes.

It is also worth remembering that the Soviet Union comprised a number of states and regions with quite different levels of development and social systems. In some respects it was a mix of modern and pre-modern social relationships. In some places, and at some times, the culture surrounding Soviet institutions influenced them into an even more intense pre-modernism. Simis, for example, describes the war of rival clans in the ruling elite of Uzbekistan in the 1970s, which used state offices as weapons and the control of such offices for enrichment (1982: 60–4).

When corruption began to be identified as a major problem in communist states in the 1980s (Holmes 1993: 134–9; cf. Clark 1993: 15), it seems likely that the behaviour of officials remained much the same as in the earlier Soviet period. But by then the standards had changed. There was a growing sense that officials should serve the public, and not themselves, the Communist Party, history or some other rationalization for the abstracted 'proletariat' that had earlier sufficed. It was a change in standards that may have been more readily taken up by ordinary people than by bureaucrats, as the evidence of perceptions of corruption in communist states suggests. Nevertheless, throughout the communist period there were officials dedicated to communism and to their nation, officials who shunned the excessive consumption of many of their colleagues. But they operated within a system built on secrecy and privilege – with regard to food and housing, health care, travel and holidays – and around networks of patronage, that were taken largely as granted, and within which their abstemiousness was a personal choice, without systemic consequences. Perhaps only one official ultimately made a real difference, and that because his choice forced ideal and reality into confrontation: Mikhail Gorbachev.

CORRUPTION IN POSTCOMMUNISM

Postcommunist societies, emerging from the communist system after the revolutions of 1989, are in transition to legal-rational forms of authority. It is not just a question of the operation of a – or even the same – bureaucracy in different contexts, Soviet and democratic, as might be assumed from the ready identification of Soviet state organization as 'bureaucratic'. Rather, it is a question of creating a new type of bureaucracy, a new type of state, and a new relationship between state and citizens. The new bureaucracy represents a new approach to the basic organization, functions and expectations of bureaucracy. The presence, and the discussion, of corruption is symptomatic of a larger change in the character and consequent organization of the postcommunist administrative system.

Although it is impossible to quantify precisely, corruption seems endemic in many postcommunist states, and particularly in the states of the former Soviet Union. We know this through anecdote, through surveys of citizens and through corruption perception indices. Corruption is such a problem because it retards the development of democracy and of the market, both of which are important for the quality of life of the citizens of postcommunism.

Why has postcommunism become such a breeding ground for corrupt behaviour? There was, as we have seen, a legacy of 'corruption' under communism (largely unacknowledged), due to a lack of professional administration, and the lack of a clear distinction between public and private spheres as officials used their offices for personal benefit, but believed – or pretended to believe – that they were acting in the public interest. Also playing a role was the unleashing of market forces, including a profiteering mentality, into societies where the restraints that attend developed markets are not functioning. There were few legal restraints, and perhaps little will, to restrain and channel greed. Likewise, there was little sense of professionalism among civil servants, with the limits that imposes. And there was little spiritual restraint. Despite the resurgence of the Russian Orthodox Church in Russia, and the Catholic Church in some of the East Central European states, there was little counterweight to consumerism. Pope John Paul II lectured postcommunist Poles on this very point, to their annoyance.

Another major reason why postcommunism has seen the rise of corruption is that in the era of privatization there were enormous opportunities for taking advantage of the sale of public property (Mauro 1998). Sokolov (1998) – an auditor of the Account Chamber of the Russian Federation – highlights the sort of corruption that happened in the course of privatization. And he underlines the lack of convictions for breaches of even the new laws, by insisting that there is still no independent judiciary.

The citizens of postcommunism believe that corruption in their states is increasing (Grodeland et al. 1998). Some have identified a collapse of the old value systems, and the rise of explicitly self-aggrandizing values (described as 'the moral chaos and economic pressures of the transition'), that points to the hybrid nature of transitional societies, when things are out of kilter. Surveys show that there is not a great difference between the way people in former Soviet Union (FSU) and East Central Europe (ECE) judge their ability to influence political outcomes through elections (though it is 10 percent lower in the FSU); but there is a great difference in the expectation of citizens to fair treatment by officials. 'Citizens in the FSU were 39 per cent less likely than those in ECE to expect fair treatment from officials without recourse to bribes or contacts' (Miller et al. 1997: 183–4). And this finding did not simply reflect habits of complaint; there was indeed a substantial difference in treatment of citizens by public officials in the Ukraine as compared with the Czech Republic.

Ledeneva (1998) argues that among the most important changes of the transition are, first, that the Soviet practice of *blat* shifted from the everyday life of ordinary citizens to networks of former *nomenklatura*, now businessmen; and second, that in the lives of ordinary citizens, 'influence' shifted to outright bribery.

Organized crime and endemic corruption are major problems in Ukraine, threatening its stability and undermining its transition to a market economy (Shelley 1998). They deter foreign and domestic investment, and exacerbate the problems of capital flight. Citizens' trust in government institutions is very low, but Shelley argues that Ukraine has failed to adopt the legal infrastructure necessary to combat crime and corruption. Indeed, some politicians have strong criminal connections, and become politicians in order to benefit from the immunity from prosecution it gives them.

Corruption happens at the top in postcommunist states. Here, among senior officials and politicians, it sets a bad example to more junior government officials, and sends very bad signals to foreign investors and aid donors. Corruption also occurs at the bottom. Here, among officials of various ranks, corruption is driven by a mix of need, greed and a lack of professionalism. The remedies here include paying officials properly and regularly (their employers currently assume that they will take bribes to supplement their salaries), making transactions between officials and citizens more transparent to the public and to higher officials, making such transactions simpler and with less discretion available to the official, and ensuring that there is a paper trail of all transactions.

But the problem, and its solutions, are more than procedural. Andras Sajo (1998) explains corruption in East Central Europe as 'structural', in the sense 'that it is part and parcel of the region's emerging clientelistic social structures'. This clientelism, he argues, is not simply a series of unrelated, individual acts, but a social phenomenon. He sees 'striking similarities between postcolonial and postcommunist societies', especially in connection with nation-building in the aftermath of an imperial legacy. Ultimately, the effects of corruption are negative: 'even if it smoothes the operations of an underpaid bureaucracy, mostly it perpetuates the influence of political, party-centered, client–patron structures over the distribution of resources'.

ALTERNATIVE EXPLANATIONS

I have argued that endemic political corruption is best understood as a phenomenon characteristic of the transition of public administrations to a rational-legal form of rule, and may be associated with a change in social relationships from traditional to individualistic. I shall make a contrast in this section between this conception, and corruption conceived both as a timeless problem and as another type of economic relationship.

It is customary to say that corruption is an ancient curse. There is no doubt that government officials have been abusing their position for personal gain for thousands of years. More than 2,000 years ago, in his classic treatise *Artha-sastra*, the Hindu statesman Kautilya declared that:

[The King] shall protect trade routes from harassment by courtiers, state officials, thieves and frontier guards ... [and] frontier officers shall make good what is lost ... [It] is impossible for one dealing with government funds not to taste, at least a little bit, of the King's wealth.

We can also find venal behaviour in officials frankly recorded in Samuel Pepys' diary of the 1660s. The examples could be multiplied endlessly. But corruption in the way that we commonly understand it is a relatively modern phenomenon; it denotes deviation from bureaucratic standards formulated by Weber; and its 'victims' are the public. It is modern because it assumes a public sphere that is devoted to the public interest, not simply to maintaining order and providing public works and infrastructure. What is described as ancient corruption is theft from the king or other rulers, the state being effectively their property. It is hardly surprising that officials in the Stuart court were venal, given that many of them had purchased their offices. Clarifying the distinction between public and private is therefore crucial to the contemporary usage of 'corruption'.

Another important interpretation of corruption holds it to be simply another form of exchange, able in important senses to be analysed economically. Susan Rose-Ackerman has made a major contribution to the political-economic understanding of corruption as a phenomenon which depends on a calculation of benefits and costs. On this account, the potential for corruption arises whenever a public official has discretion over a decision which incurs benefits or costs to others. At the interface between private and public sectors lie opportunities for private economic gains by public officials. Economic analysis is useful, she argues, because it 'can isolate incentives for payoffs to government agents, evaluate their consequences, and suggest reform' (Rose-Ackerman 1997: 31). Corruption varies widely in its extent and depth across countries, and even within countries; measuring it is difficult if not impossible. Rose-Ackerman examines corruption as a factor in developing countries, and even those which have growing economies, but argues that ultimately growth will be undermined as corruption spreads, and that the benefits of economic growth will be badly distributed (especially away from the 'have nots'). Her interest is both conceptual and practical.

Bribes are paid for two reasons: to obtain government benefits and to avoid costs. An effective anti-corruption strategy should both reduce the benefits and costs under the control of public agents and limit their discretion to allocate gains and impose harms. (Rose-Ackerman 1997: 34)

Rose-Ackerman treats corruption as akin to a market transaction, except one that is illegal. She notes that some countries maintain a stable corrupt system for some time, but this usually degenerates into kleptocracy. The wider the circle of officials in receipt of bribes, the more secrecy is likely to be maintained about it, and the less the threat of exposure. Yet stable corrupt societies risk an escalating cycle of bribes and payoffs, and thus degeneration.

But is corruption a way of understanding government decisions that is amenable chiefly to economic analysis? Rose-Ackerman's political-economic approach, as she describes it, combines the 'economist's concern with modeling self-interested behavior with a political scientist's recognition that political and bureaucratic institutions provide incentive structures far different from those presupposed by the competitive market paradigm' (Rose-Ackerman 1978: 3–4). The market analogy has some obvious attractions, but it needs to be qualified. A market suggests voluntary exchanges and competition, and neither of these may be present in corruption. There may be exploitation or violence involved, and there is unlikely – because of secrecy – to be a bidding war between those who bribe. We may expect in most circumstances that individuals will try to benefit themselves; but how they do so, what limits they observe, and what priorities, is a complex and highly contextual matter.

Though corruption occurs everywhere, it is a fundamental problem in societies that are 'transitional' between traditional, pre-modern, or communist forms of order and the Weberian form of legal-rational order. People in positions of authority in such societies are caught between two value systems. There is no obvious recipe for eradicating endemic corruption in transitional societies; it is part of the general process of change, though it can doubtless be assisted by a cocktail of practical measures including reduced government enterprise, transparent decision-making, organizational oversight, attempts to inculcate professionalism into public officers, and paying appropriate salaries to public officers. Ultimately, the eradication of endemic corruption depends on the development of a strong civil society to impose clear standards on political authorities, and demand better of them. And civil society cannot be conjured into existence; its self-recognition is not automatic; it must be built up by slow, cooperative efforts.

CONCLUSIONS

Corruption is a major negative factor in any country, in terms of economic growth, government legitimacy and general human security. It is a fundamental problem in many developing countries and especially in some postcommunist ones. And despite the increased recognition of the problems it creates, corruption is perhaps more extensive than it ever was (Tanzi 1998). The purpose of this chapter is not to deny that corruption can be identified, nor to diminish the problems it creates, nor to undermine the many practical proposals that have been developed to deal with it. What this chapter does suggest, however, is that corruption needs to be understood in relation to its social context, and that it is a different type of problem in (for want of better terms) 'developed' and 'transitional' societies. The transitional societies discussed here are the postcommunist states and particularly the former Soviet Union because, like the postcolonial states of the 1950s and 1960s, many of them exhibit significant patterns of informal and traditional behaviours that affect the relations between public officials and citizens. The corruption in these societies is endemic, and the solutions to it must be sought not just in procedural terms but in political and social leadership.

The line between incidental and endemic corruption may be difficult to draw, and it may not be a simple quantitative one, but it seems a useful distinction to make. Incidental corruption takes place against a background of established rational-legal authority; endemic corruption takes place where rational-legal authority is not yet predominant (and may delay its elevation). There may be a substantial amount of incidental corruption, but it is of a different order to endemic corruption because the norms in the latter case are unclear.

The procedural approach to reducing the problem of corruption in rational-legal systems is by now well-established. But the larger problems associated with endemic corruption occur where tensions exist between the different types of social relationship which are assumed by traditional and modern forms of ruling. Officials in transitional regimes should not be regarded as intrinsically evil or culturally predisposed to corruption. Rather, they are responding

– perhaps even in inconsistent ways – to the different demands and opportunities thrown up by the transition period. Among those opportunities are the bribes on offer from foreign companies.

The consequences of endemic corruption for locals and outsiders alike are deleterious. Yet Westerners barging into transitional societies, complaining of the gap between official pronouncements and everyday realities, and expecting general conformity with rational-legal norms, display a cultural myopia that tends to compound the problem. That does not mean that the anti-corruption movement is simply an advance brigade for a globalizing market economy (Bukovansky 2002).

Dealing with transitional situations and the endemic corruption that may develop in them is an enormous challenge, and goes beyond procedural remedies. Its most important factor is leadership, the ability to set an example of public service and to convince other public officials, subordinates and citizens of the need to separate public and private considerations. Leadership also means denying perhaps the greatest temptation in transitional situations: an appeal to the standards of traditional social relationships. It is well to rail against the paternalism, insensitivity and sometimes hypocrisy, of Western states and companies. But strong states, economic prosperity and increased human security can only be built on the basis of addressing corruption, not cloaking it with patriotism.

REFERENCES

Abramovici, P. (2000) Corruption: A Necessary Evil?, *Africa News Service*, 1 December 2000. Available online <www.globalpolicy.org/nations/corrupt/2000/1201pa.htm>. Accessed 7 November 2004.

Andreski, S. (1968) Kleptocracy or Corruption as a System of Government in Africa, in S. Andreski (ed.) *The African Predicament* (New York: Atherton).

Backman, M. (1999) *Asian Eclipse: Exposing the Dark Side of Business in Asia* (Singapore: J. Wiley & Sons).

Berliner, J.S. (1957) *Factory and Manager in the USSR* (Cambridge, MA: Harvard University Press).

Bertsch, G.K., R.P. Clark and D.M. Wod (1991) *Power and Policy in Three Worlds* (New York: Macmillan).

Bukovansky, M. (2002) *Corruption Is Bad: Normative Dimensions of the Anti-corruption Movement* (Canberra: Department of International Relations, RSPAS, ANU. Working paper 2002/5).

Clark, W.A. (1993) *Crime and Punishment in Soviet Officialdom: Combating Corruption in the Political Elite, 1965–1990* (Armonk, NY: M.E. Sharpe).

Cohen, A. (1995) Crime without Punishment, *Journal of Democracy*, Vol. 6, No. 2: 34–45.

Dobel, J. (1978) The Corruption of a State, *American Political Science Review*, Vol. 72: 958–73.

Eigen, P. (1996) Field Reports: Combatting Corruption Around the World, *Journal of Democracy*, Vol. 7, No. 1: 158–68.

Forbes, M. (2001) My Government Is Corrupt, PNG Leader Admits, *Sydney Morning Herald* , 27 July.

Fortescue, S. (1986) *The Communist Party and Soviet Science* (London: Macmillan).

Friedrich, C.J. (1972) *The Pathology of Politics: Violence, Betrayal, Corruption, Secrecy, and Propaganda* (New York: Harper & Row).

Friedrich, C.J. and Z.K. Brzezinski (1965) *Totalitarian Dictatorship and Autocracy* (2nd edn, Cambridge, MA: Harvard University Press).

Grabosky, P. and P. Larmour (2000) Public Sector Corruption and its Control. *Trends and Issues in Crime and Criminal Justice* No. 143 (Canberra: Australian Institute of Criminology).

Grodeland, A.B., T.Y. Koshechkina and W.L. Miller (1998) Foolish to Give and Yet More Foolish not to Take – In-depth Interviews with Post-communist Citizens on their Everyday Use of Bribes and Contacts, *Europe-Asia Studies*, Vol. 50, No. 4: 651–77.

Henderson, K.E. (1998) Corruption: What Can be Done About It?, *Demokratizatsiya*, Vol. 6, No. 4. Available online <www.demokratizatsiya. org>. Accessed 4 December 2000.

Heywood, P. (1997) Political Corruption: Problems and Perspectives, in P. Heywood (ed.) *Political Corruption*, pp. 1–19 (Oxford: Blackwell).

Holmes, L. (1993) *The End of Communist Power: Anti-corruption Campaigns and Legitimation Crisis* (Melbourne: Melbourne University Press).

Huntington, S.P. (1968) *Political Order in Changing Societies* (New Haven, CT: Yale University Press).

Klitgaard, R. (1988) *Controlling Corruption* (Berkeley, CA: University of California Press).

Klitgaard, R., R. Maclean-Abaroa and H. Lindsey Parris (2000) *Corrupt Cities: A Practical Guide to Cure and Prevention* (Oakland, CA: ICS Press).

Komlenovic, U. (1997) State and Mafia in Yugoslavia, *East European Constitutional Review*, Vol. 6, No. 4. Available online <www.law.nyu.edu/ eecr/vol6num4>. Accessed November 2004.

LaPalombara, J. (1994) Structural and Institutional Aspects of Corruption, *Social Research*, Vol. 61, No. 2: 325–50.

Ledeneva, A.V. (1998) *Russia's Economy of Favours: Blat, Networking and Informal Exchange* (Cambridge: Cambridge University Press).

Lyall, K. (2001) Mahathir's Deputy in Plea to End Corruption, *The Australian*, 21 June.

Mauro, P. (1998) Corruption: Causes, Consequences, and Agenda for Further Research, *Finance and Development*, Vol. 35, No. 1. Available online <www. worldbank.org/fandd/english/0398/articles/010398.htm>. Accessed November 2004.

Mauss, M. (1970) *The Gift: Forms and Functions of Exchange in Archaic Societies* (translated I. Cunnison. London: Cohen & West).

Miller, W.L., T. Koshechkina and A. Grodeland (1997) How Citizens Cope with Postcommunist Officials: Evidence from Focus Group Discussions in Ukraine and the Czech Republic, in P. Heywood (ed.) *Political Corruption*, pp. 181–209 (Oxford: Blackwell).

Mungiu-Pippidi, A. (1997) Breaking Free at Last: Tales of Corruption from the Postcommunist Balkans, *East European Constitutional Review*, Vol. 6, No. 4.

Available online <www.law.nyu.edu/eecr/vol6num4>. Accessed November 2004.

Myrdal, G. (1970) *The Challenge of World Poverty* (New York: Random House).

Nye, J. (1970 [1967]). Corruption and Political Development: A Cost–Benefit Analysis, in A.J. Heidenheimer (ed.) *Political Corruption: Readings in Comparative Analysis*, pp. 564–78 (New York: Holt, Rinehart & Winston).

Pakulski, J. (1986) Bureaucracy and the Soviet System, *Studies in Comparative Communism*, Vol. 19, No. 1: 3–24.

Payne, R. (1975) *The Corrupt Society: From Ancient Greece to Present-day America* (New York: Praeger).

Rigby, T.H. (1976) Politics in Mono-organizational Society, in A.C. Janos (ed.), *Authoritarian Politics in Communist Europe: Uniformity and Diversity in One-party States*, pp. 31–80 (Research Series no. 28, Berkeley CA: Institute of International Studies, University of California).

—— (1980) A Conceptual Approach to Authority, Power and Policy in the Soviet Union, in T.H. Rigby, A. Brown and P. Reddaway (eds) *Authority, Power and Policy in the USSR*, pp. 9–31 (London: Macmillan).

Rose-Ackerman, S. (1978) *Corruption: A Study in Political Economy* (New York: Academic Press).

—— (1997) The Political Economy of Corruption, in K.A. Elliott (ed.) *Corruption and the Global Economy*, pp. 31–60 (Washington, DC: Institute for International Economics).

—— (1999) *Corruption and Government: Causes, Consequences, and Reform* (New York: Cambridge University Press).

Sajo, A. (1998) Corruption, Clientelism, and the Future of the Constitutional State in Eastern Europe, *East European Constitutional Review*, Vol. 7, No. 2. Available online <www.law.nyu.edu/eecr/vol7num2/special/special.html>. Accessed 24 October 2000.

Schwartz, C.A. (1979) Corruption and Political Development in the USSR, *Comparative Politics*, Vol. 11: 425–42.

Shelley, L.I. (1998) Organized Crime and Corruption in Ukraine: Impediments to the Development of a Free Market Economy, *Demokratizatsiya*, Vol. 6, No. 4: 648–63. Available online <www.demokratizatsiya.org>. Accessed 4 December 2000.

Simis, K.M. (1982) *USSR: The Corrupt Society. The Secret World of Soviet Capitalism* (translated J. Edwards and M. Schneider, New York: Simon & Schuster).

Smith, H. (1976) *The Russians* (New York: Quadrangle).

Sokolov, V. (1998) Privatization, Corruption, and Reform in Present-day Russia, *Demokratizatsiya*, Vol. 6, No. 4: 664–80. Available online <www.demokratizatsiya.org>. Accessed 4 December 2000.

Tanzi, V. (1998) Corruption Around the World: Causes, Consequences, Scope and Cures, *International Monetary Fund Staff Papers*, Vol. 45, No. 4: 559–94. Available online <web6.infotrac.galegroup.com/itw/infomark/307/104/14786195w3/purl=rc1_EIM_0_A54064603&dyn=4!xrn_7_0_A54064603?sw_aep=adfa>. Accessed 1 November 2000.

Weber, M. (1948) *From Max Weber: Essays in Sociology* (translated H.H. Gerth and C. Wright Mills. London: Routledge & Kegan Paul).

5 CORRUPTION, PROPERTY RESTITUTION AND ROMANIANNESS

Filippo M. Zerilli

Social scientists, and particularly scholars of economics and political science often distinguish between *normal* or *physiologic* corrupt forms and behaviours that are judged *endemic* or *pathologic*, that is systemic to a particular cultural milieu. Not surprisingly, while everyone seems to agree that corruption is a social phenomenon widespread in all societies, its manifestations in 'Third World', 'undeveloped', 'developing' or 'transitional' societies are often viewed as an integral part of their economic, cultural and political organization (e.g. Lovell 2004; Mungiu-Pippidi 2002: 161–6, 214). From this perspective, corruption is represented as inherent in societies in which democracy and market economy are commonly judged to be insufficiently or imperfectly developed. Therefore, conventionally suggested remedies for corruption are trapped in a circular argument: if corruption is pathologic or endemic where democracy and market economy are weak and undeveloped then we simply have to strengthen the latter (building civil society, supporting privatization, good governance programmes, etc.) in order to 'struggle against corruption'. Obviously anti-corruption discourse and ideology is far more complex and diversified than this.[1] Nevertheless, in conventional anti-corruption discourse societies where corruption is represented as pathological are often depicted as if they lacked certain fundamental features. This might be called a 'rhetoric of deficiency': nation-states under scrutiny are conceptualized as missing those requisites that are judged essential to democratic and economically proficient societies. Accordingly, corruption seems to cover a social space that in 'normal' conditions would be occupied by something else.

An ethnographic understanding of the local discourses and practices of corruption should help us challenge such an essentialist and ideological view of corruption and point out its pitfalls. Furthermore, a local understanding of corrupt practices should contribute to a more open definition of the phenomenon. What is too often missing in corruption literature, is in fact precisely how corruption is locally perceived by social actors directly involved in allegedly corrupt practices in a specific place and time (see, however, Gupta 1995; Zinn 2001). The aim is to reach a useful comprehension of corruption, both as symbolic and social practice by studying how and why it works in specific social contexts by way of sharing 'the immediate, direct, vivid impression of the lives of Peter, Paul, and John, of single, real individuals' as Antonio Gramsci once said in one of his letters from prison (in Crehan 2002: 165). Studying corruption ethnographically should also offer insights about how 'the state' is experienced and conceptualized by 'real people' in their everyday lives, discourses and practices, and how this eventually produces and transforms their personal and social identities.

Interestingly, talking and making jokes about corruption is commonplace in today's Romania,[2] discursive practice in which many persons appear to be involved daily. This is not say that corruption permeates the everyday life of Romanian citizens, even though many would probably argue that it does. Rather, just like 'Europe', 'democracy', 'privatization', 'private property' or 'market economy' (see Verdery 1996, *passim*), 'corruption' has became a symbol *in* and eventually *of* post-socialist Romania. Certainly a public symbol (being widely diffused by mass media and electoral propaganda, among others) but at the same time a very private and intimate one. Its privacy and intimacy does not solely refer to the occult and illegal dimension of corrupt practices. It also refers to the idea of corruption as a social practice (de)generated from Romanian *ancient customs*. Thus, the extension of corruption as a socially meaningful symbol in post-socialist Romania is particularly salient not only because TV and the press are filled with cases of corruption daily, but also because it is given a certain socio-historical depth that suggests deep, ambiguous and multiple genealogies. Corruption as a present social practice is in fact locally thought and experienced as something related to (or even developed from) a wide range of older social practices and ideas, whether this past is socialist or pre-socialist. Consequently, talking about corruption generates a good number of conflicting stereotypes with regards to what *being* and *acting* as a Romanian actually means. More precisely, discourses on corruption tend to hide, and at the same time reveal (self-)representations of Romanian (im)moral behavior, including attitudes towards justice, legality, trust, interest, solidarity, generosity, altruism, reciprocity and accountability, among many others.

Accordingly the reader should not find it surprising that I do not employ the conventional definition of corruption.[3] Nor do I enter the controversial 'definitional dilemma' (see Ceobanu 1998: Ch. 2.1) in order to advance a new definition of corruption. Through fieldwork conducted in Bucharest I would explore the way people talk, represent and eventually practise corruption by using it in order to signify and communicate within specific social contexts and discursive fields. Using heterogeneous materials dispersed in different locales and temporalities, social actors differently positioned create in fact diverse and often conflicting images of corruption (and Romanianness) to be played out in particular social contexts with different 'political' purposes.

The remaining part of this chapter is divided into three sections. I start by discussing how people actually talk about corruption in everyday life, especially by using irony. Then I focus on property restitution law-cases and how corrupt practices are experienced, conceptualized, and used by social actors that are directly involved. The last section focuses on local explanations of corruption, and explores their relation to the illegal behaviour that is often represented as a typical trait of Romanian identity. I conclude by suggesting that an ethnographic understanding of what corruption is and how it works, both as a symbol and social practice in specific social fields could bring new considerations to the anti-corruption policy debate.

TALKING CORRUPTION THROUGH IRONY:
THREE ETHNOGRAPHIC VIGNETTES

A friend of mine recalled how his cousin, a manager for a computer enterprise located in Cluj-Napoca (the main urban centre in Transylvania), during a Sunday family lunch openly declared that his company was regularly bribing the City Hall functionaries in order to get contracts. According to my friend, his family members were not surprised at all, and certainly nobody suggested that local authorities be informed. The fact was perceived as something unpleasant and surely unfair but nevertheless accepted because 'this is how the system works'. Interestingly, within the context of the family lunch atmosphere the episode immediately functioned as a vehicle for ironic comments and jokes about corruption and its pervasiveness in Romania.

A second vignette is about a well-known professor at the University of Iasi, the main town of the north-eastern Romanian region of Moldova. His widespread reputation among students is due neither to his scholarly work nor to his teaching ability. He is so well-known because, in order to pass his examinations, candidates are expected to fill his wine-cellar with a particular brand of wine and honey. The attention of those of us listening to the story shifted from the illegal action to the bribe-taker's peculiar request and soon slipped into ironic comments. Certainly most of the listeners would have agreed that the professor's actions were immoral but his passion and good taste for wine gave him a curious if not appealing aura.

A last vignette is about a woman, the head of a publishing house who was in the hospital in Bucharest because she needed a relatively simple medical operation (for appendicitis). Before she entered the hospital, she said she knew that she was supposed to give something (money) to nurses (for injections), the anaesthetist and, last but not least, to the surgeon himself. She stressed that she was only doing what everyone else would have done. Actually the anaesthetist, a young man with literary aspirations and a friend of the woman, refused to accept any money. The 'funny part' here is that a few months later the patient's publishing house produced a book of his poems.

Although these stories were told and collected at different times and places, all of them are characterized by the frequent recourse to irony. This is not by mere chance. A rhetorical device provided with multiple socially meaningful implications (see Fernandez and Huber 2001), irony is a good way to communicate by implicit reference without saying something directly. There are good reasons for the use of irony when talking about social practices that are widely judged as 'pathological', but still recognized as 'normal' in a specific context. Irony serves well the purpose of relativizing without minimizing and, more importantly, of keeping a distance without assuming moralistic attitudes. It is a good tactic to show (to oneself as to others) how 'anomaly' is in fact provided with a 'normative' character.

But irony is not simply used to protect themselves and others from the ethnographer's invading gaze. As I was told, irony and jokes about corruption are often present at local level, even when the ethnographer is not present. Here, it serves more precisely to underline the gap that exists between corruption as something imposed upon personal choice, and corruption seen as a deliberate option. It must be stressed that all our vignettes create images of corruption from the point of view of the bribe-givers. Contrary to the bribe-takers (who are viewed as profiting by their institutional position) bribe-givers perceived themselves as the 'victims' of these mutual agreements. Even if bribe-givers do not blame their counterparts, by playing irony 'at home', they underline the socially established character of such agreements and, more importantly, they point out their coercive nature. In so doing, they reveal the asymmetric structure of the power relations between bribe-givers and bribe-takers. Contrary to assumptions often taken for granted in corruption literature, the willingness to engage in corrupt practices is not (perceived by the actors themselves as) a deliberate choice. In the stories above, the bribe-givers do not conceive of themselves as rational actors, making their own choices in order to attain some selfish purpose or utilitarian goal. This is not to say, of course, that their actions are illogical or irrational. By contrast, by using irony they show that they are well aware of how their actions respond to widely shared social logics. Logics they refuse in principle, but nonetheless willy-nilly feel they have to accept if they want to gain access to basic public social services. In fact, we are talking about people who are expected to bribe in order to exercise elementary social rights, such as working, studying or obtaining medical assistance. If they want to play, as one of them said, they have to 'accept the rules of the game' (see Stefan 2001, also mocking on this point). For most of them, to refuse to engage in such practices (that is, by not 'offering'), or to struggle against them (that is to denounce) means taking the risk of not having access to these social rights. Discursive practices that – for analytical reasons – I subsume under the single register of irony could then be seen as a way of exercising a kind of 'passive resistance' against a system of unwritten rules, as one informant nicely put it.

Jokes and ironic comments on corrupt practices also play a fundamental role by subtly questioning whether we can actually consider a given practice as *real* corruption. Here the aim is neither simply to re-inscribe the illegal practices into social contexts that show their coercive power, nor to draw a line between bribe-givers and bribe-takers according to their different degree of moral responsibility, but rather suggest that the 'real corruption' is played out someplace else. To quote one informant, it is situated at 'another level'. On this point, see Zafiu's discussion of a Romanian 'corruption lexicon' (1993), and the multiple linguistic games underlying each story. Suffice it to say that the 'official' term *mita* explicitly employed by the Penal Code to cover offences of bribe offering was never used.[4] More precisely, it was often used but mainly ironically, that is, to represent the described actions for what they are not. When I asked one informant why they did not use the term *mita* for the given examples, she said, '*mita* is more official', and it is used to indicate 'corruption at a higher level'. The term *mita* is in fact the 'formal' term for bribery, but in everyday discourse it is mainly associated with corrupt offences perpetrated by 'politicians or judges' and does not apply to 'ordinary citizens'. Of course the bribe-taking protagonists of our vignettes were entrusted with public duties and responsibilities, but, as one of them suggests 'there are public institutions that are *more public than others*' (my emphasis). That is to say that the opposition 'public vs private' on which the conventional definition of corruption is based is differently modulated when corruption is directly experienced at the grassroots. 'Real corruption' tends to be located within what is often perceived as the 'more public institutions', that is the Parliament and the judiciary.[5] So, the distinction between 'passive corruption' (bribe-offering) and 'active corruption' (bribe-taking) is recognized but not morally stigmatized within a network of social relations working at the local level, but a sharp moral divide is posited between what is considered 'small' or daily corrupt practices played out by 'ordinary citizens', and 'real corruption' where institutional actors such as politicians and judges play a leading role. From this point of view, bribe-givers and bribe-takers involved in 'petty corruption' can join each other in blaming 'the state' as the primary and genuine source of corruption.

USING CORRUPTION IN THE STRUGGLE FOR PROPERTY RIGHTS: TWO ETHNOGRAPHIC CASES

In this section I present and discuss two different law-cases regarding property restitution, a conflicting and politicized issue in post-socialist Romania that has received much media coverage. According to legal sources, more than 80 percent of civil law cases in recent years directly concern property rights and particularly property restitution. In this context it is not surprising to find many people fighting for property rights through different means, including corruption.

The first case is about a former owner whose corruption attempt failed.

Case 1. Ion Popescu is a 62-year-old architect who is now retired. He lives in Bucharest where he has recovered a family house after a long and distressing law-case (as he said: 'It cost me three heart attacks'). Nevertheless, Popescu considers that in Bucharest, between 1990 and 1993, the judgments of the courts concerning property restitution were generally 'fair' (that is, from his point of view, in favour of the former owners). In 1993 he decided to seek restoration through civil justice of another family house located in a well-known small provincial and tourist town in the Prahova Valley (around 130 km north of Bucharest). At the very beginning his opponent in the trial was the town's City Hall, in fact the state institution that had been managing the house since the 1950 nationalization (Decree no. 92/50). The legal actions Popescu brought forth were unsuccessful, as the first two court judgments (*fond* and *apel*) favoured City Hall. According to the Procedural Civil Code Popescu still had a third – and last – means of recourse. Meanwhile, according to Law 112/95, the City Hall sold the house to the tenant who inhabited it at the time, a local politician who had formerly worked at the City Hall. As is the case with many other tenants who had lived in his house during socialism, Popescu knows him well. According to Popescu the house could not legally be sold as the City Hall could not be considered the legitimate owner. Nevertheless, the house was sold to this tenant and when Popescu decided to appeal against the last court's judgment the tenant himself was admitted as a party to the trial. Fully convinced that 'in the Prahova region not a single case of restitution could be won without bribery', Popescu arranged with his lawyer to offer a significant sum of money (US \$4,500) to influence the three members of the court. The money was kept in the lawyer's hands until the delivery of the sentence that, once again, went against Popescu. The lawyer returned the money to Popescu who concluded, 'certainly the counterpart [the new owner] had offered more' than he had.

As a Romanian judge once said to Katherine Verdery, 'there are two Romanian views of law: those who win a case in court say justice was done and the law is impartial, whereas those who lose say justice is corrupt and the judge was bribed' (1996: 222). From one side or another every court's judgment is then perceived as resulting from illegal agreements between one of the two parties and the judge(s). Certainly, the climate of suspicion and conspiracy that shaped everyday life and social relations during socialism (e.g. Liiceanu and Sélim 1999), continues to play an important role in contemporary Romania. Paradoxically, from this point of view bribe-offering is often described as a way of gaining access to fair judgment. This is especially the case of the former owners: through a recurrent dramatic representation of the suffering experienced during socialism (confiscation, persecution, exile, etc.), supported by a dominant neoliberal exclusive property rights discourse and ideology (see Zerilli 2002: 61–2), they can even invoke corruption as a way of obtaining justice. Accordingly, for Ion Popescu, any judicial sentence pronounced against property restitution is perceived as 'a new expropriation', 'a second nationalization' or, more prosaically, 'a theft'. While the offence of bribe-offering committed by tenants is judged fraudulent and immoral, as perpetrating 'communist rule', former owners represent themselves as repairing injustice by bribing. Representing himself as a bribe-offerer, Popescu is actually communicating and defining his peculiar social identity (as a former owner) in contrast to that of those who are currently benefiting from ties with the communist regime established during socialism (the tenants of nationalized houses).

Like many other former owners, Popescu nourishes doubts about the correct functioning of the judiciary in his country. He is convinced that a good number of Romanian judges are still influenced by what he calls 'communist mentality'. Nevertheless, he does not blame the legal system per se. He tends rather to identify specific responsibilities at the local level. When asked if once he had exhausted national remedies he would address his law case to the European Court in Strasbourg (as many other former owners did), he responded that 'damages should not be compensated by the Romanian state but by those who are guilty'. According to Popescu, to obtain compensation from 'the state' would be immoral, implying that Romanian society itself would thus be unjustly condemned. Why should 'we' – the Romanians – pay for the crimes perpetrated by communists?, asks Popescu. This conceptualization also reflects the particular judicial structure of Popescu's law case in the Prahova region. In fact, while many other former owners found themselves competing against state institutions, Popescu faced a 'new owner' in court. Actually, he participated in a struggle in which two private individuals confronted each other, while 'the state' was supposed to mediate between them by way of the judiciary. I am not able to conclude so far that when state institutions are directly involved as party to the trial, the social actors are discouraged from engaging in corrupt practices. But I guess it is not by chance that it was precisely when the 'new owner' was admitted to Popescu's law case that he decided to use bribery. When a third subject obtains (or threatens) to intervene in court, bribing apparently becomes a 'legitimate' weapon. In fact, the recurrent explanation 'I bribe because the other is bribing' is not a simple self-justification. In property restitution law cases when litigation shifts from a 'private vs public' judicial structure to a 'private vs private' one, then the social actors tend to represent themselves as authorized to mobilize their network of social relations in order to influence the court's judgment, as also happened in the next case I will discuss.

If in property rights litigation a 'private vs private' judicial structure seems locally a more 'appropriate' terrain for bribing judges, every act of corruption should also be cast in a specific context. As Popescu's case shows, material and symbolic resources that might explain a corruption attempt in the Prahova region's law courts in 1997, are not necessarily mobilized if the same person is facing litigation in Bucharest's law courts in the early 1990s. As any social actor involved in a law case for property rights would argue, from 1989 up to 2001 various political and legal events diffused by mass media and transnational institutions have widely influenced public perception, and eventually also judges' attitudes towards property restitution.

The second ethnographic case also concerns a former owner seeking restoration of property rights. Relying on an informant's exegesis, I will stress how corruption can be used not only 'to obtain justice', as in Popescu's case, but also in order to define and secure social distinction.

Case 2. Elisa Koelner is a retired Romanian lady of German origin whose apartment was confiscated from her family during socialism, in 1977 (Decree no. 223/1974). According to Law 112/95 regulations Elisa applied to obtain restitution in kind. Her request was accepted in 1998 but two years later, based on the argument that for the same apartment the Romanian state had already paid compensation to the German state, Bucharest City Hall summoned Elisa to court. The court's judgment in the first and second instance favoured City Hall. Assisted by a lawyer specializing in property restitution, Elisa decided to appeal. In the meantime, as the apartment was occupied by a state tenant named Stefana Sassu, Elisa called her to court for eviction. Elisa and Stefana know each other, though when they meet (in court) they systematically ignore each other. According to a petition that Elisa addressed to Bucharest City Hall, Stefana has good relations with City Hall functionaries who protect her. In her petition, Elisa also alludes to the influence Stefana has upon them, as well as on the judge called to pronounce a sentence on the eviction law case. As

I was told by an informant from Bucharest City Hall (a young lawyer who in fact had friendly relations with Stefana), the evening before the court's judgment of third instance (*curtea de apel*), Elisa rang Stefana to inform her that 'she had no chance of winning because she [Elisa] had bribed the judges'. The day after, the court's judgment was made in Elisa's favour.

While I was having dinner with my key informant Mihail, a young lawyer temporarily working as a public officer at the Bucharest City Hall, I asked him if he hadn't been surprised by the phone call Elisa made to Stefana on the evening before the trial. Actually, I was trying to understand the meaning of what other informants and I considered to be most curious in her story, that is her phone call to Stefana that revealed what is generally supposed to be kept secret (i.e. bribery). Without hesitation Mihail said: 'No, it is perfectly normal!', and immediately added, smiling maliciously: 'Filippo, you know "Miorita", don't you?', arguing that this would be a sufficient and self-evident explanation. So, what is 'Miorita', why and in what sense did my friend Mihail use it as a metaphor of Romanian 'natural' tendency to act *in a certain way*? And more generally, to what extent does 'Miorita' work locally as an explanatory device for corrupt practices and tolerant attitudes towards illegal behaviour?

In short, 'Miorita' is a Romanian folk poem which tells the story of a shepherd who is warned by his 'small and pretty' lamb, called Miorita, that two other shepherds intend to murder him in order to take his rich and beautiful flocks of sheep. The young shepherd, instead of resisting, accepts his fate and looks forward to his death as a sacred marriage with the whole of nature. While a hundred different versions of the poem actually exist (see Fochi 1964), 'Miorita' is widely recognized as, to quote Mircea Eliade, the authentic creation of 'Romanian popular genius' (Eliade 1992 [1943]: 49). Others see it as the genuine expression of the 'Romanian soul' (L. Blaga), or as the moral basis of 'Romanian spirituality' (A. Fochi). Among the countless re-readings, the majority of the interpreters have centred their analysis on the protagonist, on his stoic acceptance of death and his sacred marriage with nature.[6] Interestingly, till very recently much less attention was devoted to the other two shepherds who connived to murder the good one.

In his provocative and heretical reading of 'Miorita', Mihail was precisely arguing the relevance of envy, conspiracy, theft and even murder to represent Romanian identity. Reversing the stereotyped image produced by historically more authorized interpretations of 'Miorita', Mihail presented 'the Romanians' not as fatalists passively awaiting their destiny, but rather as active venal subjects corroded by envy and ready to act illegally in order to secure their neighbour's possessions.[7]

After dinner, asked to comment in detail why Elisa should have made a phone call to Stefana the evening before the trial, Mihail responded, first, because in so doing Elisa 'was not taking any risks', second, because in this way she was intimidating Stefana and discouraging her from engaging in new legal action, and finally because this was the simplest and most efficient way to show Stefana that 'Elisa had influential connections' (Mihail's paraphrases). To be sure, as another informant accurately observes, 'before you bribe you have to know who you are going to bribe. I am not going to bribe someone completely unknown... the network of relations comes before the act of bribing'. In communicating to Stefana that she had bought the judges (it does not matter whether she actually had or not), Elisa implied that 'she has connections' (*are relatii*), that she is actually able to mobilize (not only) economic capital but also social relations capable of supporting her legal or even illegal actions. From this perspective her phone call is no longer surprising: through it, Elisa was symbolically using corruption as a weapon, as well as to define and affirm her identity as a former owner. Quite paradoxically, bribery works here as a blameless social value, as the actors playing it are not ashamed but rather proud of it. Similarly, a recommended person in Romania (someone *are pile*) is often a person that holds a certain social prestige, a person to be respected or feared.

In corruption literature, a lack of trust in state institutions, notably in the judiciary, is often invoked in order to explain or even justify corrupt behaviour. Cultural observers of corrupt practices also tend to frame illegal actions within a cultural code, or to consider them as part of a moral system relatively autonomous from the legally legitimated morality. Fieldwork among Romanian former owners suggests that bribery can also be conceived as a way of 'settling accounts' (Borneman 1997), that is repairing injustices and restoring a more equal social order. The cases discussed indicate also that 'real persons' directly involved in litigation have precise views concerning where, when and why it is worth engaging in corrupt practices. That is to say that particular legal, political and economic circumstances, along with personal evaluations, could have pushed some social actors to act illegally, while others would have refrained from doing so. Moreover, corruption also works as a weapon to be shown in order to redefine identities and social relations within a specific field of struggle. To be sure, as for the protagonists in the ethnographic vignettes referred to in the previous section, people facing litigation for property rights share the opinion that the most serious illegal abuses are committed at a 'higher level', that is by politicians, former *securist* agents, judges themselves and, more generally, by 'those who are in power'.

CORRUPTION AND ROMANIANNESS: EXPLORING LOCAL
EXPLANATIONS

A good number of different historical and ethnographic sources
attest to the historical depth of a local representation according to
which illegal behaviour (notably theft) can work as a stereotype for
Romanian identity (e.g. Verdery 1983: vi). Obviously, this apparently
historically well-established (self-)representation has in itself a
certain contested history that should be analysed to show how it
was produced, perceived and reproduced with different purposes
and through different agencies in various historical moments and
places. In this section I explore how and why this stereotypic image
of 'Romanians as thieves' is locally reactivated while differently
articulated in current discourses of corruption.[8]

A first intriguing suggestion comes from documentary sources, a
sardonic short article that appeared in a recent issue of the cultural
magazine *Dilema*, the thematic section of which was (again) ironically
entitled 'The Merits and Faults of Corruption'. The author, Irina
Nicolau, a distinguished Romanian ethnologist, museographer, and
friend, who unfortunately died prematurely, puts it this way:

> Here in our country people have always stolen. Here as everywhere. [...]
> Anyhow, in Romania, before communism people used to steal, but it was
> considered to be a shameful act. Then the glorious Soviet army arrives, offering
> us liberty and the no less glorious communism. A golden age began for theft.
> For 45 years the state stole grandiosely: land, water, forests, all kinds of values,
> lives. Hey, they stole so well, so incredibly well, that even 11 years after
> the fall of communism people still don't get back what belonged to them.
> (Nicolau 2001)

It is actually common to find people in and outside Romania who put
the blame on the perpetuation of several malfunctioning mechanisms
of the communist regime as the primary source nourishing today's
corruption. While Irina nicely stresses how communism made of
theft an institutionalized practice, interestingly suggesting that it
has re-framed corruption as a social value (as in Elisa Koelner's case
mentioned above), many other cultural observers would agree with the
distinguished Romanian historian Neagu Djuvara who has recently
argued that 'the most tragic legacy of communism is that during
half a century it has broken our [Romanian] soul' (2000: 225). Quite
paradoxically, from this point of view 'communism' (and surely anti-
communism) represents a major line of the current re-articulation of
self-representation of Romanianness. It does not really matter if this
takes place through a nostalgic discourse (e.g. 'life was better during
communism') or by way of blaming communism's cultural legacy, as
in the Djuvara example. In both cases, communism works as a symbol
of a shared moral order, which is perceived as radically different from

that which characterizes Romanian society before and after it. I am not saying that communist ideology has not exercised any influence on today's discourse and practices of corruption. I am rather trying to suggest that communism, like other historical phases of Romanian cultural history, while differently (politically) interpreted is often used to explain illegal practices by way of assuming or refusing its *otherness* as part of the Romanian soul.

Along with communism, another historical period of Romanian history induces many people to establish a direct link between Romanianness and corrupt behaviour. This is the historically controversial Ottoman domination in Romania between the second half of the fifteenth century and the late eighteenth century (see Panaite 2000). Turkish and/or Phanariote (Greek) practices and concepts are in fact frequently evoked, both in academic and popular discourse on corruption, in order to explain the very roots of various illegal behaviours understood as 'traditional practice' (one informant), or in many cases as a 'genetic illness' (another informant) affecting the nation as a whole.[9] To be sure, each informant according to her/his different knowledge, education and purpose is able to go into more or less detail in describing Turkish and/or Phanariote traditional cultural practices which are considered relevant in explaining or understanding contemporary corrupt practices. For example, one of them shows that he is well informed about the concept of *pesches*, a word of Turkish origin, which denotes a practice that – according to that informant – continues to affect the clientelistic political allocation of key managing roles within Romanian public administration. Another informant talked of an 'Oriental practice' characterized by the act of giving without any utilitarian goal, covered by the word/concept of *hatâr* (something close to gift). More commonly, in popular discourse and writings Phanariote and Turkish practices are matched and subsumed together under the same larger label: the 'Oriental-Balkan' heritage. This is also the case in scholarly work, as a recent legal study of legal offences of corruption conducted by a collective of Romanian academics attests: 'to eliminate corruption means to take educational measures, especially *to get rid of the Oriental-Balkan mentality* and people's tolerant attitude towards petty corruption' (Mrejeru et al. 2000: 5, my emphasis). As in the case of communism, once reified as a single and homogeneous entity the Oriental-Balkan historical heritage could be later constructed both as the 'dark side' of Romanianness or, on the contrary, as the imagined place of an uncorrupted past. The following quote is taken from an e-mail message another informant sent me after I asked him to explain the difference between *spaga* (bribe) and *bacsis* (tip):

Favour (*favor*) and bribe (*spaga*) are unnatural, impostors. They have abusively grown on the basis of decades of oriental gestures, such as tip (*bacsis*) and gift (*hatâr*). And nowadays people justify [illegal] practices in their names. There are for instance people who say that it is natural to ask or to carry out a favour, to take or to give a bribe. Nothing is further from the truth. All naturalness disappears when you start to offer something to a person who is supposed to do something for you. Favours and bribes change you, they distort you, they are gestures that create tension and keep you in permanent fear of maybe not obtaining what you expect.

The critical appreciation of contemporary immoral practices is supported by an idealized world of altruism and mutual generosity which is also constructed by using ancient Oriental traditions, here a symbol of a natural uncorrupted social order where the custom of 'giving without keeping' was apparently the rule. Besides this, the last sentence of the quote is intriguing in as much as it invites a closer examination of what I observed above, that is the frequent recourse to the irony register in everyday conversation about 'small' or 'petty' corruption. Far from being 'funny', as some informants suggest when *talking* about corruption, to engage *physically* in such actions is often conceived as a very sad, painful and 'distorting' experience.

By way of documentary and ethnographic sources we have seen how 'Miorita', 'communism' and 'Ottoman rule' can operate in Romania as rhetorical devices that create different images of corruption that establish a relationship between illegal behaviour and Romanian-ness – although articulated in different ways. People who use them are no doubt also involved in complex politics of othering, that is, they are engaged in different ways of constructing their own social and personal identities (and otherness) according to their particular interests, values, social tastes and world-views. Interestingly, while they are produced within specific local contexts all these images work by using a similar pattern, and by implicitly locating a *beginning* somewhere in the past that should help to explain the current profusion of corrupt practices. From this perspective they all seem to quite adequately fit the model of 'structural nostalgia', as coined by Michael Herzfeld: 'this is a collective representation of an Edenic order – a time before time – in which the balanced perfection of social relations has not yet suffered the decay that affects everything human' (Herzfeld 1997: 109). As Herzfeld himself observes, while 'for the state the model legitimizes intervention as an act of restoring a formerly perfect social order', for 'the lawless, the model offers evidence of a condition of moral corruption that makes engagement with the state an acceptable, pragmatic accommodation' (1997: 109).

CONCLUSION

For obvious reasons it is complicated to study corruption by way of 'participant-observation', and notably to grasp the bribe-giver's or bribe-taker's point of view. In Romania, the presumed pervasiveness of corruption within important social fields of action (such as work, education and health), means that people often use irony in order to communicate (outside and inside 'the community') and play with the asymmetric structure of power relations underlying corrupt practices at different levels. Within the specific field of property restitution, individual case narratives not only confirm that there are no 'absolute moralities' (see Pardo 2000: 21–3), they also show that moral attitudes towards corrupt behaviour often shift in time and place according to personal experience, occasional circumstances and collective histories. Former owners seeking restoration of property rights, while on the one hand blaming corruption per se, can also 'legitimately' have recourse to it in order to repair the crimes perpetrated by 'communism'. In so doing they signify and define their own social and moral identities by showing how the self (personal and collective) and the other (including the state) may be dynamically and politically constructed in corruption discourse and practice. Moreover, if corruption has become a potent symbol *in* and *of* post-socialist Romania this is also due to several widespread stereotyped images that establish an historical connection between illegal behaviour and national identity. Manipulating different aspects of Romanian cultural history as rhetorical devices (the Ottoman domination, communism or a folkloric poem), people construct particular and conflicting images of corruption and explain its causes. I do not argue that these images and explanations are irrelevant to an understanding of how corruption works in given social fields. Rather, I point out how behind this sort of explanation there often lurks an essentialist discourse that naturalizes corruption, suggesting that its roots are located somewhere in pure essences, whether 'our own' or those of 'others'. To make of corruption a 'natural' consequence of social life could be an innocent game in which all of us, as citizens and social scientists are involved on a daily basis. Nevertheless, in many cases this process of naturalization serves to legitimize specific politics of othering, producing harmful social and political consequences (such as exclusion and discrimination). All this should lead us at least to be doubtful of interpretations that tend to frame corrupt practices within a 'cultural code' without paying attention to local tactics and representations of the social actors themselves. More generally, I argue that in demystifying popular as well as academic processes of reifying corruption (or theft) as 'cultural', anthropologists could effectively participate in the collective work required to understand as well as deal with the phenomenon of corrupt practices. In order to do this, we have to refer back and forth between multiple agencies (individual and collective) and multiple systems (local, national, transnational), and focus on their continuous interplay. In so doing our contribution as social researchers would not be limited to pointing out the functioning of a local 'culture of corruption', an essentialist notion often lurking behind anthropological analysis. We could rather contribute by complicating the picture, pointing out ambiguities and contradictions that permeate the social fields where corrupt practices are played out (or not), legally sanctioned and interpreted, differently evaluated, and socially communicated in various social fields and discursive formations, each of which is provided with a specific and changing degree of socio-historical legitimacy.

NOTES

I would like to thank Mira and Nicu, Ina and Irina, Mihail and Cristina, Dan and Sanda, Radu, Adrian, Mihaela P., and Mihaela S. whose stories were the most valuable source in understanding what 'corruption' means in contemporary Romania. I also wish to thank the editors, and especially Peter Schneider, for their helpful comments and suggestions in order to sharpen the argument of a lónger version of this chapter (see Zerilli 2003). Sites and informants' names are modified in the text to avoid identification. All translations from Romanian texts and conversations are my own.

1. Obviously, anti-corruption discourse has in itself a social and ideological dimension that should also be ethnographically investigated (see Sampson 2004). While I am not pursuing here this line of approach, I assume that a sensitive 'global ethnography' (see Burawoy 2001) of those transnational institutions producing anti-corruption discourse and policies would reveal that far from being pathologic somewhere and physiologic somewhere else, generally speaking corruption is part of a wider range of 'occult economies' that shape and are shaped by the 'culture of neoliberalism' in its millennial features (see Comaroff and Comaroff 2001: 19–28 particularly).

2. Corruption and anti-corruption policies have been, and actually are widely debated in Romanian society especially since the elaboration of a bill in 1998, that subsequently led to the adoption of Law 78/2000 ('Law on Preventing, Detecting and Punishing Acts of Corruption') according to specific recommendations provided by United Nations and Council of Europe (see Pruna 2000).

3. Political scientists and transnational institutions engaged in anti-corruption policies such as the World Bank or NGO Transparency International conventionally define corruption as 'the abuse of public office for private gain'. This definition relies on the opposition between 'public' and 'private', a legalistic one which has been shown to be problematic in specific ethnographic contexts, as also shown in the next section.

4. In the Romanian Penal Code the very word corruption (*coruptie*) is explicitly mentioned only in two cases: the first refers to 'sexual corruption' (*coruptie sexuala*, Article 202) and the second to the 'corruption exerted on a person to make false statements in justice' (*coruperea unui persoane de a da declaratii mincinoase în fata justitiei*, Article 261). Nevertheless, it is commonly accepted within the penal doctrine and practice to consider that the notion of corruption is extended to various offences, and particularly

that of 'bribe-taking' (*luare de mita*, Article 254), 'bribe-offering' (*darea de mita*, Article 255), 'receiving unjustified advantages' (*primirea de foloase necuvenite*, Article 256) and 'trade of influence' (*traficul de influenta*, Article 257) (see Banciu and Radulescu 1994: 171–2). Formerly defined as 'office or related to office offences' within the Penal Code, these offences are now formally recognized as 'corruption offences' by Law 78/2000.

5. Not surprisingly, a recent World Bank survey about corruption in Romania shows that at the 'household' level people perceive (in this order) the Parliament, the judiciary, the ministries, and the government as the institutions where corruption is most widespread (see Anderson et al. 2001: 5).

6. An influential role was played by the philosophical exegesis offered by Lucian Blaga (1944 [1936]) to whom we also owe the famous notion of '*mioritic* space'.

7. Interestingly, the 'orthodox' interpretation of 'Miorita' (the one that draws essentially on the stoic acceptance of death by the protagonist) concludes that Romanians have a 'fatalistic attitude' and a 'contemplative character'. This identity trait of Romanianness is actually another powerful stereotyped image which also plays a leading role in explaining corrupt practices, especially from the bribe-givers' point of view: representing themselves as embedded in a system of unwritten rules that they cannot refuse to accept (see section above), bribe-givers justify their participation in the game by explicitly evoking *mioritic* features and images such as passiveness, inertia, attitudes of observing and gossiping instead of acting and making decisions.

8. It is worth mentioning that during fieldwork, in August 2002 this stereotyped image was being reproduced in French national newspapers such as *Le Monde* or *Libération*.

9. A recent public-opinion poll on corruption conducted in Bucharest states that 28 percent of the people interviewed mentioned 'national traditions' among the principal causes of corruption (see Baboi-Stroe and Tiganescu 2000: 7). Unfortunately, the authors do not go further in detailing what kind of 'national traditions' their sample is referring to.

REFERENCES

Anderson, J., B. Cosmaciuc, P. Dininio, B. Spector and P. Zoido-Lobaton (2001) *Diagnostic Surveys of Corruption in Romania*. Available online <http://www.transparency.ro>. Accessed July 2002.

Baboi-Stroe, A. and O. Tiganescu (2000) *Sondaj de opinie la nivelul municipiului Bucuresti privind fenomenul coruptiei*. Available online at <http://www.transparency.ro>. Accessed July 2002.

Banciu, D. and S. Radulescu (1994) *Coruptia si crima organizata în România* (Bucuresti: 'Continent XXI').

Blaga, L. (1944 [1936]) Spatiul mioritic, in L. Blaga, *Trilogia culturii* (Bucuresti: Fundatia Regala pentru Literatura si Arta).

Borneman, J. (1997) *Settling Accounts* (Princeton, NJ: Princeton University Press).

Burawoy, M. (ed.) (2001) *Global Ethnography*. Thematic Issue of *Ethnography*, Vol. 2, No. 2.

Ceobanu, A.M. (1998) When Socialism Meets Capitalism, MA thesis, University of Nebraska. Available online at <http://www.transparency.ro>. Accessed July 2002.

Comaroff, J. and J. Comaroff (eds) (2001), *Millennial Capitalism and the Culture of Neoliberalism* (Durham, NC and London: Duke University Press).

Crehan, K. (2002) *Gramsci, Culture and Anthropology* (London: Pluto Press).

Djuvara, N. (2000) *O scurta istorie a românilor povestita celor tineri* (Bucuresti: Humanitas).

Eliade, M. (1992 [1943]) *Les Roumains. Précis historique.* (Bucuresti: Roza Vînturilor).

Fernandez, J.W. and M. Taylor Huber (eds) (2001) *Irony in Action* (Chicago: University of Chicago Press).

Fochi, A. (1964) *Miorita* (Bucuresti: Editura Academiei R.P.R.).

Gupta, A. (1995) Blurred Boundaries, *American Ethnologist*, Vol. 22, No. 2: 375–402.

Herzfeld, M. (1997) *Cultural Intimacy* (New York and London: Routledge).

Liiceanu, A. and M. Sélim (1999) Entretien avec Aurora Liiceanu, *Journal des Anthropologues*, No. 77–8: 53–65.

Lovell, D.W. (2004) Corruption as a Transitional Phenomenon: Understanding Endemic Corruption in Postcommunist States, Chapter 4, this volume.

Mrejeru, T., D. Florescu, D. Safta and M. Safta (2000) *Infractiunile de coruptie* (Bucuresti: All Beck).

Mungiu-Pippidi, A. (2002) *Politica dupa comunism* (Bucuresti: Humanitas).

Nicolau, I. (2001) Hotia la români. Înainte si dupa 23 August, *Dilema* (Special Issue: Foloasele si ponoasele coruptiei), No. 448, 28 Sept. – 4 Oct.

Panaite, V. (2000) *The Ottoman Law of War and Peace* (New York: Columbia University Press).

Pardo, I. (ed.) (2000) *Morals of Legitimacy* (New York and Oxford: Berghahn Books).

Pruna, R.A. (2000) *Legal Anti-corruption Measures in the Romanian Public Sector.* Accessed online <http://www.transparency.ro>. July 2002.

Sampson, S. (2004) Integrity Warriors: Global Morality and the Anti-corruption Movement in the Balkans, Chapter 6, this volume.

Stefan, C. (2001) Sistemul asta... *Dilema* (Special Issue: Foloasele si ponoasele coruptiei), No. 448, 28 Sept. – 4 Oct.

Verdery, K. (1983) *Transylvanian Villagers* (Berkeley: University of California Press).

—— (1996) *What Was Socialism, and What Comes Next?* (Princeton, NJ: Princeton University Press).

Zafiu, R. (1993) Din lexicul coruptiei (I), *Luceafarul*, No. 48: 4; 'Din lexicul coruptiei (II)'. *Luceafarul*, No. 49: 4.

Zerilli, F.M. (2002) Sentiments and/as Property Rights, *Focaal*, No. 39: 57–71.

—— (2003) Playing (with) bribery, in C. Papa, G. Pizza and F.M. Zerilli (eds) *La Ricerca antropologica in Romania* (Napoli: ESI).

Zinn, D.L. (2001) *La Raccomandazione* (Roma: Donzelli).

PART II

Institutionalized Corruption and Institutions of Anti-corruption

6 INTEGRITY WARRIORS: GLOBAL MORALITY AND THE ANTI-CORRUPTION MOVEMENT IN THE BALKANS

Steven Sampson

INTRODUCTION: THE ANTHROPOLOGY OF VIRTUE

There is something going on out there. It is a movement toward increasing morality, ethics and simply 'doing the right thing' in human affairs. This movement goes under several labels: 'global governance', 'oversight', 'accountability', 'transparency', or what Mary Robinson has termed 'ethical globalization'. The loudest voice in this accountability movement appears to come from 'global civil society', the conglomerate of non-governmental interest groups and organizations who exert pressure on governments and transnational corporations to change policies or reveal their true motives. This voice often invokes its grassroots character, yet it would be misleading to think that the impetus towards accountability comes solely from below. Governments, large international organizations and transnational corporations are not simply *reacting* to pressure or trying to save face. Among these organs of global elite power as well, we see a new-found interest in doing good, or at least doing better. We see it among governments, in the corporations, within the World Bank, and in the programmes of the Davos crowd. Both from below (global civil society) and from above ('them'), there seems to be a wave of virtue out there.

Evidence for this can be seen in governments making public promises to do good, in the international organizations' efforts to promote accountability, in private companies talking about integrity and ethics, and in the success of civil society networks who successfully push and prod these actors via their awareness-raising activities, lobbying, advocacy, whistle-blowing and public demonstrations.

One part of this move toward governance, accountability and transparency is the fight against corruption. The struggle against corruption is now transnational in two respects. First, it is springing up all over, from finance ministries in Belgium to aid offices in Kenya to city government in Colombia. Second, it is now the object of global coordination. Ethical globalization and ethics management are now at the forefront of corporate activity. The high level of publicity given to recent business scandals such as Enron, Arthur Andersen, WorldCom and Halliburton in Iraq, indicates that the ethical issue is not simply window dressing. Every major government now has a high-level anti-corruption unit, an action plan, and various campaigns in the works.

Anti-corruption activities, I would argue, are part of a general trend toward global ethics and moral justification in human affairs. We see this trend in various spheres of political and social life, from the development of codes of conduct to courses in corporate ethics. We also see it in the increasing dominance of human rights programmes in foreign policy, in the establishment of truth and reconciliation commissions, and in efforts to construct national integrity systems as part of anti-corruption. Why is this happening? Why, in the midst of no-holds-barred neoliberal efficiency and organizational downsizing, do we also find more institutions consciously trying to 'do the right thing'? Why is everyone trying to act so honestly? What has happened that social relations should now be so transparent and accountable?

One could account for this trend by asserting that there has been some kind general progress in human affairs. In a post-Holocaust, post-totalitarian world, we can certainly observe the influence of human rights practices. Efforts to ensure dignity, democracy and equality have made even the most marginal groups aware of their rights, and the most powerful corporations and governments responsive to them. This argument would assume that we are in some kind of new era, an era of dignity, and that progress has forced the privileged classes, ruthless corporations and unresponsive governments to ensure these rights by treating people in a dignified fashion.

The problem with this kind of argument, that things are getting better, is that it coexists with manifest evidence that things are also getting worse. Along with struggles for human rights and dignity for minority or marginal groups, we thus see ever more vicious examples of human neglect and human misery: the so-called 'new wars' targeting civilian populations, ethnic cleansing and genocide, trafficking of women, children and refugees, new forms of slavery, child abuse, unscrupulous terrorist attacks, the ruthless sale of human organs, 'the politics of the belly' among venal African dictators, transnational organized crime networks, diamond wars using child soldiers, unabashed corporate embezzlement and innumerable other examples of debasement of moral standards and human dignity.

In this latter group of negative phenomena lies 'the rise' in global corruption. Whether corruption has in fact increased is difficult to discern, since measures of corruption are notoriously difficult to validate. There is certainly a rise in the issue of corruption as a topic of public concern. Integrity, ethics and responsibility have become integral parts of public policy. The 'C-word', as it was once called at the World Bank, is now up front. The Bank itself is at the forefront of anti-corruption efforts (Stapenhurst and Kpundeh 1999). Governments, corporations and aid organizations are all being held accountable. Open tendering procedures, open financial accounts and open recruitment are all the order of the day. The key to integrity is accountability.

The anti-corruption movement has now entered this sphere of integrity and accountability. Anti-corruption is not just a set of policy measures enacted by governments to prevent bribery and punish nepotism. It is also a moral force, reflecting the indignation among ordinary people and among articulate elites that things are not right. Anti-corruption entails not only making governments or aid programmes more effective, but also making people more honest, raising people's consciousness to a new level. Anti-corruption is thus a moral, even religious force. This is why some activists within Transparency International, the leading anti-corruption organization, see themselves as 'integrity warriors' (see <www.transparency.org>). Responding to unscrupulous transnational forces of immorality and profiteering, the struggle against corruption is an effort to restore standards that were lost, the standards of morality and responsibility which connote what we call 'community'. There is now an emergent 'anti-corruption community', acting on behalf of 'global civil society'. The anti-corruption community struggles for accountability from faceless bureaucracies and secretive corporations. It is now so extensive that it includes groups normally at odds with each other: grassroots activists pursuing social justice, enlightened corporations who believe that ethics is good business, neoliberal governments who see corruption as a brake on trade, and international aid organizations who want their donor funds to be more effective. The fight against corruption is thus more than just the 'tactics' of governments or corporations who want to look good: it is a moral crusade.

This chapter deals largely with the civil society actors behind the anti-corruption movement. The idea of 'a global civil society' or 'a global community' as a social actor is not unproblematic. These terms take on a rhetorical form which makes them little more than wishful thinking. How can there be a global civil society without a global state? Where is the global citizenship consisting of clear rights and enforceable obligations? To what unit do these global citizens belong? Who, or what is their point of reference? If global citizenship consists only of marching in demonstrations or being connected to the Internet, what happens to citizenship if I can just remove my name from the e-mail list? Where are my obligations then?

Nevertheless, some social movements have the power to mobilize large numbers of people from diverse social classes to achieve common goals. This mobilization takes place as a reaction to specific events in specific places, but also in transnational forums unbounded by place. In this sense, such 'movements' create a quasi-form of community solidarity. Anti-corruption is becoming one of these movements. Even more than women's rights, environmental protection or the rights of the child, to name three such global movements with varying local dynamics, the movement for anti-corruption is one of the few platforms which can bring virtually all of us together. After all, who can be *for* corruption?

ANTI-CORRUPTION GOES GLOBAL

Corruption is conventionally defined as the abuse of public office for private gain (though recent definitions, stimulated by the Enron and Wall Street scandals, now extend corruption to be the abuse of any sort of 'entrusted authority', as would occur by a board chairman). Corruption is a complex social practice with its own specific local variations. An understanding of corruption entails an understanding of the social contexts that produce and sustain it, such that a change of these contexts would also cause changes in patterns of corruption. Corruption, in other words, has a history. To this history must be added a discursive element: the rhetoric of corruption, accusations of corruption, claims of 'endemic corruption' and now the discourse centred upon the 'struggle against corruption.'

The struggle against corruption also has a history, both rhetorically and in terms of action plans. In the late 1970s, states as diverse as China and Mexico had anti-corruption campaigns and anti-corruption offices. The US government enacted the world's first strict anti-corruption act in foreign trade in 1977, penalizing companies that gave bribes. These campaigns, however, had little effect until the late 1990s, when corruption suddenly became a major issue.

In the last five or six years, anti-corruption practices have diffused transnationally and have become organized globally. We have seen the emergence of a *world of anti-corruption* with its own actors, strategies, resources and practices, with its heroes, victims and villains. Unlike corruption, which is locally grounded and moves internationally, this new world of anti-corruption seems to be more globalized and coordinated from its inception. Whereas corruption begins locally and spreads, anti-corruption begins at the top and then penetrates locally. The particular problem I will deal with in this chapter is why this struggle against corruption has become so prominent, becoming even a cornerstone of international development initiatives and United States foreign policy. After all, corruption has been around since the very beginning of the public sphere, and philosophers, citizens and leaders have always complained about corruption (Hindess 2001: 5, citing Aristotle). For decades we have known that billions of dollars have been diverted by various corrupt practices, including bribery of judges, false contracts, padded development projects, dishonest officials and nepotistic arrangements. Why have anti-corruption initiatives become so prominent in the last few years? What is it that took so long for anti-corruption to 'arrive' as a global accountability issue?

Two possible explanations come to mind: one centred on moral progress, the other on system rationality. The moral explanation is that anti-corruption is just the next step in a project to make the world a better, more just place. This is the rhetoric of 'ethical globalization'. The fight against corruption is virtuous, and those who form part of the 'anti-corruption community' are thus 'integrity warriors'. The second explanation focuses on the need to increase system rationality: fighting corruption, it is argued, will make market economies more efficient, state administration more effective, and development resources more accessible. Let us for the moment assume that both these imperatives, the moral and the rational, are operating. If this is the case, we might say that we find ourselves in a conjuncture of anti-corruption. Such conjunctures provide interesting 'windows' for understanding how global and local processes intersect, be they processes of global economic restructuring or processes of accountability linked to respect for human rights and global justice.

Since anti-corruption has become globalized, I will explore the issue of corruption and anti-corruption in terms of globalization. Here globalization is understood as a dual process that entails first transnational economic exchange and, second, the cultural process in which certain discourses, symbols, practices and understanding of the world seem to diffuse, and are thereupon manipulated by local actors in pursuit of specific projects. The 'anti-corruption movement' is one such project. It can thus be both a goal, something to be achieved in moral or systemic terms, and a means of pursuing one's own private strategies or those of one's group. Anti-corruption is thus an objective and a tactic.

STUDYING ANTI-CORRUPTION: GLOBAL AND LOCAL SCENES

In the past decade, I have been involved in both research and consulting on various aspects of democracy assistance in Southeast

Europe. In these dual capacities, I have observed how the rhetoric of 'anti-corruption', what I will call 'anti-corruptionism', is now penetrating the Balkan aid practices and local political life. In focusing on global anti-corruption and how it operates in the Balkans, I will describe the nature of the global anti-corruption activity, centring on international meetings, conventions, agreements and on one particularly successful anti-corruption organization, Transparency International (TI). TI has been at the forefront of anti-corruption initiatives, though it is only beginning its activities in Southeast Europe. TI is interesting because of its seemingly unparalleled success in making an impact on the major public actors and in dominating the anti-corruption discourse. How and why was TI so successful and what does this say about the global anti-corruption movement? This research is only in its initial stage, and my data will be based partly on a perusal of the massive anti-corruption literature, attendance at the world anti-corruption conferences in Prague in October 2001 and Seoul in May 2003, where I interviewed many anti-corruption activists, and a brief visit to TI's London office for research and documentation. I have also participated in other anti-corruption forums in Latvia, Sweden and Denmark. With these data, I attempt to present some aspects of the global anti-corruption scene, including the anti-corruption landscape in Romania, where I worked recently. Like other parts of Southeast Europe where I conducted fieldwork, Romania has been notorious for corrupt practices spanning various political regimes. Today it is experiencing an upsurge of anti-corruption initiatives emanating from both governmental and non-governmental actors. This upsurge comes as a result of public outcry against corrupt officials, pressure from international donors for accountability and the demands of EU association/membership. Pursuing anti-corruption has led to a whole set of practices revolving around the formulation and implementation of national and regional anti-corruption programmes.

This combination of public, private, international and civil society actors makes the world of anti-corruption into a complex social force of its own, and worth understanding anthropologically. On the basis of the documentation and field study, my preliminary conclusion is that an understanding of the anti-corruption 'industry' can help us understand how knowledge and practice are produced in a globalized setting. This production has a moral aspect: it is about virtue and efficiency in the same 'package'. Moreover, an understanding of anti-corruption can help us to understand the emerging dynamics of global citizenship. This global citizenship is founded upon an imagined global moral order. It is about doing what is necessary and what is good. Understanding anti-corruption as a global morality discourse linked to neoliberal rationality can help us understand why anti-corruption has emerged on the scene in the past five or six years, together with other movements for global justice, governance and accountability. Anthropology is about studying how people engage with the world. In this sense, 'doing good' comes in waves. There are conjunctures of virtue, and perhaps we are now in one such conjuncture. Hence, this chapter is a step toward outlining a general anthropology of virtue.

ANTI-CORRUPTION AS A GRANT CATEGORY

Virtue is not just about ideas. It is about obtaining the resources to struggle for one's ideas. 'Civil society development' and 'democracy promotion' are very much tied to 'Funding Virtue', to use the title of a recent book (Ottoway and Carothers 2000). Anti-corruption is therefore an interesting case of this production of virtue, of goodwill, of the struggle for integrity in human affairs which characterizes other global movements for rights, environment and justice. This movement attempts to establish and enforce ethical codes, to regulate virtue (Brien 2001).

In pursuing virtue, this struggle for resources is relentless. Organizations are constantly attempting to procure money for projects, and hence developing funding strategies. Anti-corruption is now at the stage where what were once moral campaigns and virtuous ideas must now be converted into grant categories and technical assistance contracts. This trend is hardly new. We have seen the way in which struggles for human dignity and mobilizing grassroots movements to achieve change have now evolved into programme areas and budget lines for 'human rights' and 'civil society'. Similar trends are occurring with anti-corruption, especially in the Balkans, where international donors bring their own agendas and priorities, where there are foreign aid organizations, humanitarian NGOs, training needs assessments, political foundations and private consulting companies all specializing in governance and anti-corruption.

This trend is what I call the *projectization* of anti-corruption. Projectization is not necessarily to be condemned, but it does throw a new light on how we should understand the pursuit of virtue. Virtue, like morality, can thus be viewed as a specific kind of social process. Anthropologists who study NGOs, for example, are often members or supporters of the goals of these organizations. They may therefore overlook (or even refuse to acknowledge) more unpleasant phenomena of power and manipulation behind them. It is in this sense that we should also examine other movements for global morality and virtue, including the anti-corruption movement. We need to examine 'global morality' not just as an ideological stream but as a social process. It is a process by which virtue is transformed into a specific activity called a project – one that includes formulating a funding strategy, approaching donors, analysing stakeholders, hiring consultants, developing NGOs, conducting project appraisals, making evaluations... and yes, on to the next project. Anti-corruption activities can therefore lead to and reinforce an entire complex of discursive practices which may have little to do with fighting corruption as such. Anti-corruptionism, as I will show here, is a stage in which moral projects are intertwined with money and power. This is the world of anti-corruption.

ANTI-CORRUPTION AS A WORLD

As part of the general wave of openness, struggle for dignity, transparency and accountability, anti-corruption has developed its own discourse, actors and sets of practices. That anti-corruption has arrived is evidenced by its 400,000 hits on Google, up from 115,000 in early 2003, but far below the 6.4 million hits if one searches for 'human rights'. Nevertheless, there now exist several 'anti-corruption gateways' run by well-funded NGOs and companies. There are intergovernmental organizations, world conferences, anti-corruption web portals, World Bank offices, government reports and NGO projects dedicated to corruption. There are '*aides mémoires*' written by development agencies, anti-corruption training courses for government officials and, in the UK one can now obtain an MA in 'Fraud Studies'. In sum, one can conclude that anti-corruption has become 'a world'.

A 'world', as anthropologists might define it, could be equated with Bourdieu's 'field'. It involves a set of actors whose practices are carried out under various structural constraints. These actors attempt to control or channel resources to achieve their strategies. This world has its own special terminology, jargon and rhetoric, and it bases its appeal on adherence to certain legal, economic and moral norms. The world of anti-corruption has its own ritual events, its foundation myths and its own folklore, a kind of mirror image of Myrdal's 'folklore of corruption' from 35 years ago (1968: 355–77).

Anti-corruption is more than just high-sounding talk and World Bank aid projects. It can also constitute a political platform for ambitious politicians or ex-military officers who want to 'clean up' government. Anti-corruption is invariably a part of most military coups, and as part of the good governance rhetoric, an obligatory anti-corruption programme is now one of the conditions written into most foreign aid cooperation agreements.

In the world of anti-corruption, diverse actors normally at odds with each other can come together in the same moral crusade. There are anti-corruption campaigns conducted among large private companies and government agencies, anti-corruption conferences bringing together activists and world leaders, and there is a growing anti-corruption 'movement' led by Transparency International, whose international lobbying is backed by nearly a hundred local branches and dedicated local activists. It is significant that anti-corruption measures can make headlines, and that every corruption scandal not only fills newspapers but places pressure on politicians 'to do something'.

As anti-corruption has become a 'world', it has also become amenable to cross-national comparison using presumably objective measures. There is thus an emerging industry of corruption measurement, bribe-payers' indices, opacity indices, indices of 'state capture', all of which pale in importance to Transparency International's Corruption Perceptions Index.

Since corruption is tied not only to individual strategies and opportunities, but also to manipulation of value systems and legal norms, the anti-corruption discourse also revolves around a moral–legal nexus. Combating corruption is thus viewed as a multi-pronged effort of government, the private sector and civil society to change institutions, pass new laws, crack down on dishonest officials and raise awareness of citizens. Anti-corruption is economic openness, political will and moral commitment. Just as we can compare the various forms of corruption in different societies, we can also compare the forms of anti-corruption.

In the morally charged atmosphere of anti-corruption, there are heroes, villains and innocent victims. The heroes are the 'integrity warriors' who expose corruption or fight abuse; they may be journalists, lawyers and community leaders. One such hero is the Norwegian prosecutor Eva Jolie, who helped expose the massive French corruption scandals by officials in Paris. Another such hero is Peter Eigen, the most prominent among the founders of Transparency International (TI). A former World Bank expert in Africa, Eigen has tirelessly worked to build up TI as the leading non-governmental anti-corruption player. Mr Eigen is in no way a grassroots activist, but by travelling around the world to spread his message of anti-corruption, he has encouraged local activists to expose government or police abuse while helping to build the global anti-corruption community.

The villains in this anti-corruption narrative are the corrupt officials or venal government leaders, especially in the developing world, who not only take the occasional bribe but who systematically plunder their treasuries. These grand villains are assisted by the lackadaisical officials who refuse to enact or enforce anti-corruption legislation. In consort with them are the bureaucrats and the foreign donor agencies who are not forceful enough in their demands for honesty, or not effective enough in monitoring their donated funds.

As Transparency International activists are fond of pointing out, discussion of corruption used to be taboo in development discourse (Galtung 2000; see also the TI website). Donor accusations that Third World regimes were pilfering aid were considered interference in these countries' internal affairs, even racism.

Finally, the anti-corruption drama has its hapless victims: the ordinary citizens confronting unresponsive bureaucrats, the legal clients who must bribe a lawyer or judge, the hospital patients who must pay off a nurse, the students who must bribe their teachers, the women and children who are unprotected by corrupt police, etc. In the eyes of the anti-corruption community, corruption is a 'violation of human rights', corruption is 'the opposite of democracy', 'corruption is a tax on the poor', etc.

One might at first sight see the anti-corruption discourse as similar to the other global discourses on human rights, women's rights, democracy, environmental protection, cultural self-determination, etc. Yet in all these latter projects, there are legal, political and philosophical issues in which there are clearly demarcated interests: women's rights advocates, for example, must struggle against 'cultural traditions' by which women are subjected to family or male dominance. The universal aspects of human rights have had to struggle with doctrines of non-interference in a nation's internal affairs or cultural understandings of the individual and the collective. Environmental protection policies must continually deal with legitimate interests of fostering economic growth to the detriment of natural resources. Corruption and anti-corruption have no such 'balance'. There is no 'corruption lobby' against which anti-corruption advocates mobilize. There are no openly identified vested interests which can be fought. There are no 'procorruption forces'. While there is considerable research being carried out on the causes and consequences of corruption (see Andvig and Fjeldstad et al. 2002), there is little reflection on how one might research anti-corruption.

An anti-corruption *research* agenda differs from descriptions of anti-corruption strategies or measures. Anti-corruption research might include the following questions: what groups/institutions occupy themselves with the 'struggle against corruption'? To what extent is corruption viewed as a legal, economic, moral and/or political issue? Which definitions are dominant in the public and policy discourse? To what extent is anti-corruption implemented as effective actions, i.e., doing right, versus simply façade measures, that is, feeling good about doing right? Which groups in society mobilize against corruption, both informally and as interest organizations? Which political formations use anti-corruption as part of their platforms and how do they do this? Who accuses whom of corruption? What is the effect of such accusations on the parties involved and on society as a whole? When is it taboo to talk about corruption and when is it nearly a duty? And to what extent is anti-corruptionism a genuine crusade, versus an instrument by which actors compete for organizational resources, international donor grants, etc.? In short, what does all this anti-corruption activity 'mean'?

The world of anti-corruption is not self-contained. It is a world where players struggle to influence others. These others are the large international donor institutions such as the World Bank or UNDP (United Nations Development Programme), the international business community, acting under such rubrics as the Global Compact, and the local politicians who are pressured to enact stricter laws and regulations on the private sector and on civil servants. The goal of anti-corruption activity is to get these various institutions 'on board', so that the corrupt politicians or unaccountable companies can be isolated or shamed into better governance. In the terms used by global civil society, which are also the terms used by the anti-corruption movement, placing pressure on powerful institutions involves 'coalition-building'. One of the most successful of these coalition builders is Transparency International. The success of TI has been its ability to mobilize these players into a common mission, despite the obvious differences of interests between them. TI has done this by both challenging and accommodating themselves to the other players.

THREE ANTI-CORRUPTION SITES

In the remainder of this chapter, I outline three sites where the anti-corruption world unfolds. First, the international anti-corruption meetings, in which activists, donors and officials exchange ideas and decide priorities. Second, the global NGO Transparency International which, with headquarters in Berlin and nearly 100 branches, attempts to set the agenda for anti-corruption activism. Third, an example from Romania will serve to illustrate the complexities of the anti-corruption world so that we can see how global virtue and anti-corruption interact.

Site 1. 'Together against corruption': The International Anti-corruption Conference

Every two years, two major anti-corruption events are held. One is the Global Forum on Anti-corruption, a meeting of governmental representatives, delegations and experts whch discuss anti-corruption policy. The Global Forum is a closed gathering only for government delegates and other invitees. The second event is the

International Anti-Corruption Conference (IACC), which is open to all those interested in fighting cooperation, including grass roots organizations.

The Tenth International Anti-Corruption Conference was held in October 2001 in Prague, some five months after the Global Forum (see Transparency International 2002). The IACC was billed as a grassroots conference, with TI playing the secretariat role. Among the IACC's 1,300 paying participants were representatives from 133 countries and, more importantly, from all the major international players, including 'the Bank', the UNDP, major development aid organizations, Interpol, local government officials and a diverse group of Northern and Southern NGOs. The theme of the conference was 'Together Against Corruption: Designing Strategies, Assessing Impact, Reforming Corrupt Institutions'.

The conference was a major event, with Vaclav Havel giving the opening address in Prague Castle, with invitations, security checks and black-tied waiters. At the International Conference Centre were exhibition stands of major international institutions and publishers in the world of development economics and statistics. Celebrity speeches were given by the Mexican President Vincente Fox, the financier George Soros, the French prosecutor Eva Jolie (who received an award) and innumerable government ministers and officials, even from the People's Republic of China. Underlining the importance of this event were the access conditions: the participation fee for the three days was no less than US $890. Being used to academic conference fees, I mentioned my dissatisfaction to one of my fellow participants, an Interpol delegate. Nonchalantly, he remarked: 'This is nothing, at police conferences you pay $500 per day.' So much for the grassroots element.

Our conference packets, along with a programme of 200 presentations, contained a ticket to the 'Art Against Corruption' exhibition in Prague and a plastic whistle to symbolize one of the conference themes: protection of 'whistle-blowers' who expose corruption. At the panels, government officials, aid experts, lawyers and activists presented papers on topics as diverse as corruption in aid programmes, corruption in health, corruption in education, corruption among NGOs, anti-corruption legislation, parliamentary oversight, the role of the media, and ethics in the private sector. With the Enron/Arthur Andersen scandal just breaking, private sector oversight was a major topic of discussion. There was a variety of area presentations focusing on corruption and anti-corruption in post-communist Europe, Latin America, Asia and Africa. There were a few presentations on corruption research in which World Bank experts operationalized the concept of 'state capture', and in which TI staff members gave details about the Corruption Perceptions Index.

Among the activist-oriented panels in the conference, a major theme was 'coalition-building', here understood as the pragmatic cooperation with the powers that be. Coalition-building is conceived as the opposite of confrontation. Corruption may be related to market reforms, but anti-corruption activity should not be linked to anti-globalization demonstrations. Anti-corruption NGOs had to become more professional. Hence, the Conference statement explains:

Ours is a powerful coalition which has grown increasingly in size and strength over the course of past Conferences. We are committed to building global standards of transparency and accountability not only for governments but also for the private sector, civil society and international institutions alike. We do this in the belief that we are contributing to improving the welfare of people throughout the world, particularly the poor, and see these standards as fundamental to achieving acceptable levels of social justice buttressed by the Rule of Law. We must encourage others to embrace transparency and accountability, but we ourselves must ensure that our own practices also meet these standards. (<www.10iacc.org> and Transparency International 2002a)

The tendency toward professionalism over activism was evidenced at one session, when one of the panellists, from an ecological policy group, mentioned how successful they had been in their periodic meetings with 'Jim' at 'the Bank' and how Jim had given assurances that anti-corruption was placed at the top of the Bank's agenda. For the uninitiated, Jim is James Wolfensohn, the affable chairman of the World Bank. One can speculate how far from grassroots such organizations have come when they are on a first -name basis with one of the major personages representing the icon of global capitalism.

One of my most striking impressions of the conference was its moral atmosphere. Most of the participants were in Prague not only because they wanted to acquire knowledge about anti-corruption strategies or learn about projects but because they were genuinely committed to wiping out corruption. The latter was especially true of certain North American delegates (American and Canadian) who had anti-corruption activity as an avocation. The moral aspects were present in some of the surprising mixture of panels which brought together such diverse actors as the 'ethics officer' of the mining company Rio Tinto, a vice-president from Royal Dutch Shell, an activist from the NGO Global Witness who has successfully fought to enforce a ban on 'conflict diamonds', the financier George Soros and Mexican President Vincente Fox. All are against corruption not only because it hurts people or is bad for business, but because it is 'bad', period.

The Prague Anti-corruption Conference was a tremendous public relations success for Transparency International. TI chairman Peter Eigen was cordially thanked and enthusiastically applauded by all the delegates during each plenary session. Like other plenary speakers, Eigen was emphatic in saying that coalition-building was essential, that fighting corruption is not just a government activity but demands cooperation from international institutions to fight corruption's global nature; it demands the support of the international business community; anti-corruption requires that development assistance agencies and development NGOs maintain standards in order to keep Third World leaders honest; and, finally, support for civil society is also necessary. Anti-corruption has thus become everyone's responsibility.

The conference was not without tensions, centred largely on the discussion of 'conditionality' in aid to Third World countries and how to enforce this. Anti-corruption was viewed by some Third World delegates as a political tactic to keep Third World recipient countries in line, as the latest incarnation of the Bank's structural adjustment programme. As in so many gatherings where development is discussed, much of the discussion centred on what 'the donors' should do, that corruption started with them, and that the local Third World politician who pocketed a contract was but a symptom of a larger problem.

The Tenth International Anti-Corruption Conference was followed 19 months later by the Eleventh Conference, a four-day gathering held in Seoul. South Korea had been undergoing a major corruption clean-up over the past years, and the conference was clearly meant to reveal the new face of the country, including its anti-corruption initiatives. The conference was marketed as a grassroots gathering, but it was not without its exorbitant participation fee of $800. As a result of prohibitive travel costs, and due to restrictions connected with SARS, many delegates from East Asia and Third World countries did not attend. There were about 1,000 delegates, 200 of them from Korea itself, and a disproportionately large number of Anglo-Americans and West Europeans (though no French).

Nevertheless, the Seoul gathering was a milestone because it was directly followed by the more established Global Forum which only government delegates and experts could attend. Just prior to this gathering was Transparency International's General Assembly, attended by about 120 delegates. The vast majority of the non-governmental participants were somehow connected to TI.

As in Prague, participants in Seoul were treated to an elaborate opening ceremony in a grand conference centre under government patronage and a cultural evening sponsored by the Ministry of Justice and the City of Seoul. The theme of the Eleventh Conference was 'Different Cultures, Common Values' and the focus was again on themes such as private sector governance, public sector management, the role of civil society, international corruption, measuring corruption and building ethics. To symbolize the ethical aspect, the opening address was given by theologian Hans Kung, one of the foremost leaders in the global ethics movement. The South Korean prime minister, a former activist in Transparency International, also spoke. As in Prague, the core of the anti-corruption activists are British, American, Canadian and European. On the heels of the Enron scandal, the conference contained renewed emphasis on controlling corporate corruption. Whereas corruption used to be about corrupt public servants, it was now a question of controlling any kind of abuse of 'entrusted authority', including that of a corporate board room.

Like Prague, the Seoul conference was an organizational triumph for Transparency International and for its director Peter Eigen, who was celebrated at every turn. TI had a large booth at the conference to exhibit CORIS, its anti-corruption portal and database. TI's presence was embodied in the many staff members from the Berlin and London offices, and additional heads of national affiliates who had received some travel funds via TI. Peter Eigen was present at all the major ceremonies on the podium.

International conferences function as channels of information, forums for network-building and sites of rites of solidarity. Some of these anti-corruption conferences, such as the Global Forum and the Anti-corruption Summit (held in 2000 in Arlington) are closed affairs. Others, such as the IACCs, are issue-centred and open to all, thus bringing together a varied group of specialists, bureaucrats and activists. Unlike traditional academic conferences, there is no specific experience among the participants that marks them as members. They have paid (or their governments have paid) a fee and they attend. The conferences are not the high points of an organization, but the venue for a 'movement'. In this case, donors, activists and officials are brought together. At the helm of the 'movement', however, remains Transparency International.

Site 2. Global Civil Society: Transparency International

Transparency International is a Berlin-based NGO with 85 independent national affiliates. TI's Berlin office has 40 staff members, and administers €6 million of project funds raised largely from European governments and development agencies and from private foundations. TI provides information, training, support and strategy for its affiliates while it attends international anti-corruption forums. TI was founded in 1993 by a small group led by former World Bank official Peter Eigen. Eigen had been disturbed by the widespread bureaucratic corruption in Kenya development projects and the failure of the development agencies to remedy the situation (for more on TI's early history see Galtung 2000 and TI's own website). The core founders of TI were a small group of disgruntled lawyers, diplomats and development experts who were critical of shady international business transactions and corrupt development projects. Today, TI has now achieved a near monopoly position among non-governmental groups in the global struggle against corruption. From its core of founders and its original chapters (in Kenya, Bangladesh, the USA, the UK, Germany and Ecuador), TI has become a global organization, with national affiliates on every continent, and a key player within the NGO sector in the field of anti-corruption and public sector accountability. TI is often the only representative of civil society to participate in governmental or intergovernmental forums on cooperation. It is the primary reference point for corruption research and training for the World Bank and other development agencies.

Over the years, and under the influence of its board, which contains lawyers, former diplomats, journalists and aid officials, TI has launched a variety of initiatives to promote anti-corruption campaigns, has supported its branch offices in their own projects by distributing literature and providing translations, and has participated with various development agencies in formulating anti-corruption policies.

Major projects promoted by TI include: the *Source Book in Corruption*, a description of corrupt practices and measures to fight them (Pope 2000; see also <http://www.transparency.org/sourcebook/index.html>); the *Global Corruption Report*, an annual report on corrupt practices and sectors around the world (Transparency International 2001, 2003, 2004 and <http://www.transparency.org/toolkits/index.html>); the *Corruption Fighters' Tool Kit*, a catalogue of methods used by NGOs to fight corruption in various countries (<http://www.transparency.org/toolkits/index.html>); an anti-corruption database containing articles and a daily news bulletin about corruption around the world, regional reports and strategy papers; and the development and promotion of a National Integrity System for fighting corruption.

The National Integrity System, developed chiefly by Jeremy Pope in the London office, approaches corruption as a systemic problem of inadequate laws, inefficient institutions, lack of monitoring and control, and shortcomings in public attitudes (see for example Pope 1999, 2000; Langseth et al. 1999). As such, building an integrity strategy means attacking on all these fronts: new laws, accountable institutions, civil servant training, building 'islands of integrity' within government, establishing 'integrity pacts' between government ministries to ensure proper conduct in procurement and administration, developing codes of conduct for the private sector, and conducting campaigns to build a public culture of honesty (on integrity pacts see <www.transparency.org>). Civil society, the rule of law and a free press are prerequisites for the success of such a strategy, the result of which is the signing of Integrity Pacts with certain ministries or government organs to act honestly. With TI providing expertise, governments are encouraged to develop anti-corruption strategies and action plans and to involve all relevant actors in the struggle against corruption.

While TI's mandate is to help fight corruption, its most successful PR tool, its 'brand', is the Corruption Perceptions Index (CPI). Appearing each fall, the CPI ranks countries according to their level of corruption using a variety of indices and public opinion surveys. Generally, the Scandinavian countries, north-west Europe, New Zealand, Australia and Singapore are ranked as the least corrupt, followed by certain Far Eastern Countries and Central Europe, and then a mix of richer or poorer countries in Latin America, Asia, Central Asia, Africa. At the bottom of the list are West Africa, Central Asia, Nigeria, Bangladesh and Indonesia. Since corruption as such is difficult to measure, and since the CPI is a *perceptions* index, the CPI data base endeavours to provide detailed explanations for the way in which corruption perception actually reflects corruption; this is done by using the comparison between countries and comparing rankings from year to year. In this way one can conclude that the corruption situation is improving or worsening in certain countries or regions. Release of the CPI is a major news event in most countries, and politicians in lower-ranking countries may cite the CPI as proof that the current political party should be replaced. The success of the CPI has now spawned new indices, such as the Bribe Payers Index or BPI.

TI has up to 100 national affiliates (full, probationary, focal points). The local units, in order to avoid becoming embroiled in local politics, are not supposed to engage themselves in local corruption cases but are rather supposed to influence policy-making. In this way they differ from the more activist Amnesty International or Human Rights Watch groups, which are often high-profile and confrontational in their strategy. Moreover, local TI affiliates are not permitted to engage in consulting activities or bid for contracts. They can cooperate with other organizations in developing programmes, but unlike other professional NGOs, they do not bid on contracts or offer services for fees. This latter policy is a problem for many local branches that exist under uncertain financial conditions.

TI's staff in Berlin provide their branch affiliates with materials and capacity-building. They organize the biannual Anti-Corruption Conference and also take on various consulting tasks for governments or foundations (though TI resolutely refused to bid on consulting contracts). In TI's own understanding, the national chapters (NCs) 'are the owners of the organizations; the Secretariat its "servant"' (<www.transparency.org/about_ti/history.html>). The NCs tackle bribery, graft and other abuses of power, with each chapter adapting to the specific conditions of their country of location. 'What had begun as an organization has quickly flowered into a powerful global movement.'

The success of TI lies in its so-called 'coalition strategy'. Here TI has straddled the line between interest organization and global movement. Few NGOs can boast having trained the World Bank at all-day conferences, but TI has. The challenge for TI is thus matching the global project of its elite founders with the concrete needs of the local organizations. Moreover, TI's fundraising has not always met the more acute needs of its affiliates, with funding having declined in 2003 for various reasons.

With limited funds, there is the dilemma of the local organizations scrambling for support and a relatively expensive central office unable to support the national affiliates, but which at the same time does not permit them to pursue lucrative consulting contracts.

TI has now gotten through its growing pains and has also developed its own strategic planning culture, complete with weekend retreats and scenario planning. At the annual meeting, held in Seoul just prior to the International Anti-Corruption Conference, the 120 TI members in attendance were divided into groups to conduct scenario planning. The issue was whether TI should develop as a consulting group, as an activist organization, or as a network of interest groups.

A second conflict, which occurred at the annual meeting, had to do with the role of the original active members, versus the emerging national chapters. After a major controversy, the statutes have now been revised, and it is the affiliates who have control.

A third major change has been the split between TI's Berlin office, under the tutelage of Peter Eigen, and Jeremy Pope, who headed TI's Centre for Research and Innovation in London. Pope, a TI co-founder, had developed one of TI's major project tools, the National Integrity System. Following the split, the London office remained, but Pope and his colleague Frederik Galtung left to form TIRI, an independent NGO whose mission is to 'help counter corruption by assisting in the building and remodelling of institutions and practices' (<www.tiri.org>). TIRI argues that corruption fighting must now go beyond conventions and protocols. Now is the time for action, programmes and tools. Galtung, who has been with TI since its founding and who started TI's research unit, has thus issued a critique of the Corruption Perceptions Index (<www.tiri.org/documents/CPI-questions.pdf>).

TI is an international NGO with excellent relations with all major international donors and organizations. Even the World Bank, whom Eigen had quit in disgust for their refusal to engage corruption, became a patron, employing Eigen and Pope as consultants to develop an anti-corruption strategy. Today TI focuses on ensuring that anti-corruption provisions are part of every international aid document or protocol on organized crime. TI's mark is visible on several anti-corruption documents, and no major governmental or intergovernmental initiatives take place without in some way involving TI. This is truly a unique achievement. At present, a major initiative of TI is developing codes of conduct for international business and for the private sector in Western countries. Having focused on corruption in international aid and the Third World, TI had tended to overlook the corruption going on in its very backyard (in which recent corruption scandals in German, French and Belgian political life have figured prominently). Following the Enron scandal, TI has now tried to broaden its working definition of corruption from 'abuse by public officials for private gain' to 'the abuse of *entrusted power* for private gain'. This expanded definition makes it more necessary to form the broad-based coalitions of government, civil society and private sector which TI has pursued. The definition of corruption has now expanded in local affiliates as well. The TI chapter in Denmark, for instance, has recently removed the definition of corruption from its statutes, concluding that it constituted an impediment to its work. Corruption is now whatever TI defines it to be.

TI's various activities are carried out using funds donated by others. In this sense, TI is a sophisticated project unit. Project culture takes its point of departure in international priorities and major donors. TI itself is a link between the priorities of donors and the local organizations. In this sense, anti-corruption is but the latest manifestation of project life, and TI-Berlin is a clearing house for that traffic in resources which is project life.

TI's strategy is implemented through large-scale and short-term projects. Like other projects, anti-corruption entails the transfer of resources – money and ideas – to other countries that need them. When issues become attached to activities and money, we have projectization, and projectization is a common activity in all kinds of international democracy promotion (Sampson 1996). In the Balkans, corrupt societies recovering from communism and/or civil war, there are massive inputs of Western/EU assistance. Here as in other development situations, project society takes on a special significance. Anti-corruptionism is but the latest influence in this process by which project society embeds itself. What, then, is this project society?

Project society entails a special kind of activity: short-term activities with a budget and a time schedule. Projects always end, ostensibly to be replaced by policy, but normally to be replaced by yet another project. Project society entails a special kind of structure, beginning with the donor, the project identification mission, the appraisal, the selection of an implementing partner, the disbursement of funds, the monitoring, the evaluation and, of course, the next project. Project society is about the allocation of resources in an organized, at times bureaucratic, fashion. There is no project without a project application, a waiting period, a preliminary assessment, and the monitoring and accounting procedures that follow. The practices of project society demand a special kind of language, functioning almost like the wooden language of Stalinism. Passing on knowledge is called 'training'. Passing on knowledge to selected cadres is called 'training of trainers' or TOT. Getting better at something is called 'capacity-building'. Being able to say what you want to do is a 'mission statement'. When we understand what's going on we speak of 'transparency'. Trying to find out what's going on is called 'networking'. Figuring out who will benefit is 'stakeholder analysis'. Finding the money is called 'fundraising'. Making sure you don't waste it is called 'donor coordination'. Surviving after the money runs out is called 'sustainability'. People with money who don't see results are suffering from 'donor fatigue'. Taking your money somewhere else is an 'exit strategy'. Failure to find a recipient is called 'absorption problems'. And when there are too many donors and not enough recipients, you have 'donor constipation'. Participation in this world of projects requires understanding what are the latest key words and concepts which can magically generate money: this year its 'empowerment', then 'good governance', now 'income generation', but don't forget 'trafficking' and now, 'anti-corruption'. Behind this is the ubiquitous 'partnership', in which cooperation can be commenced, or just as quickly stopped if partners do not fulfil their obligations. In anti-corruption projects, the goal is to mobilize civil society by 'awareness raising', or to strengthen organizational effectiveness via 'capacity-building'. Capacity-building can involve humans, organizations or institutions. In capacity-building for anti-corruption, the ultimate goal is to create NGOs which are not only service providers but can also carry out 'advocacy', that is, influence decision-makers. In trying to help people in the Balkans get rid of corruption, it has now created a new funding category 'Anti-corruption'. The triumph of global virtue is the existence of an anti-corruption budget line in virtually every major aid project. This budget category is so recent that in Kosovo during 2003, one NGO anti-corruption project did not receive enough project applications to fill it, while in other areas there was bitter competition.

Project society, here in its anti-corruption variant, is about traffic in scarce resources: traffic in money, knowledge, people and ideas. Project life is about what people do with these resources. It is a world with a premium on the most abstract of knowledge. Hence, those who manipulate symbols and concepts can occupy strategic positions in the chain of resource allocations; they become as important as those donors and programmes which actually help people with concrete problems. Project managers are entrepreneurs in launching and using concepts, including concepts such as 'governance', 'transparency' and 'accountability'. The role of TI-Berlin in this network is thus crucial. They can both discover, mediate and transform concepts.

It is this world of projects that 'the anti-corruption community' is bringing to the Balkans, and it is the ideas and practices of this world that permeate down to a specific group of Balkan project managers and staff, their 'local partners' or 'counterpart organizations'. This is the process by which a global 'anti-corruption community' is created.

As anti-corruption penetrates the Balkans, there will also be resource opportunism. There will be a lot of anti-corruption projects. The question remains, however, whether these projects will actually reduce the amount of corruption.

Projects are part of the activity of global movements. But they are also a means by which NGOs can show that they are professional, and earn the respect, and resources, of major donors. TI has certainly succeeded here, with its experts and lobbyists seeking to influence the major development organizations, governments and private sector actors. At the same time they cooperate with them in coalition-building. At any TI gathering, there will be the customary mantras warning of the danger of neoliberalism and unrestricted corporate power, but representatives of these same corporations will be present to talk about business ethics and codes of conduct. This rather close relationship with the global capitalist elite tends to be limited to the central office in Berlin and can bring benefits to these companies in the form of PR. Private corporations and development agencies see no benefits in dealing with tiny chapters of TI in the Third World or Eastern Europe.

An example: Romania's anti-corruption scene

Southeast Europe was known for endemic corruption long before the communist period. Under the Ottoman Empire, various corrupt practices flourished, and it was widely considered that holding public office was simply a means for Balkan officials to enrich themselves. Throughout Southeast Europe, the weak state apparatus allowed for the mobilization of family, political and ethnic ties in the informal sector (Sampson 1983, 1986). The communist period was plagued by widespread nepotism, bribery, and the accompanying political abuse. These practices continued, and in some ways increased, with the demise of the communist state, the subsequent privatization process and the input of Western aid and business investments. In Romania, privatization and democratization were delayed, the bureaucracy was moribund and many politicians were former officials of the communist regime. This has led to a continuing stream of petty and grand corruption scandals in which politicians became wealthy, ministries gave out contracts without tender, goods were smuggled through the airport and factories were bought at rock-bottom prices. Petty corruption became grand corruption. Comparing various Balkan countries, the structure of these corrupt networks might differ due to ethnic, regional or political alliances – clan groups might overshadow networks; and some officials might be more venal than others – but in general the processes and accompanying social pathologies were quite similar across the region. Corrupt practices and accusations of corruption are now part of the political scene in every Southeast European country. Here I use Romania as an example of what such an anti-corruption scene might look like.

Ordinary Romanians need only glance at newspapers to become livid about corruption. Their experiences of corruption involve the use of bribes to obtain services, or recalling instances of nepotism and favoritism. 'Everyone is corrupt' explains a retired lawyer. 'We are not in a normal world', says another. 'The system has no mechanism to promote good people' so that 'everyone is out for their own interests.' Corruption exists in Romania because of 'lack of political will'. By not prosecuting anyone, it 'sends a signal'. It is these frustrations that are mobilized by various actors in the anti-corruption landscape that is Romania.

Public voices against corruption can come through various channels, including NGOs, websites, print media and various anti-corruption events. Romania has an Internet *anticoruptie* site where individuals can submit complaints. Most of these concern abuse by police or local bureaucrats regarding land or property disputes. The *anticoruptie* portal even contains a list where one can cast a vote for the top ten most corrupt Romanians. Typical of the messages on the list is the following, by a man from the town of Buzau speaking in the capacity of 'a free citizen, without political affiliation'. 'In Buzau county', he says, 'there exists a heavy and opaque administrative system, corrupt functionaries and much bureaucracy.' He describes how demonstrators came to the town hall holding placards and shouting slogans: 'We have a corrupt prefect', 'We have a corrupt mayor', 'Down with corruption in Buzau', 'Down with Bureaucracy', 'We want reform not theft', 'Romania: the most corrupt country in Europe', 'Shame on the corrupt ones', 'We elected you and we voted for you, but you cheated us', 'We want democracy not bureaucracy'. The author then details his arrest by Buzau police for disturbing public order, his harassment and warnings during interrogations, and formally makes a claim for 10 million lei (US $280) compensatory damages. Such protests, appearing daily in all Romanian media, touch on all the main themes of the anti-corruption scene in Southeastern Europe. Not only has corruption become more brazen in the new era, but the government is complicit. But for Romanians, waiting in line to 'enter Europe', corruption is also an international issue: the whole world is watching.

In Romania as well as elsewhere in Southeastern Europe, surveys of corruption show high levels of abuse within the state property fund, in the administration of Western aid, in tax assessment and in the customs service. For ordinary citizens, the health system and the court system are particularly notorious for the solicitation of bribes and for sustaining people's perception that only by paying can one receive effective services. Doctors and nurses, police and judges, teachers and rectors, bureaucrats and customs officers all seem to be taking bribes. In politics and the media, and within ministries of foreign trade, corruption is said to be rampant. As a result, Romanians seem to expect that these payments take place, and that any advantageous treatment must occur because of a payment or favour rather than respect for abstract principles. Data from World Bank and Transparency International surveys place Romania among the most corrupt countries in Europe.

Given the prevalence and high perception of corruption, it is not surprising to see many actors operating on the Romanian anti-corruption stage, including the media, the government, the opposition parties, international actors, local anti-corruption agencies and that all-embracing category now called 'civil society'. With their various resources, the media or some NGOs may struggle to uncover corruption; anti-corruption agencies or NGOs may try to raise public awareness; while certain politicians may even criticize those who expose corruption as politically motivated or uninformed. On the anti-corruption stage the various actors try to point out the guilty, propose measures to fight corruption and pronounce on the effectiveness of these measures as well.

The world of Romanian anti-corruption thus contains various groups of actors: aside from the political institutions are the disgruntled citizens who come together into groups, networks and coalitions; and the media which focuses on uncovering scandal, identifying the guilty, and drawing conclusions as to Romanians' fate in Europe. In Romania as elsewhere, corruption and anti-corruption are intimately tied together with accusations of corruption, and even more importantly, counter-accusations. There are governmental and 'independent' agencies assigned to fight corruption. There are political competitors who use corruption accusations as a platform. There are foreign donors and financial institutions who decide to prioritize corruption or transparency, who castigate the Romanian government for not doing enough and who dispense funds among NGOs to combat corruption; the struggle for funds is not without its own intrigues. As 'extras' on this stage, ordinary Romanians are using the discourse of corruption as a lament about their own experience and their inability to deal with it. Corruption is thus a particular form of talk (Ries 1998; Zerilli, Chapter 5, this volume), an all-embracing trope, like Transition, Mafia and Globalization. Corruption, or accusations of corruption, have become a narrative about social decay and citizens' lack of confidence in their public institutions and poitical leaders. In this sense, corruption resembles witchcraft; it explains forces over which we have no control and can become a vehicle for social conflict through accusations or rooting out evil. Like witchcraft, corruption is latent within each institution and individual.

In this scene of corruption, the various actors in the anti-corruption landscape each have their sets of resources. The resources of these actors include money, rhetoric, public knowledge, secret knowledge and political parties and parliamentarians. Access to international discourses, donors, networks and conferences is part of this scene, such that there is a traffic in these resources across borders. The anti-corruption scene involves various theories of what corruption is, how and why it is sustained, and how it should be combated. Not to be forgotten are the various anti-corruption rituals, sponsored by both government and society. These would include the various press conferences, the statistical presentations of hardworking campaigns, the public events such as the opening of anti-corruption units, the demonstrations against them, the individual appeals of frustrated citizens, the televised debates, etc. Corruption arrests are not just law enforcement, they are 'signals' to be sent by the authorities that certain kinds of behaviour will not be tolerated. Through the sensation-hungry media, the signals are sent to the political opposition, to the public and to the international actors who can decide on aid priorities and even credit ratings. The Romanian world of anti-corruption is thus a complex intersection of moral intrigues, citizens' desires for justice and political jockeying for power. It is a world – both transparent and opaque – of citizen laments, high-profile actions and of government declarations.

CONCLUSIONS: THE ANTHROPOLOGY OF ANTI-CORRUPTION

Lessons from the anti-corruption scene in Romania could certainly be extended to other Balkan countries. Some of the actors would change, some laments would have a different style, some interaction between actors would differ and the leitmotifs of declining trust, that 'everyone is doing it', that 'outsiders are watching us', etc. might differ. Nevertheless, there is an uncanny resemblance between anti-corruption scenes across Southeastern Europe, especially in the way in which anti-corruption enters through outside projects and interacts with local laments and political intrigues. I would therefore postulate that it is through corruption and anti-corruption that we might find certain similarities in understanding how the people of Southeast Europe relate to their formal institutions, on the one hand trying to get around them, on the other insisting that these institutions function properly so as to control unchecked personal aggrandizement by those in power.

The local experiences of corruption and anti-corruption, however, are intimately tied to the various international actors and their desire for a more effective global economy, for the enforcement of legal sanctions across borders, and to the general climate of pursuing global justice and integrity in human affairs. Hence, the anti-corruption conferences, the lobbying activities of organizations like Transparency International, and the various international anti-corruption treaties all have an influence on how a local anti-corruption scene unfolds.

In this sense, let me conclude this description by raising not 'lessons learned' but 'questions raised'.

First, *what does it mean to say that anti-corruption is a 'world'*? It is only to say that we must understand anti-corruption in terms of local human experience together with external inputs and practices. Global civil society and global morality are not just 'outside forces' or 'flows of meaning' somehow penetrating stable societies. The global is also a set of concrete practices. Global anti-corruption is embodied by its world congresses, donor meetings, coalition-building activities, press releases, etc. This world of anti-corruption includes, as we saw in Romania, a variety of domestic and external actors, each with their own sets of social networks and institutional resources.

Second, *anti-corruption is not innocent.* Insofar as anti-corruption is one tool for controlling resources and maintaining control over others, we should expect that even the most unscrupulous regimes and leaders will develop anti-corruption agencies and strategies to please donors and obtain funds, just as they have developed façade environmental agencies, façade NGOs, and 'conveyor belt' organizations of women, youth and peace. One should assume that anti-corruption agencies can themselves be corrupt, just as we find that those organs fighting what is called 'organized crime' can themselves be linked to organized crime. Anti-corruption is not innocent.

Third, *how can we integrate moral projects with political strategies?* The rise of global ethics, accountability and practices of virtue, is in itself an interesting social process. It may even constitute a historical turning point, as with the rise of human rights as a force in foreign policy, used to save lives in some situations and used cynically in others to pursue more dubious military projects. It is thus incumbent upon anti-corruption research to examine anti-corruption in a benign, critical and reflective manner. This means asking some very simple questions: Who are the players? What do they want? Why do they want it? Who wins and who loses in this game? To quote a much maligned specialist in political dynamics, V.I. Lenin: *'Kto? Kovo?'*, 'Who? To whom?' The instruments of anti-corruption are not just morally charged concepts, but concrete resources of aid programmes and political patronage. Should we conclude that the anti-corruption actors are simply manipulating a concept? Of course! Are there any exceptions to this 'rule'? No. All concepts with any moral content are manipulated by their proponents and by their opponents. Yet this does not rule out morality and integrity as driving forces in human affairs.

Fourth, *how do we do research with morally valued projects?* It is a common problem for those doing research on politically correct issues (civil society, anti-racism, indigenous people's rights, anti-corruption) to let down their critical guard. Those who research NGOs, for example, find themselves becoming involved with their organization, the goals of which they might share, and this may prevent them from seeing the full dynamics of the organization. Civil society may talk about grassroots and horizontal structures, but the dynamics from the inside may be something quite different. For those researching anti-corruption activities, we must be clear about the conflicts between global elites and grassroots, between the moral imperatives of fighting against corruption and the grant-getting intrigues involved in procuring funds for projects. Such conflicts may be pushed under the rug by 'the anti-corruption community'. Anti-corruption, like other communities, has its taboos.

This last problem is particularly pertinent for Transparency International, which openly expresses its willingness for critique, but like any organization, also has its own internal conflicts and differences. These came out clearly during the most recent general assembly as a controversy over the role of the individual founding members versus that of the national chapters. It also emerged in the split between the main office in Berlin and the research unit in London, where the two leading staff eventually founded a competing NGO. The question, perhaps, is not why these conflicts took place, but rather, why they took so long to emerge.

Fifth, *anti-corruption research is a reflective project.* Anti-corruption is a practice, that is, people doing things in the world. But anti-corruption is also anti-corruption*ism*, an ideology grounded on an understanding of ethics, integrity, justice, morality and accountability. As rhetoric, people will use anti-corruption to pursue their own interests just as the most corrupt leaders have used the most morally correct phrases to pursue theirs: who has not been exposed to the chatter about 'decentralization', 'public access', 'local democracy', 'coordination', 'empowerment', 'human rights' and, before that, 'socialism'. Anti-corruption, too, is not innocent. It can be manipulated to serve the interest of even the most unscrupulous actors. An anthropology of anti-corruption needs to sketch out these interests, especially those that highlight a phenomenon which was once kept hidden. Our task as academics is to reveal the interests at stake, to show how people articulate their interests and how people pursue them. Discourse analysis, of whatever variety, is a handy tool, but it is clearly not enough. We not only need to understand what kind of signals are being sent, but how they are received. We need not only to understand corruption laments and anti-corruption rhetoric, that is, anti-corruptionism, but anti-corruption practices.

Finally, *donors and projects*. The need to understand anti-corruption is intimately tied to the need to better understand how donors operate. How do priorities become projects, how are budget lines established, what do donors want and what kinds of projectization processes take place (Sampson 2003a, 2003b)? Being a donor is about giving gifts. Surely anthropologists can make a contribution here (Sampson 2002). Most important, we need a fuller understanding of the anti-corruption community in its moral, political and economic aspects.

Social science has always operated from the axiom that things are not what they seem. This is particularly true for the world of anti-corruption, where the ethical mission may blind us to more concrete, everyday dynamics. An anthropology of virtue, of which anti-corruption is but one example, requires us to understand that 'accountability' and 'civil society' may operate simultaneously as ethical ballast and as tactical slogans. In the world of anti-corruption, one can pursue virtue and integrity while being ruthless and partisan. The world of anti-corruption, for all its transparency, thus remains opaque. It is a world that anthropologists can elucidate.

NOTE

Research funding for this project has been provided by the Swedish Research Council for Social Science (Vetenskapsrådet) and is ongoing. Earlier versions of this chapter have been presented at various forums: Third Conference on Post-Communist Anthropology (Copenhagen), the European Association of Social Anthropology meetings (Copenhagen), the Amsterdam Social Science Centrum Conference on Corruption, the University of East Anglia conference on Constructing Corruption, and at seminars here in Lund. I am grateful for these institutions and colleagues for their valuable feedback. Thanks also to the staff of TI Romania for valuable assistance. Finally, I wish to thank Cris Shore and Dieter Haller for their extraordinary patience in allowing me to complete this chapter.

REFERENCES

Andvig, J.C. and Odd-Helge Fjeldstad, with I. Amundsen, T.K. Sissener and T. Soreide (2002) *Corruption: A Review of Contemporary Research*, NUPI report no. 268 (Bergen, Norway: Christian Michelsen Institute).

Brien, A. (2001) Regulating Virtue: Formulating, Engendering and Enforcing Corporate Ethical Codes, in P. Larmour and N. Wolanin (eds) *Corruption and Anti-corruption*, pp. 62–81 (Canberra: Asia Pacific Press).

Galtung, F. (2000) A Global Network to Curb Corruption: The Experience of Transparency International, in A. Florini (ed.) *The Third Force: The Rise of Transnational Civil Society*, pp. 17–48 (Washington: Carnegie Endowment for International Peace).

Hindess, B. (2001) Good Government and Corruption, in P. Larmour and N. Wolanin (eds) *Corruption and Anti-corruption*, pp. 1–10 (Canberra: Asia Pacific Press).

Langseth, P., R. Stapenhurst and J. Pope (1999) National Integrity Systems, in R. Stapenhurst and S. Kpundeh (eds) *Curbing Corruption: Toward a Model for Building National Integrity*, pp. 127–49 (Washington: World Bank).

Myrdal, G. (1968) *Asian Drama*, Vol. 2 (New York: Twentieth Century Fund).

Ottoway, M. and T. Carothers (2000) *Funding Virtue: Civil Society Aid and Democracy Promotion* (Washington: Carnegie Endowment for International Peace).

Pope, J. (1999) Elements of a Successful Anti-corruption Strategy, in R. Stapenhurst and S. Kpundeh (eds) *Curbing Corruption: Toward a Model for Building National Integrity*, pp. 97–104 (Washington: World Bank).

—— (2000) *TI Source Book 2000. Confronting Corruption: The Elements of a National Integrity System* (Berlin: Transparency International).

Ries, N. (1998) *Russian Talk: Culture and Conversation during Perestroika* (Ithaca, NY: Cornell University Press).

Sampson, S. (1983) Bureaucracy and Corruption as Anthropological Problems: A Case Study from Romania, *Folk* (Copenhagen), Vol. 25: 30–55.

—— (1986) The Informal Sector in Eastern Europe, *Telos*, Vol. 66: 44–66.

—— (1996) The Social Life of Projects: Importing Civil Society to Albania, in C. Hann and E. Dunn (eds) *Civil Society: Challenging Western Models*, pp. 121–42 (London: Routledge).

—— (2001) What Is a Donor? *Newsletter, European Association of Social Anthroplogy*, January: 5–8.

—— (2003a) Trouble Spots: Projects, Bandits and State Fragmentation, in J. Friedman (ed.) *Globalization, the State and Violence*, pp. 309–42 (Palo Alto, CA: Altamira Press).

—— (2003b) From Forms to Norms: Global Projects and Local Practices in the Balkan NGO Scene, *Journal of Human Rights*, Vol. 2: 329–38.

Stapenhurst, R. and S. Kpundeh (eds) (1999) *Curbing Corruption: Toward a Model for Building National Integrity*. (Washington: World Bank).

Transparency International (2001–03) *Annual Reports* (Berlin: Transparency International).

—— (2001) *Global Corruption Report* (Berlin: Transparency International).

—— (2002) *Summary of the 10th IACC Proceedings* (Berlin: Transparency International).

—— (2003) *Global Corruption Report* (Berlin: Transparency International) (also <www.globalcorruptionreport.org>).

—— (2004) *Global Corruption Report 2004* (London: Pluto Press).

7 CULTURE AND CORRUPTION IN THE EU: REFLECTIONS ON FRAUD, NEPOTISM AND CRONYISM IN THE EUROPEAN COMMISSION

Cris Shore

INTRODUCTION: MODERNITY, CORRUPTION AND THE EU

A major theme in the international study of fraud and corruption concerns understanding the conditions that enable these practices to flourish. It is widely assumed that corruption thrives mostly in contexts where bureaucratic norms and rational administrative structures are either absent or underdeveloped. Hence, endemic corruption is perceived as the 'pathology' of developing, 'transitional' or Third World societies. Broadly speaking, this argument rests on a Weberian stereotype of bureaucracy as a legal-rational mode of organization where behaviour of officials is governed by formal, codified and transparent rules; recruitment is based on merit and technical competence; where there exists a hierarchical division of duties and responsibilities, and impersonal relationships between officials and their clients; and where there is a clear separation between private and official income. These ideas are regarded as defining features of modernity and have become central to the image and self-image of the West's advanced industrial societies (Herzfeld 1992). By contrast, corruption – a personal and particularistic mode of behaviour that is typically clandestine and entails a violation of the rules – represents the antithesis of these principles of transparency, efficiency and modernity.

This chapter tests these assumptions by analysing corruption in a highly bureaucratic setting, that of the European Commission, the civil service of the European Union (EU). My focus is on events surrounding the corruption scandal that precipitated the resignation of the European Commission in March 1999, which occurred as I was completing an ethnographic study of EU civil servants in Brussels[1] and subsequent debates over fraud, accountability and institutional reform in the European Union. The main questions I want to address are how should we *interpret* that scandal and, beyond this, how did politicians and officials in Brussels explain it? My argument is that nepotism, fraud and corruption in the EU can only be properly understood in terms of the 'organizational culture' of its administration, and that the scandal of 1999 highlights problems of cohesion and accountability that may be common to other international and multicultural organizations where shared administrative norms and codes of conduct – and proper mechanisms of accountability – are lacking. Much of the debate also centres on identifying the causes of endemic corruption in international organizations – and whether embedded cultural norms are more important than institutional rules and procedures (Pujas and Rhodes 1999). I suggest that *both* are important, but in the case of a novel and multicultural body like the European Commission, part of the problem lies precisely in reaching consensus over what those norms and ethics of public administration should be. These tensions are compounded by problems of transparency and accountability that are specific to the EU. This leads to a final question: how successful will the Commission be in its efforts to reform itself?

First, however, let me put this debate in a wider context and explain why I became interested in fraud and corruption and why the discourse of anti-corruption has come to feature so prominently in discussions about the EU. One immediate answer is because the corruption debate has focused attention once again on unresolved tensions of governance and accountability in the EU. The European Commission has long prided itself on the uniqueness of its civil service, which it claims represents a new and distinctly 'European' model of public administration commensurate with the EU's ideals concerning transnational cooperation and supranational governance, and its image of itself as an organization whose purpose is 'to ensure that its citizens can live in peace, freedom and prosperity' (CEC 2002: 4). However, the resignation of the Santer Commission on 16 March 1999, following a scathing Committee of Independent Experts (CIE) investigation into fraud, nepotism and corruption (discussed below) raises fundamental question about this experiment in 'supranationalism' and the need for institutional reform. The report also opens up an important debate about morality and the ethics of public administration in Europe. If, as David Parkin (1985) observed, morality is most clearly seen in its transgression, the way people *react* to such transgression can reveal even greater insight into cultural (or national) differences between systems of classification.

There is also a wider context to these debates that may be of more historical, comparative and global interest. A cursory review of the major international news stories over the past few years would suggest that fraud and corruption have become major problems throughout the world of international organizations, not only in 'rogue' US corporations like Enron, Xerox and WorldCom, but in bodies whose rationale has little to do with profit maximization or shareholder value: UNESCO (Henley 1999), the United Nations (Halper 1996), the international football association UEFA and the International Olympic Confederation have all recently been mired in corruption scandals. Equally, there has been a rash of political sleaze scandals involving parties and governments not only in poor or developing countries like Mexico, Pakistan and Peru, but in many of the leading 'G7' nation-states (including Germany, France and Italy) who have most leverage in defining and promoting 'good governance' through their trade and aid policies.

These scandals appear to be part of a wider pattern. Whether corruption is *actually* increasing, however, is hard to gauge given the absence of any reliable yardstick for measuring the phenomenon cross-culturally. Moreover, in many contexts, accusations of corruption may have increased largely because, in the new climate of public intolerance to old nepotistic practices, such accusations and counter-accusations have become part of the way politicians compete for legitimacy and votes against their opponents. Like witchcraft accusations in seventeenth century New England, there may be a complex set of reasons for accusing others of malfeasance. However, the increasing prominence of the term 'corruption' – and the labelling of activities as 'corrupt' that were previously accepted as normal – may also relate to a wider crisis of 'trust' that is characteristic of what Beck (1992) and others call 'risk society'. The preoccupation with rooting out public-sector corruption, like the current obsession with introducing regimes of 'accountability' through numerical measurements and indices of 'productivity' and 'performance', is part of a more general search for assurance and certainty through 'rituals of verification' (Power 1997) and the imperatives of modern 'audit culture' (Strathern 2000).

THE EU CIVIL SERVICE IN BRUSSELS: A CRUCIBLE FOR FORGING EUROPEAN MAN?

I should begin by saying that I did not set out to research corruption; it was something I encountered during fieldwork. In 1995 I went to Brussels to carry out a two-year research project examining the EU civil service in the context of debates about 'European identity' and the EU goal of forging 'ever-closer union amongst the peoples of Europe'. In Brussels, as I discovered, European integration is typically conceived of as a 'project', one that goes under the label of 'European construction' *('la construction européenne')* – a revealingly mechanical and modernist metaphor that sums up precisely the way many EU policy-makers conceptualize integration; not as a spontaneous or organic process to be shaped from below by the peoples of Europe, but rather as a blueprint (the so-called 'Monnet vision') to be executed from above by a strategically placed technocratic elite.

The project of 'European Construction' has two main dimensions: first, the 'Europeanization' of the masses (and here my research examined the various policies, political technologies, 'cultural actions' and symbols used by EU elites to create a collective European identity in order to bind the divided nations of Europe); and second, the Europeanization of the elites themselves, or integration 'at the core'. That is, the creation of a new political class of committed Europeans who would become, to adapt a phrase from Benedict Anderson (1983) the '"Creole pioneers" of Europeanism' to lead the EU's emerging supranational political system.

The key questions I wanted to answer were what sort of 'organizational culture' has the EU created within its own institutional heartlands in Brussels, and to what extent does the EU civil service embody the kind of 'European ethos' and identity espoused in its official documents? I also wanted to test the assumption that 'once appointed, officials will tend to acquire a loyalty to the EU institutions' rather than their respective nation-states (Smith 1983: 248) – a process that Westlake (1994) refers to as 'Cotta's Law'. According to leading integration theorists including Ernst Haas (1958), the experience of working together within European institutions would have a 'positive spill-over effect on the psychology of [European] elites' (Webb 1983: 17–18). They predicted that prolonged exposure and intermingling among national officials and politicians within the EU would result in a steady transfer of loyalties from the nation-state to Europe. This shift in allegiance, as Michael O'Neill (1996: 42) describes it, is the beginning of a process of 'cognitive change' that will culminate in the birth of supranational cadres embodying a new type of 'European consciousness'. European construction, thus conceived, is an ambitious project of social and political engineering aimed at forging a new type of European subjectivity.

In Brussels, as I discovered, the local idiom to describe this process was *engrenage*, a French term that translates roughly as 'gearing' or 'enmeshing'.[2] I also learned that this process had been skilfully anticipated long ago by Jean Monnet, the EU's official 'Founding Father', whose memoirs enthusiastically describe the European civil service as a 'laboratory' for the creation of a new kind of 'European Man'.[3] This raises a further question of major theoretical and empirical significance: to what extent might EU institutions function as crucibles for the creation of a new type of 'European' subjectivity, or what Paul Valery and others have termed *Homo Europaeus* (see Shore 1999)?

The term 'supranationalism' epitomized this Europeanist ethos. Technically, supranationalism is simply a legal concept that refers to the unique competencies of Community institutions and their autonomy from national and international institutions and laws. Robert Schuman popularized the term in 1951 when he used it to describe the character and functions of the High Authority of the ECSC – the precursor of the Commission.[4] As Monnet and Schuman saw it, supranational bodies would control the excesses of nation-states by removing their power over iron and steel production and atomic energy – the 'sinews of war'. This was seen as the beginning of a process that would bind Germany and France together so tightly as to make war, quite literally, impossible.

However, like most political concepts, supranationalism also embodies a series of normative and ideological assumptions. Foremost among these is idea that the EU institutions create spaces of identity that somehow transcend the cultural logic of nationalism – and that Europe's de-territorialized, de-nationalized supranational civil servants somehow embody a 'higher' set of principles: a distinctly 'European' ethos and morality that stands above the more primitive and parochial nation-state. What sort of administrative culture, therefore, has the EU created within its civil service? And to what extent is the Commission a repository for these 'Europeanist' ideals and values?

THE EUROPEAN COMMISSION'S ADMINISTRATIVE CULTURE: INSIDER/EMIC PERSPECTIVES

The official view – the picture the Commission likes to give of itself – is that the EU institutions are the living embodiment of the EU (and Enlightenment) ideals of reason, progress, modernity and universalism against the particularism and integralism of the nation-state (Delanty 2002; Holmes 2000). In the words of David Williamson (1994), its former Secretary-General, the Commission is 'a lean machine' – small, dynamic, highly efficient and dedicated to serving the Community interest. Typically, it portrays itself as something unique in the world of international organizations: 'cosmopolitan', 'multinational', 'multilingual' – but with its own distinctive ethos, identity and, most important of all, autonomy. It is worth noting here that for most officials, a job in the Commission has traditionally meant a job for life: that new Commissioners swear an oath of allegiance to the European Communities, and that the *Staff Regulations* (1993) impose obligations on officials to uphold and defend the 'Community interest'.[5] The Commission was also typically described as a 'cultural melting pot': a hybrid body combining all that is best from the different national civil services: a 'culture of compromise' as Bellier (1994) describes it. Finally, it is represented as a civil service composed of Europe's 'brightest and best': highly trained and motivated staff committed to the European idea who together constitute an meritocracy of talent at the service of Europe.

Does the empirical evidence support this, and what does the Commission's 'organizational culture' look like from an anthropological perspective?[6] The official picture is partially accurate. The Commission is certainly small, multilingual and multinational: an administration employing barely 24,000 staff, most of whom work in the 47 or so EU offices and buildings in Brussels. However, four factors stood out as particularly salient.

1. Despite talk of 'hybridity' and cosmopolitanism, the Commission's administrative norms and practices are still predominantly francophone. This is hardly surprising given that Monnet explicitly modelled its precursor, the High Authority of the ECSC, on the French civil service and that the French language was, and remains, the lingua franca of everyday administration (although English is now more commonly used as the language of policy in most Directorate-Generals, or 'DGs').

2. There exists still a very strong ethos and *esprit de corps*. Staff would invariably refer to the Commission as 'The House' (*la maison*) – and usually with a great sense of affection (the phrase 'we in the House' was one I heard quite frequently by staff of all nationalities). Evidently, the Commission has succeeded in generating a strong sense of identity and loyalty among its *fonctionnaires*. This affection was often expressed in conversations and interviews with staff, as was the obverse; a hostility towards those who would bring the 'House' into disrepute.

3. There was an interesting 'spillover' between the way the Commission represents itself publicly, and the way staff represented (and 'narrated') themselves privately. That is, individuals were clearly influenced by the Commission's definition of itself as 'conscience of the Community', 'defender of the European interest' and 'dynamo of the integration process'. Staff tended to see themselves as part of an elite corps of 'policy-makers', intellectuals and diplomats rather than mere 'public servants'. (Indeed, the French translation of 'civil servant' – *fonctionnaire* – means something quite different). This vanguard self-image may also reflect the fact that a large percentage of staff are from elite educational institutions and have legal training: something that the EU recruitment process encourages. The origins of the Commission might also explain its ethos, particularly the fact that in the early days, Walter Hallstein had consciously sought

to instil a supranational ideology and sense of élan within the organization. What I found is that that this sense of mission and commitment to the European ideal persists, even among new recruits (Spence 1994).

4. Finally, my study confirmed what many integration theorists had predicted: that prolonged exposure and intermingling among national officials *does* lead to a progressive shift in role perceptions and identification – a point corroborated by many interviewees, who typically spoke about how their experience of working in the Commission had changed their outlook and made them more self-consciously 'European' (Shore 2000).

Is this evidence of genuine and sustained 'cognitive change' or simply an ephemeral, corporate loyalty of the kind one might find in any multinational or international organization? My research suggested the former and concluded that *engrenage* does work. Within the EU institutions a process of identity-formation is taking place that is, in many ways, akin to the process of 'ethnicity' (Cohen 1974; Eriksen 1993). What we are witnessing here is the transformation of a social *category* into a self-recognizing and self-defined *group*: a 'community' with its own particular identity and ethos. Several other factors have contributed to this process. Foremost among these are the common experience of exile (*depaysement*) and social distance from the host population and the relative 'ghettoization' of EU expatriates in Brussels (most of whom work in its compact, densely built 'European Quarter' and commute from its affluent suburbs to the south); the shared sense of 'mission', of working together 'for Europe'; and the ideology of European integration that still informs (and legitimizes) most of what the EU does. Added to this is the common lifestyle, high salaries and quasi-diplomatic status of the EU *fonctionnaire* and, perhaps most important of all, the free education that all children of EU officials are offered in the prestigious European School system (Swan 1996).

My point here is that officials are largely insulated from their host society, a point many complained about. They inhabit an institutional space that isolates them from the native population and ordinary people in their countries of origin. Their situation is thus akin to that of diplomats and colonial administrators: they are *in* Brussels, but not *of* it.

FORMAL VERSUS INFORMAL STRUCTURES: THE COMMISSION'S PARALLEL ADMINISTRATIVE SYSTEM

So far I have concentrated on the 'integrative' mechanisms that unite EU officials as a cohesive group. However, bureaucracies rarely conform to the Weberian ideal-type. My research also identified a vibrant, anti-Weberian 'informal' system of administration based on private interests, personal networks and 'pragmatic' codes of conduct.[7] For many observers, particularly Keith Middlemas (1995) and his team, this 'informal system' is something to be celebrated and encouraged. The EU's system of personal networks, they argue, is precisely what gives it its dynamism and flexibility,[8] enabling it to cut through the red tape of formal bureaucracy.

Staff themselves, however, did not share this optimistic picture and were keen to point out its less salutary features, particularly the problems of cronyism and political patronage. I first observed this in 1996 when a dispute erupted between management and staff at the Committee of the Regions (CoR) – the institution created under the Maastricht Treaty primarily to 'bring Europe closer to its citizens'. Less than two years after its inception the CoR had become a local byword in Brussels for nepotism and empire-building,[9] so much so that its staff were threatening to strike and had already picketed its inaugural plenary session that February. The source of their grievance was the abuse of the 'fast-track' recruitment system by the CoR's energetic president, Jacques Blanc (president of the Languedoc-Roussillon region and a former French agricultural minister), who had allegedly filled many of the senior posts in its bureaucracy with friends and cronies. Frank Patterson, vice-president of 'Union Syndicale' – the largest of the EU staff unions – told me that over half of the 90 new posts had been allocated in this 'corrupt and feudal manner'. The 'fast-track' system allowed normal recruitment procedures to be bypassed. Instead, a series of 'closed shop' interviews for favourites had been held, some lasting a mere 30 minutes. The row triggered several strikes and the unions subsequently took their case to the Court of First Instance which, after two years of deliberation, eventually upheld their complaints.[10]

Subsequent interviews and research indicated that this episode was not a-typical. The following accounts from my field-notes are indicative of the way the Commission's organizational culture appears to seasoned insiders.

INTERVIEW WITH PASCALE-BENÔIT FOGER
15 February 1996 (Grade 'A4')[11]

47 years old. Former Director of Personnel in DG 9. Currently head of Recruitment and Personnel in DG 12 (the Directorate-General for Education, Training and Research, headed by Edith Cresson). Son of a French army officer. Grew up in Eastern France, Germany and the USA. Educated in a French lycée and European School. Has worked for the Commission for 20 years, since leaving the University (Nancy), where he studied law. He says he was originally interested in the UN, but realized that it 'wasn't going anywhere' and passed the EU concours while at university. Divorced, with two children.

CS: What makes the Commission civil service different from other administrations?

PF: It is a very new organization. People say it's based on the French and German civil service – that it is very formal, top down and hierarchical – but it's really a blend of traditions, and there are no rules ... a 'model in the making'. We've taken bits from all of the different member states. The French system is probably the best geared to the needs of the Commission. Next is the Belgian system – although the Belgian civil service is the worst example to follow; it's highly politicized and basically rotten. You can't become a civil servant unless you're politically affiliated. Most of the Belgian university high-fliers try to get into the Commission. Many of their professors have been in the Commission. The British are not well prepared; your university system is not 'European-minded' enough.

I was quite suited for the Commission because we moved around so much. It was like my family background. You have to be adaptable: you have to accept the project you've been working on for the past five years may be scrapped and buried forever and then understand what are the new priorities.

The highest degree of frustration I find comes from French colleagues. They're the ones who complain the most. They can't bear the lack of rules. But this is what makes the Commission such a great and interesting administration. For example, I never use the *Guide de Service*. We say 'if it exists on paper, it means it is a problem'. If I need something, I just call on the people I know. It's unfair to call it a system of *piston*.[12] It is more about networking and using personal contacts – and it probably stems from the Italian way of working.

We discuss the role of networks in promotions:

PF: If you're not an *Enarque*,[13] a Catholic, a Socialist or 'upper class' it is difficult to make your way here. What I mean by 'class' is a network system: You either have to belong to the Catholic Left, the Socialist Party, be from the ENA, or from the École d'Agronomie. If you don't belong to any of these, it's difficult to advance your career. Under Delors, the French got all the best jobs. But Delors was a disaster for the Commission. He killed it ... The problem here is 'Parkinson's Law'. The Commission is not monitored enough by Parliament or the Court of Auditors. No internal audit has ever been carried out. For example, DG 1A spent billions of ecu hiring external staff for its TACIS and PHARE programmes[14] – who then gave contracts only to their friends and cronies. For many people, the Commission has become giant piggy-bank distributing money to member states. I used to be quite committed to the European idea. Now I don't believe in it at all.

CS: So what is the solution?

PF: Scare people. We still don't sack people who do no work. For example, in disciplinary cases, the accused often turn up with a lawyer to defend them and the Commission ends up as the accused. There are some very good staff lawyers in Brussels – I should know: we use them as well.

Another problem is that the organigram has grown simply to make room for enlargement states. We've created some totally useless units, especially in the area of middle management. DG 22, 23 and 24 were created simply so that new member states could have their own Director-General. All the reports in the past recommended major reforms, but nothing is ever done. Why? Because every government wants its own A1s and A2s[15] – they all want power. That creates problems of demoralization [the 'gilded cage' syndrome]. We're in danger of losing talented staff because there is no proper career management. We don't train and manage staff properly. The normal career path stops at A4. You can reach that in 15 years. So what do you do for the next 20 years?

Foger points to himself as a case in point. I suggest he could always look for another job. He laughs.

Where would I find another 9 to 5 job that I enjoy, that puts me in good company, and that pays 350,000 BF a month take-home? I'd have to be managing direction of a big French company to get an equivalent salary.

INTERVIEW WITH GERHARDT PAUWELS
(Grade: A1 – Director-General) 7 March 1996

Born in Antwerp (Flemish). Went to the Catholic University in Brussels. Joined the Commission in 1958. Worked for four or five different DGs (including DG 9, Administration, where he was Head of Personnel).

CS: How would you describe the internal 'culture' of the Commission?

GP: You British see it as a 'French' system: it is not French, it is the continental system ... To understand the EU administration you should read the history of the Middle Ages. The Commission is not a single or unified body. We have no boss. Even Santer is just a colleague among 20 Commissioners. There are over 30 departments, each very independent and with their own boss – like the medieval barons. The only difference between the Commissioners and Director-Generals is that we get to stay longer: they are here for four or five years, we stay for 35 – if we are clever.

There has never been a personnel policy. We never had any training or staff development policy in the Commission; the salary was considered to be enough ... The Commission needs to recruit clever people who are mentally flexible. We don't need academics; we can't use them: they are too rational: they live in their mind. You need to be irrational: a compromiser. The best compromises are the most irrational ones – look at the Union, how do you think it has survived all these years? The British – with their Anglo-Saxon, anti-patronage culture – fail to grasp the networking dynamics of the Commission's internal culture: the smaller countries are better adapted to appreciating and playing this system because they are more used to compromises. That's why there are so many more senior officials from the smaller countries. They really have a lot of power thanks to the Commission.

I ask about 'Mafias' within the Commission.

CS: Yes, there is a French Mafia, but there is also an English Mafia ... You have mafias everywhere: there is a mafia *des trois étoirles*, an Opus Dei mafia, a socialist and communist mafia, a freemasons mafia – yes, Emile Noel was a Freemason – a pederast mafia [**a what? I ask**] A what-do-you-call-it, a homosexual mafia: yes, that was very influential. The important thing is that they neutralize each other – that was my aim when I worked in DG 9. The trick is to find out which mafias exist and who belongs to them. Once you recognize these networks you can begin to work with them ... At the beginning there were only about ten of us who were aware of this.

CS: So what 'mafia' did you belong to?

GP: I went to the Catholic University in Brussels. I am also from Antwerp – there were five of us from the same college in Antwerp who joined the Commission (all of us now are either Directors or Director-Generals). I have no party card. That helped because the Christian Democrats thought I was one of them. But the Socialists and Liberals also helped me. I never joined a union – only the manual labourers and secretaries are really unionized. But you are clever: I don't usually talk like this. Perhaps I have said too much.

The implication here is that beneath the surface of bureaucratic rationality, the Commission is much more complex and messy in its everyday practices. In fact, so pervasive is this system of personal networks that insiders call it a 'parallel system of administration' with its own rules, codes and career paths (Spence 1994: 65). The

characteristics of this 'informal system' include many features typical
of the French civil service: a highly politicized senior management,
closely linked to parties in power, an institutionalized system of
national quotas, a powerful *cabinet* system (whose members act
as bastions of national interest, and who constantly interfere in
staffing matters), and a host of informal methods (*parachutage* and
piston: political cronyism; fly-by-night titularization exams and
rigged *concours*) used to circumvent the formal rules and procedures.
Interestingly, staff unions were particularly scathing about former
President Jacques Delors who they blamed for encouraging these
practices.[16] Most people I spoke with recognized that this was the
reality of 'how the House works' and accepted it as a *fait accompli*.
Typically, they justified it on the grounds that the formal system
simply didn't work: that you needed to 'bend the rules' just to get
things done.

A STATE WITHIN A STATE: ADMINISTRATIVE CULTURE AND CORRUPTION

Following publication of a report on 15 March 1999 by a five-member
Committee of Independent Experts (or *'Comité des Sages'*), entitled
*Allegations Regarding Fraud, Mismanagement and Nepotism in the
European Commission*, the entire College of Commissioners resigned.
What began in 1998 as a routine dispute in the European Parliament
over signing off the accounts in the EU's annual budget escalated
into a humiliating defeat for the President and his colleagues – and
plunged the Commission into the most serious political crisis in its
42-year history. But the episode also gives a critical insight into the
complex relationship between the Commission and the European
Parliament – and the administrative cultures of both institutions.

The CIE Report focused on just six areas of Commission activity
– including tourism, the Humanitarian Aid Office, vocational training
programmes, and the Commission Security Office. In each of these
spending programmes it found evidence of administrative failure,
financial irregularities, mismanagement and nepotism – including
(as the Commission's anti-fraud unit UCLAF had previously revealed)
the 'disappearance' of £600 million worth of funds from the
humanitarian aid budget,[17] and some £17 billion in structural fund
projects that the Commission was unable to account for because it
was not Commission practice to keep records of expenditure (*Daily
Telegraph* 9 Oct. 1998; *Sunday Business* 18 Oct. 1998). Elsewhere the
report noted:

a catalogue of instances of fraudulently altered tender specifications and
disregard for lower tenders, fictitious and double invoicing, inflated fees;

unjustified and illegal payments, non-existent reports, simple fraud where a staff member wrote cheques payable to herself, clear cases of favouritism in employment, and evasion of tax and social security obligations ... 'ghost personnel' who could not be accounted for, a low level of overall competence and a pervasive sub-culture of petty graft, favouritism and criminality. (MacMullen 1999: 711)

Perhaps the most serious case of corruption was found in the Commission's own security office – which answers directly to the President. The report portrayed a shadowy inner world of clientelism and corruption where collusion between security officials and the Belgian police was rife. The Security Office had become 'a state within a state' (1999: 105): 'a private club for former police officers from Brussels ... for whom special recruitment "competitions" were arranged' (1999: 102). It had developed a 'kind of "regulation free zone"'; a 'sub-culture' that was 'characterised by personal relationships, a system of "give-and-take" and a withdrawal from the overall system of control and surveillance' (1999: 102. Even more shocking was the revelation that the Security Service had put the Commission's own internal anti-fraud unit (UCLAF) under surveillance in order to block its investigations.

The report was particularly scathing about the Commission's lack of accountability. In a damning paragraph it concluded:

It is becoming difficult to find anyone who has even the slightest sense of responsibility. However, that sense of responsibility is essential. It must be demonstrated, first and foremost, by the Commissioners individually and the Commission as a body. The temptation to deprive the concept of responsibility of all substance is a dangerous one. That concept is the ultimate manifestation of democracy. (CIE 1999: 144)

While no individual Commissioners were found to have personally benefited from fraudulent dealings involving Community funds, the Commission President (Jacques Santer), the Vice-President (Manuel Marín) and the Commissioner for Education and Training (Edith Cresson – a former French Prime Minister) were singled out for particular criticism. Cresson had appointed her long-standing personal friend and dentist, Mr Berthelot, to a highly paid post as 'Visiting Scientist' in DG 12. Mr Bertherlot possessed none of the scientific qualifications required, his appointment was manifestly irregular, his contract was extended beyond its legal limit, and he produced no work for the Commission. His only discernible activity was constant visits to the town of Châtellerault – where Cresson had remained mayor until the end of 1997 – at the request of the Commissioner.

The reactions of senior Commissioners to the report were equally revealing. The blunt language of the report had clearly shocked the Commission, which had expected the report to lay the whole issue to rest. In a press conference held immediately after the report's release, Jacques Santer expressed anger and indignation, declaring that he was 'offended' by the report, and its 'wholly unjustified' tone, and that he himself was 'whiter than white' (*Financial Times* 17 March 1999: 2). Edith Cresson refused to accept responsibility for any wrongdoing. When questioned by MEPs she retorted 'Are we supposed to work only with people we do not know?' (*The Times* 16 March 1999) Prior to the report's publication she had initiated legal proceedings against two newspapers (*Libération* and the *Financial Times*), which, she alleged, were engaged in a right-wing-led campaign against her. Asked by the Labour MEP Michael Tappin whether she would resign on account of 'the atmosphere of illegality and cronyism which profits the family and friends of your circle?', her reply was that she was being hounded only because she had tried 'to do something for Europe'. She subsequently told France 2 Television that she had no reason to resign as the Commission had been found collectively responsible. To compound this defiant stance, she then went on to dismiss the charges against her as part of an Anglo-German 'conspiracy' and a 'German-inspired bid to damage France' (*Financial Times* 17 March 1999; *The Times* 17 March 1999). Even more astonishing were reports that many officials within the Commission privately agreed that Cresson had been a victim of an 'Anglo-Saxon political crusade' against the southern culture of state administration – a view corroborated by the findings of an earlier anthropological study commissioned by the Commission's own think tank, the Cellule de Prospective (McDonald 1998). As Cresson declared, to the embarrassment of French colleagues, she was 'guilty of no behaviour that is not standard in French administrative culture' (*The Times* 16 March 1999: 13). These reactions only inflamed public outrage and media hostility (although criticism was significantly more muted in southern Europe).

Following the demise of the Santer Commission, European leaders called for an urgent and fundamental 'root and branch reform' of the Commission's administration. The new Commission under Romano Prodi made institutional reform its virtual *raison d'être*, speeding up the preparation of three Codes of Conduct 'for a European Political and Administrative Culture' that had been set in motion in 1995. To the earlier policies of 'Sound and Efficient Management' ('SEM'), and 'Modernisation of Administration and Personnel' (MAP 2000) have now been added a raft of new initiatives designed to make its recruitment and operational practices more open, democratic and transparent. The former British Labour Party leader Neil Kinnock, and Vice-President of the Commission, was given the brief of carrying out these reforms, a task some have compared to cleaning out the Augean Stables, the fifth 'Labour of Hercules'. However, as we shall see, these reforms have not put a lid on the scandal or prevented further damaging allegations of corruption from arising elsewhere in the administration.

INTERPRETING EU CORRUPTION: EMIC VERSUS ETIC EXPLANATIONS

The Commission's own explanation stressed chronic understaffing and blamed external contractors and non-statutory staff (i.e. those 'outside' the House). Many in the Commission also argued that the campaign for reform is really a covert attempt to weaken the autonomy of the Commission spearheaded by 'anti-Europeans' who want to re-nationalize the administration, and that the level of fraud is no greater than that found in any other national administration anyway. These arguments have little foundation: first, the Commission had enthusiastically launched these programmes in full knowledge of its limited resources and had not even requested extra staff (MacMullen 1999). Second, fraud and mismanagement were found to be endemic – and not only among non-statutory staff. What the report exposed was arguably just the tip of the iceberg. Third, proclaiming itself 'Europe's conscience' and 'defender of the Community interest' begs the question 'What is the European interest?' and what legitimacy do public officials have to claim this? Finally, the scale of fraud and budgetary misuse in the EU is by no means insignificant, particularly in the Common Agricultural Policy (CAP), the EU's most established policy area.[18] To quote from one group of British Labour MPs:

Apart from the fact that about half the EU budget is spent on the Common Agricultural Policy – itself a deeply irrational and wasteful use of resources – on a straight accounting basis, staggering sums are not spent as intended. About 5% of the EU budget is lost to various forms of fraud – from non-existent tobacco farms to imaginary decontamination plans to help deal with Chernobyl – while another 5% is misappropriated, and not spent on the programmes for which it was designed. The 10% of the EU budget which the European Court of Auditors accepts is misspent amounts to about £5 billion every year. (LESC 1999)

The impression conveyed by the report was that of a 'clean north' crusading against a 'corrupt south' within the EU institutions, reflecting profoundly different standards of public behaviour among member state nationals – a view strongly supported by many media commentators and political scientists. However, 'corruption' is a relative concept whose meanings shift from one context to another.[19] As the Paris correspondent for *The Economist* observed: 'As far as most of the French are concerned Cresson did little wrong by giving a job to her dentist' and that those lucky enough to win a slice of power would be considered mean not to help friends and relatives (*The Economist* 1999: 46). As Europeanist anthropologists know, there exists a vast anthropological literature on patronage and clientelism and 'Mediterranean values' going back many years that makes precisely this point (see Davis 1977: Herzfeld 1992). But how fair is this view? Can we speak of a 'clash of cultures' in Europe between the 'ambassadors' of northern and southern systems of public administration?[20] If so, where does one locate France and Belgium (two countries perhaps most deeply mired in problems of political sleaze and grand corruption) in such a schema? Interestingly, this is the conclusion reached by Pujas and Rhodes (1999), two political scientists at the European University Institute, in a major comparative study of Western European administrations. They suggest that growth of corruption in the Commission arises from a combination of factors, many of which are intrinsic to the way the EU's bureaucracy is organized. Foremost among these are the extreme politicization of the bureaucracy; the Commission's social and political 'distance' from the public; its culture of secrecy and internal solidarity against external scrutiny'; and its inadequate mechanisms of financial accountability. However, the key point they make is that institutions and rules are far more important for understanding corruption than arguments about 'embedded social norms'. In many respects, the EU's administrative rules and arrangements actually *lend* themselves to fraud and misuse. The Committee of Independent Experts drew a similar conclusion:

the *de facto* tolerance of irregular employment practices represents a serious danger for the Commission in that it presents an opportunity for fraud and creates an institutional culture which is unacceptable. The truth is that, if a 'system' is in itself inadequate, it incites irregularity. (CIE 1999: 61)

This accusation goes far beyond any suggestion that corruption is a marginal problem confined to dishonest individuals. It suggests that the problem is structural and systemic: that the EU's administrative regime actively encourages fraudulent and corrupt practice.

Two further facts support this conclusion. The first is that in order to conduct its inquiry in the first place, the CIE had to call for a suspension of the *Staff Regulations* – particularly Article 17, on 'confidentiality' which had long served to gag potential whistle-blowers. Second, most of the evidence upon which the inquiry was based was supplied by a middle-ranking Dutch official, Paul Van Buitenen, working in the EU's anti-fraud unit (formerly known as 'UCLAF'). But for Van Buitenen's disclosures to certain Green Party MEPs, none of the cronyism and entrenched corruption outlined in the CIE report would have come to light. Yet for his act of courageous public spiritedness[21] (or 'treachery' as many in the Commission saw it) Van Buitenen was suspended from his post and, as he claims, subjected to a campaign of intimidation.[22]

The question the CIE asked was 'how [could] such a sub-culture develop, exist and prevail in a section of the European civil service without being detected from within, brought to light only when a newspaper published the allegations?' (CIE 1999: 102). The answer is that the existence of fraud within the Commission *was* known about for a several years prior to the report, but was tolerated by a weak and lax European Parliament. For three consecutive years, despite warnings of 'grave irregularities' in the Commission's expenditure from the European Court of Auditors, the European Parliament granted 'discharge' for the Commission's budget. When documents leaked to the press finally compelled MEPs to take action, the initial response from the leadership of the Socialist Group was to try to protect their friends in the Commission by preventing the scandal from breaking.[23] The European Parliament was also fearful that such a scandal would damage the recently launched euro on the international currency markets. The body that was supposed to provide a watchdog over the executive on behalf of voters of Europe thus signally failed to do so because it was not in most MEPs' interests to do so – and because they were not sufficiently neutral or distanced to be able do so.

This, however, is not the way the European Parliament and its allies in the press recount the story. Even before the scandal had subsided, the events had been re-narrativized in a way that painted the European Parliament in a more favourable light, altering the wider message of the CIE report. Thus the whole episode became a tale of heroic MEPs holding to account an over-mighty executive and 'forcing it to resign' – to the general benefit of European democracy. As Pat Cox (1999), leader of the European Liberal Group of MEPs declared, this was the European Parliament 'coming of age'. In fact, it was nothing of the sort, as the account by Van Buitenen (2000) and others indicates (see Shore 2000: 171–205).

FURTHER CORRUPTION SCANDALS IN THE WAKE OF THE KINNOCK REFORMS

A key question asked today is will the Prodi and Kinnock initiatives succeed in reforming the Commission's administration and bringing about the much-heralded 'culture of transparency', 'efficiency' and 'public service'? Many EU observers are sceptical, and with good reason. In June 2000, the Commission was once again embroiled in scandal when Neil Kinnock dismissed his own chief auditor, Marta Andreasen, after only six months in the job. Andreasen had refused to sign off the Commission's annual accounts for 2001 on the grounds that the budget management process was in her words, 'out of control' and still 'vulnerable to fraud', and that there was no coherent double-entry bookkeeping system in place.[24] As some tax accountant specialists would argue, in the UK and elsewhere, recording 'advances of money against future receipts as expenses rather than as debtors receivable [is] considered a tax fraud' (Arkell 2003: 5).

Like Van Buitenen, Andreasen also claims to have been subject to a slanderous whispering campaign and harassment by EU security personnel. For his part, Mr Kinnock informed MEPs that she was being disciplined for an 'absence of loyalty' and for making 'defamatory' comments likely to damage confidence in the EU's accounting system.[25] Yet according to Jules Muis, head of the Commission's internal audit service, in a leaked confidential memo sent to Mr Kinnock in March 2003, Andreasen's criticisms of the auditing system were 'factually substantive and correct' (Banks and Cronin 2003). Paradoxically, it was Kinnock himself who had previously made the public case for a 'whistle-blowers' charter' to protect staff against such intimidation by management.

In order to regain public trust in the EU project, the Commission immediately set about implementing all of the CIE recommendations. A large number of legal texts were also adopted to improve the *Staff Regulations* and to strengthen the Commission's capacity to detect and combat internal fraud.[26] However, since the Andreasen and Van Buitenen controversies other documented cases of corruption and whistle-blowing within the EU administration have emerged, one of which involved senior officials at the European Court of Auditors itself.[27] On 22 April 2002 Robert Dougal Watt, a Scottish official at the European Court of Auditors in Luxembourg, submitted a complaint to the EU ombudsman accusing senior officials at the Court of Auditors and the Commission's anti-fraud unit (know by its French acronym 'OLAF') of 'systematic corruption and abuse', including nepotism, sexual harassment of junior staff and even links with freemasonry and organized crime. Watt (who has been on 'sick leave' and in hiding since April 2000) writes: 'I fear my life to be at risk.' He also claims that his call for the current 15 members of the Court to resign was formally endorsed by 204 of his colleagues (or 40 percent of the Court's staff) in a secret ballot.[28]

A further serious fraud scandal erupted on 9 July 2003 with the announcement that Commissioner Kinnock had launched formal disciplinary proceedings against three senior officials in the EU's data office, 'Eurostat', after evidence was disclosed of 'a vast enterprise of looting' involving double accounting, fictitious contracts and kickback fees paid into special accounts.[29] Significantly, the Eurostat Office in Luxembourg and its Director-General of 17 years, Mr Yves Franchet, had been subject to repeated allegations since 1997, and in August 2001 Paul Van Buitenen had presented a dossier of fresh complaints to Mr Kinnock, including complaints about 'serious intimidation' of Eurostat staff who dared to question the misuse of funds (*Daily Telegraph* 10 July 2003: 15).

Whatever status one attributes to these accusations, they do raise fundamental questions about the EU's ability to police itself, and the problem of '*Quis custodiet ipsos custodres?*' As David Spence (2000) predicted, reform of the Commission would seem to be a case of *plus ça change*. That was also the conclusion reached by Van Buitenen himself, who resigned from the Commission in August 2002 out of frustration and disillusionment, citing Andreasen's treatment as evidence that the EU's secretive machinery is 'inherently unreformable' as long as it remains beyond the control of elected parliamentarians (*Daily Telegraph* 27 August: 12; Evans-Pritchard 2002). This pessimism seems to be shared by other staff. In July 2003 Jules Muis, the Commission's chief auditor, announced to Parliament that he had been prevented from investigating deeply and was planning to step down next year because 'he didn't see eye to eye with the Commission on how I should do my work' (*Daily Telegraph* 10 July 2003: 15).

CONCLUSION

How, therefore, should we interpret corruption in the EU and the Commission's record of institutional reform? The evidence presented in this chapter certainly challenges the idea of the Commission as a 'cultural melting pot' in which the best practices of the different civil service traditions meld together harmoniously. It also invites us to question the dominant assumptions underlying the concept of 'supranationalism'. On the other hand, one could argue that bureaucracies are not hermetically sealed or immune from the influences of the countries in which they are located, and that the EU's administrative culture (to use John Peterson's [1997] phrase), is just a 'macrocosm' of its member states. Thus, given the widespread increase in political corruption throughout Europe, why should we be surprised to find corruption embedded within the Commission's administrative regime too? However, this explanation has significant implications for theorizing European integration. Monnet's vision for the Commission was that the 'Europeanization' of elites would create a new cadre of supranational civil servants (or 'High Authority') that would rise above the nasty and brutish self-interests of parochial nation-states. Does evidence of widespread nepotism and fraud within the Commission therefore refute this argument, and is it proof that the *engrenage* process has failed? On the contrary, collusion among EU civil servants, MEPs and politicians suggests that an *esprit de corps* has developed, not only *within* the institutions, but also *between* them. This is precisely what the Monnet method was designed to achieve: the 'Europeanization' of national elites would seem to be all too effective. Unfortunately, Monnet never considered the possibility that *engrenage* might flow the other way: that instead of a 'Europeanization' of national elites, what we might be observing is a *de facto* 'Brusselsization' of the EU and its civil service.

This chapter has argued that the encapsulated world and cultural intimacy of EU officials, journalists, politicians and business-people has created a new kind of transnational elite. To put it in sociological terms, the EU's technocratic elite appears to be transforming itself from a 'class in itself' to a 'class *for* itself'. This gives a whole new meaning to the concept of 'supranationalism'. The danger for Europe is if this emergent elite ossifies into a self-serving caste, or European *'Nomenklatura'*. Corruption – and the informal parallel system of administration in which it thrives – is one of the mechanisms by which this cultural reproduction occurs. The disclosure that former French President Mitterrand had used a secret and illegal slush funds from the state-owned oil company Elf to finance the re-election campaign of his German Christian Democrat ally, Helmut Kohl (a policy also justified in terms of the 'European interest'), adds a further dimension to this process.

The European Union has given national politicians a new platform upon which to bestride the globe, but it has not created a class of noble supranationals of the calibre that Monnet hoped to create. It has also greatly enhanced the opportunities for personal gain and the abuse of public funds. Temptation to corruption is further fuelled by the EU's lack of transparency and accountability to the 'European public' – a category that does not yet exist in any meaningful or coherent way. Ironically, as Warner's (2002) study concludes, one of the unintended side effects of European integration has been the creation of a 'common market for fraud and corruption'.

To understand corruption in international organizations we should look at what it produces as well as the structures that create it. What this case study also shows is that EU corruption is not simply a matter of a few corrupt individuals who stand outside the formal system; it is something systemic – a logical consequence of the EU's developing administrative system whose lack of accountability, as the Independent Expert report concluded, 'invites irregularities' and abuse. Thus, fraud, nepotism and cronyism are not incompatible with the ostensibly more advanced legal-rational structures of supranational bureaucracy; quite the reverse, it seems. Paradoxically, some corruption theorists would interpret these scandals as something salutary and positive. As Rose-Ackerman argues, in a newly emerging democracy corruption can be a sign of progress' as it indicates that citizens and government functionaries 'recognise that there are norms of fair dealing and competent administration and that they can be violated' (1996: 365). While it is reassuring to know that

EU *fonctionnaires* now recognize the difference between fair and fraudulent dealing, what makes reform of the European civil service so problematic is precisely the absence of democracy within the EU's emerging system of governance.

NOTES

1. I would like to thank the Economic and Social Research Council of the United Kingdom for funding that research. Fieldwork for this study was carried out between 1995 and 1997.
2. Significantly, the idiomatic phrase *'pris dans l'engrenage'* translates as 'caught up in the system'.
3. '...un nouveau type d'homme [qui] était en train de naître dans les institutions de Luxembourg comme dans un laboratoire ... c'était l'esprit européen qui était le fruit du travail en commun' (Jean Monnet 1976, *Mémoires*, cited in Spence 1994: 63).
4. This was subsequently enshrined in Article 9 of the original European Coal and Steel Community treaty.
5. Article 11 of the *Staff Regulations* poses obligations on each staff to 'conduct himself solely with the interest of the Communities in mind: he shall neither seek nor take instructions from any government, authority, organizations or persons outside his institution' (*Staff Regulations* 1993: 12).
6. This chapter both draws on, and adds to, the more detailed research findings published in Shore (2000).
7. This expression was coined by Bailey (1971), but this dualism between formal and informal rules is well documented in the anthropological literature on organizations (cf. Gellner and Hirsch 2001; Wright 1994).
8. As Middlemas explains it, the EU's 'competitive symposium' of personal linkages leads to ever-closer interdependence: 'Bargaining through networks in a densely structured game reduces friction and produces results for which the informal system may be ill attuned, even on ostensibly formal matters ... It allows for wide, flexible participation; it reduces inconsistencies; it gives rise to conventions, rather than formal rules, which can be adapted more easily over time' (Middlemas 1995: xvi).
9. 'Working for family values' and 'jobs-for-the-boys' was how most newspapers carried the story. The dispute – which continued over several years – was well documented in the *European Voice*.
10. In January 1998, however, staff again threatened industrial action over the controversial recruitment policy as the CoR had still not acted to implement the Court's ruling.
11. A pseudonym. Most interviewees insisted that interviews be conducted 'off the record' using 'journalists' rules': they were happy for their comments to be recorded, but not attributed.
12. *Piston* is the French idiom for clientelism, or obtaining jobs through political favouritism or friends in high places.
13. I.e. an alumni of the prestigious and elitist École Nationale d'Administration (or 'ENA').
14. TACIS was an EC programme launched in 1991 with the aims of providing grant-financed technical assistance to twelve countries of Eastern Europe

and Central Asia. PHARE was an aid programme also created during the 1990s. Initially it was to assist post-communist Poland and Hungary, but it was extended to ten other Central and Eastern European states. Administered by the European Commission, the PHARE programme subsequently absorbed over US $1 billion a year in EU hand-outs and became a by-word for waste and corruption.

15. The EU civil service rankings for its A-grade staff start at the rank of A7 or A8. A1 is the highest level of seniority.

16. In fact, most of these defects pre-dated Delors' presidency – and all of them were clearly identified over two decades ago in the 1979 report by Dirk Spierenburg (1979).

17. £1.5 million of which had been intended for refugees from the genocide in Rwanda and Burundi. See Vaughne Miller and Richard Ware (1999) 'The Resignation of the European Commission', House of Commons Research Paper 99/32: 11

18. A BBC *File on 4* investigation (broadcast 16 July 2002) highlighted some of the more mundane examples of CAP fraud, including the story of a Devon farmer who for years had claimed large CAP subsidies for non-existent land. The grid references he provided were in the middle of the North Sea and off the coast of Iceland. In this case, the British government had failed to check his claim. As experts have noted, part of the problem with EU funding is that no one has a sense of ownership in or loyalty to the EU grant-giving process – either from the farmers and the Ministry, or from the Commission.

19. As Pujas and Rhodes put it (1999: 670): 'What would be considered as nepotism or shameless patronage in Britain might be seen as fair practice or even a moral duty in other countries, including the countries of southern Europe.'

20. See for example Johnson (1999). My own view is that 'clash of cultures' is not a useful metaphor for conceptualizing the problem. However, I do accept that where cultures meet there is often a critical lack of fit between category systems – and this may exacerbate the problem of divided accountability. There is plenty of anecdotal evidence to suggest that concepts of probity and honesty in public affairs differ between Protestant and Catholic countries (e.g. several directors of personnel lamented the absence of a coherent human resources strategy and the virtual impossibility of introducing systems of 'performance appraisal').

21. In October 1999 the Association of European Taxpayers showered Van Buitenen with praise and gave him a whistle-blowing award (*European Voice* 21 October 1999).

22. Van Buitenen (2001) subsequently published a book-length account of his ordeal, which gives chilling details of the extent to which EU authorities were prepared to go to prevent him from disclosing his evidence.

23. For useful accounts of the political events surrounding this episode, see MacMullen (1999).

24. The accusation was subsequently endorsed in a leaked paper from the EU's Court of Auditors, which noted that despite warnings about defects in its 'Sincom 2' accounting system, the Commission had 'not taken any remedial action' (*Financial Times* 31 July 2002).

25. See *Financial Times* (8 Feb. 2002); *Daily Telegraph*, (2 August 2002). Andreasen was accused of breaching three of the EU staff regulations,

including Article 12 which states: 'An official shall abstain from any action and, in particular, any public expression of opinion which may reflect on his position.' Article 12 also requires that any individuals wishing to 'engage in outside activity' must first obtain 'permission from the appointing authority'. As critics point out, this rule functions as a very effective 'gagging clause' against internal dissent.

26. For details of these see the Commission's White Paper, 'Reforming the Commission' published in April 2000 (COM(2000) 200 final/2.

27. See *Sunday Times* (5 May 2002). In October, it was also reported that Greece's former member of the European Court of Auditors was facing legal action for alleged fraud and nepotism (Cronin 2002).

28. Watt's detailed account can be found at <http://www.justresponse.net/DougalWatt.html>.

29. For a detailed account see <http://www.cfoeurope.com/displayStory.cfm/2020389>.

REFERENCES

Anderson, B. (1983) *Imagined Communities: Reflections on the Origin and Spread of Nationalism* (London: Verso).

Arkell, C. (2003) Still Making it up in Brussels, *European Journal*, Vol. 10, No. 4: 5–6.

Beck, U. (1992) *Risk Society: Towards a New Modernity* (London: Sage).

Bailey, (ed.) (1971) *Gifts and Poison: The Politics of Reputation* (Oxford: Blackwell).

Banks, M. and D. Cronin (2003) Schreyer: No Way Back for Andreasen', *European Voice* Vol. 9 No. 10 (13–19 March): 3.

Bellier, I. (1994) Une culture de la Commission européenne? De la rencontre des cultures et du multilingualisme des fonctionnaires, in Y. Mény, P. Muller and J.C. Quermonne (eds) *Politique publiques en Europe Politique publiques en Europe* (Paris: L'Harmattan).

Cohen, A. (ed.) (1974) *Urban Ethnicity* (London: Tavistock).

CEC (Commission of the European Communities) (1999) *For a European Political and Administrative Culture: Three Codes of Conduct*. Available online <http://europa.eu.int/comm>. Accessed March 2001.

—— (2002) *Serving the People of Europe. How the European Commission Works* (Luxembourg: Office for Official Publications of the European Communities).

CIE (Committee of Independent Experts) (1999) *First Report on Allegations Regarding Fraud, Mismanagement and Nepotism in the European Commission* (Brussels: European Parliament and Commission of the European Communities).

Cronin, D. (2002) OLAF Puts Ex-auditor in Dock over Alleged Corruption, *European Voice*, Vol. 8, No. 37.

Davis, J. (1977) *People of the Mediterranean* (London: Routledge & Kegan Paul).

Delanty, G. (2002) European Identity and Architecture, *European Journal of Social Theory*, Vol. 5, No. 4: 453–66.

The Economist (1999) What's Wrong with Nepotism, Anyway? *The Economist* 20 March: 46.

Evans-Pritchard, A. (2002) Whistle-blower Admits Defeat on EU Corruption, *Daily Telegraph*, 22 August: 12.

Eriksen, T.H. (1993) *Ethnicity and Nationalism: Anthropological Perspectives* (London: Pluto Press).

Gellner, D. and E. Hirsch (eds) (2001) *Inside Organizations: Anthropologists at Work* (Oxford: Berg).

Haas, E. (1958) *The Uniting of Europe* (Oxford: Oxford University Press).

Halper, S. (1996) A Miasma of Corruption: The UN at 50, *Cato Policy Analysis* 23, 30 April.

Henley, J. (1999) *Guardian* 18 Oct.:1, 11.

Herzfeld, M. (1992) *The Social Production of Indifference: Exploring the Symbolic Roots of Western Bureaucracy* (Chicago: University of Chicago Press).

Holmes, D. (2000) *Integral Europe: Fast-capitalism, Multiculturalism, Neofascism,* (Princeton, NJ: Princeton University Press).

Johnson, R. (1999) The Nordics Versus the Latins, *The Spectator* No. 8930 (2 Oct.): 2.

LESC (Labour European Safeguards Committee) (1999) *Bulletin* May: 1.

McDonald, M. (1998) Anthropological Study of the European Commission (Unpublished report commissioned for the Cellule de Prospective, Brussels).

MacMullen, A. (1999) Political Responsibility for the Administration of Europe: The Commission's Resignation March 1999, *Parliamentary Affairs*, Vol. 52, No. 1: 703–18.

Middlemas, K. (1995) *Orchestrating Europe: The Informal Politics of European Union 1973–1995* (London: Fontana).

Miller, V. and R. Ware (1999) The Resignation of the European Commission, House of Commons Research Paper 99/32: 11.

O'Neill, M. (ed.) (1996) *The Politics of European Integration: A Reader* (London: Routledge).

Parkin, D. (1985) Introduction, in D. Parkin (ed.) *The Anthropology of Evil* (Oxford: Blackwell).

Peterson, J. (1997) The European Union: Pooled Sovereignty, Divided Accountability, *Political Studies*, Vol. 45: 559–78.

Power, M. (1997) *The Audit Society: Rituals of Verification* (Oxford: Oxford University Press).

Pujas, V. and M. Rhodes (1999) A Clash of Cultures? Corruption and the Ethics of Administration in Western Europe, *Parliamentary Affairs*, Vol. 52, No. 4: 688–703.

Rose-Ackerman, S. (1996) Democracy and 'Grand' Corruption, *International Social Science Journal*, Vol. 149: 365–81.

Shore, C. (1999) Inventing *Homo Europaeus*: The Cultural Politics of European Integration, *Ethnologia Europaea*, Vol. 29, No. 2: 53–66.

—— (2000) *Building Europe: The Cultural Politics of European Integration* (London: Routledge).

Smith, G. (1983) *Politics in Western Europe: A Comparative Analysis* (Aldershot: Gower).

Spence, D. (1994) Staff and Personnel Policy in the Commission, in G. Edwards and D. Spence (eds) *The European Commission*, pp. 62–94 (Harlow: Longman).

—— (2000) *Plus ça change, plus c'est la même chose*? Attempting to Reform the European Commission?, *Journal of European Public Policy*, Vol. 7, No. 1: 1–25.

Spierenburg, D. (1979) *Proposals for Reform of the Commission of the European Communities and its Services* (Brussels: European Commission).

Staff Regulations (1993) *Regulations of the Rules Applicable to Officials and Other Servants of the European Commission* (Luxembourg: OOPCE).

Strathern, M. (2000) Introduction: New Accountabilities, in M. Strathern (ed.) *Audit Cultures: Anthropological Studies in Accountability, Ethics and the Academy* (EASA Series) (London: Routledge).

Swan, D. (1996) *A Singular Pluralism: European Schools 1984–1994* (Dublin: Institute of Public Administration).

Van Buitenen, P. (2000) *Blowing the Whistle* (London: Politico's).

Warner, C. (2002) Creating a Common Market in Fraud and Corruption in the European Union: An Institutional Accident or a Deliberate Strategy?, *EUI Working Papers, RSC No. 2002/31* (Florence: European University Institute).

Webb, C. (1983) Theoretical Perspectives and Problems, in H. Wallace, W. Wallace and C. Webb (eds) *Policy-making in the European Community* (Chichester: John Wiley & Sons).

Westlake, M. (1994) *Britain's Emerging Euro-elite? The British in the European Parliament, 1979 – 1992* (Aldershot: Dartmouth Publications).

Williamson, D. (1994) The Looking-glass View of Europe, *Financial Times* 15 December: 25.

Wright, S. (ed.) (1994) *Anthropology of Organizations* (London/New York: Routledge).

8 CORRUPTION IN CORPORATE AMERICA: ENRON – BEFORE AND AFTER

Carol MacLennan

In the last few years, Americans have been facing news about corporate officials who have deliberately corrupted the sacred concepts of fairness, plain-dealing and honesty in business practices. Beginning with the news of Enron's demise in early 2002, we watched this Houston-based company fall apart like a house of cards, taking much of Houston with it. Once again, we have been made aware of how vulnerable our social institutions are to corrupt processes. In this recent case, the cause was the not-uncommon scheme of the new millennium: falsification of balance sheets through manipulative accounting practices in order to present a public image of sound financial health.

Americans act as if this is news. And the more we hear following Enron's exposure, the more we see corruption of business leaders is closer to a 'norm' than an aberration. We are outraged. This is a democratic society. We have laws against this behaviour, and, not to forget, ethical standards which are taught in universities and business schools that are intended to instil honest behaviour in our corporate executives.

Outrage is good. In fact, it has in the past led to laws to protect business and government offices against corrupt leaders who would use their positions to their advantage. But Americans seem to have a short memory, or perhaps a denial of the history of business malfeasance and collusion against the public interest since the industrial tide swept the nation in the late nineteenth century. Corruption in the US is not new, and it is definitely not a product of the economics of the 1980s and 1990s, as some news analysts would have us believe. What is new is the method of the corruption – stock-market oriented and in areas where the legal system has been lax or undeveloped.

This latest round of publicized corruption began with the fall of Enron, and then WorldCom, as news reports indicated that these companies were inflating (and lying about) the value of their business activities. Soon, US regulators in the Securities and Exchange Commission (SEC) found cooperative activities by accounting firms (Arthur Andersen) and major banks which amounted to fraud. The corruption continues to this day as investigations into mutual funds and tax shelters created by accountants, banks and lawyers shed light on illegal and unethical practices. What makes this recent flurry of investigations interesting is that it reveals a harm done not merely to the legal system, but to the wider American public – especially to 'the little guy'. In this case it is the middle-class investor and the large pension funds that are the future support system for elder Americans who have lost out. It is this aspect – harm to the middle and working classes – more than broken laws or sleazy ethics that riles the public. At the heart of corruption in the US is the 'unfairness' of gain marked by class divisions and culture. This is indicative of a deep tension between market and democratic values historically present in American political culture since the early republican era.

As America industrialized its economy, beginning with textile factories, railroads, and oil companies in the nineteenth century, it encountered the inevitable and fundamental conflict between the emergent values of market capitalism and democratic goals to protect the public interest. Early attempts to mute and diminish this conflict resulted in national business regulation. The Sherman Anti-Trust Act of 1890 established some protections against monopolistic predatory practices. The progressive legislation that created the Food and Drug Administration, Federal Trade Commission, and Interstate Commerce Commission furthered the national policy to protect consumers, small businesses and citizens against a business culture that flaunted its disdain for the larger public interest in the economic well-being and health and safety of the country. And the New Deal laws of the Depression era brought protection against corrupt behaviour on Wall Street and in the banks. While the US Constitution sanctifies private property rights, the US Congress has established a tradition of protecting the public interest (under the guise of minority, consumer, worker and individual citizen rights) from the corporate predation that is characteristic of a free-market industrial society. In effect, national policy has evolved to rein in the complete dominance of market values and provide a limited protection of democratic society. This history of economic regulation in a capitalist economy has also worked toward the long-term interest of securing the continued health of capitalism in the US. As revisionist historians of the 1960s and 1970s so persuasively argued, certain sectors of corporate America worked for and welcomed economic regulation as a means to stabilize industry and present capitalism from cannibalizing itself (Kolko 1977; Weinstein 1968). So, what we have is the American version of the 'welfare state', which not only provides a social safety net for the disadvantaged in the economy, but also welfare for the very rich and their corporations. And it is this regulatory system made up of government agencies such as the Federal Trade Commission (FTC), Securities and Exchange Commission (SEC), Federal Communications Commission (FCC) that everyday citizens depend upon to rein in the type of corrupt behaviour evidenced by Enron, WorldCom and, more recently, mutual funds, brokerage houses and accounting firms. So, why have these political safeguards failed to prevent corporate corruption in America?

The answer may be that we (Americans) have missed the whole point. The economy and the public do not have adequate protection against corporate predation because it is not necessarily isolated or behavioural in nature. Our regulatory system is predicated on this idea: it is only during the *moments of business failure* when the public interest is threatened and when regulations are designed to correct those *moments*. However, corruption is perhaps more than moments of broken business practices that appear in a sea of well-functioning enterprises. These moments, instead, are more pervasive than is generally accepted and they are deeply attached to the market values of corporate culture. Further, corporate (market) values are not always compatible with the democratic values of civil society as neoliberal politicians have led us to believe. Democratic values in the US demand open political processes, equality for citizens and fairness in business dealings that recognize the ideal of a 'public interest'. They are predicated on minimizing class distinctions and ensuring economic opportunity for all who are willing to work and contribute. Market values, which have their roots in a pre-industrial liberal society based upon democratic citizenship and agrarian, small business enterprises, have morphed into a new ethic of corporate capitalism which no longer resembles the business culture of the past.

Corporate behaviour in the US has become increasingly 'corrupt' and the behaviour of officials in the Enrons and WorldComs is not isolated. First, it is pervasive and institutionalized. That means, it is more than criminal behaviour by a few bad actors in an otherwise clean enterprise. It is institutionalized in the everyday world-view and processes of corporate action. Second, because institutionalized corruption in the US reflects deeper changes in market values of the economic elite, it challenges the viability of maintaining democratic society for the rest of us. This is what makes corruption in the US distinctive: a growing institutionalization in the economic sector, and the increased elevation of corrosive corporate market values over those of democratic civil society.

A new *anthropology* of corruption can help understand the everyday business practices which amount to institutionalized corruption. It can provide unique insights into the culture of corruption and suggest a research agenda that may uncover a more realistic picture of corporate culture in the US than is presented in the business press.

INSTITUTIONALIZED CORRUPTION IN AMERICA

While Americans may believe that their institutions have been relatively free from widespread corrupt behaviour because of powerful regulatory agencies, scholars have not been so optimistic. A generation of intellectuals influential in the academy and widely read by educated citizens, wrote persuasively during the 1960s and 1970s about economic and political institutions which provided a home for the type of corruption that so upsets Americans today. C. Wright Mills, William Domhoff and Ralph Nader were instrumental in engaging a generation of scholars and students in American universities during the 1970s in the study of the 'power structure' of American economic and political life. Their combined work provides significant insight into the Enron, Author Andersen, WorldCom and Halliburton misdeeds of three decades later. Anthropology's discussion of corruption in the US must review their combined contribution and build upon their main finding: corruption is more than a simple, isolated crime committed for personal gain. It is a part of corporate and political, culture – more pervasive and acceptable among elites than we realize. In short, it is *becoming institutionalized*. Corruption is something more than mere outlaw behaviour by a few corporate and political executives. What they uncovered in their investigations has come to pass more than 30 years later. A review of their work is helpful.

In his 1940 Presidential address to the American Sociological Association, Edwin Sutherland coined the term 'white collar crime' and set the stage for a new criminology of corporate America (Sutherland et al. 1985). C. Wright Mills, possibly the most highly regarded mid-century American sociologist, expanded our understanding of corporate crime as something extending beyond the anti-social deed of a criminal. In his influential and widely read *Power Elite* (1956) he showed how the social norms and institutional practices among the ruling elite in the US easily slipped into identifiable criminal behaviour. More importantly, he described a ruling class with a distinct culture which set it apart from the rest of society, enabling it to control (rule) the major economic, political and military institutions of the time. Mills' influence in the academy and beyond was profound as his ideas informed general public discussion. This was the time when then President Eisenhower coined the term 'the military-industrial complex' and cautioned against its potential abuse of power.

Mills argued that Americans were clinging to an outdated understanding of the distribution of power in the US, and Mills argued that American institutions had changed fundamentally from the Jeffersonian democratic ideals that underlay the interest group theories of Robert Dahl (1961) and others of his time. Pre-industrial America was based upon institutions that were dispersed such that 'no man had it in his power to bestow or to receive great favors'. But, concentration of economic opportunities with the rise of the trusts and limited-liability corporations fundamentally altered the landscape of power. Further, Mills pointed out, when economic power and political institutions are linked, 'public office can be used for private gain' (Mills 1956: 346). Specifically on corruption, he claims:

A great deal of American corruption – although not all of it – is simply a part of the old effort to get rich and then to become richer. But today the context in which the old drive must operate has changed. When both economic and political institutions were small and scattered – as in the simpler models of classical economics and Jeffersonian democracy – no man had it in his power to bestow or receive great favors. But when political institutions and economic opportunities are at once concentrated and linked, then public office can be used for private gain. (Mills 1956: 346)

Powerful corporations, a military in control of massively destructive weapons, and a government that centralized political power in the hands of a small ruling elite has changed the political landscape. Connections among these three sectors enabled a small class of citizens to control economic, political and military decisions without the benefit of public input. Traditional theories of 'interest group politics' – where there existed a balance of forces pressing upon the political institutions that enabled widespread representation of interests – were no longer accurate. This elite was relatively impervious to mid-level leaders (Congress, local officials, celebrities) and to the masses in wielding their authority. Meanwhile, he maintained, Americans seemed to be stuck in a romantic past, believing that our political institutions were governed by a 'balance of power' – whether in the marketplace, among individual actors, or in government institutions among different interests. His 'power elite' is essentially a ruling class in the US, a group set apart by its separate culture, access to power and ability to command resources.

While Mills was best at illustrating the institutional linkages of the powerful, William Domhoff, a social psychologist studying the culture of the American ruling class, published several path-breaking books during the 1970s that provided the detail illustrating Mills' argument about a cohesive power elite. His power structure research methods pioneered a new look at the social world of business leaders and the means by which corruptive practices are acceptable yet hidden from the rest of society. Three works – *Who Rules America?* (1967), *Higher Circles* (1970) and *Bohemian Grove* (1975) – detailed the social clubs, political party activities, schooling experiences and everyday cultural life of economic and political elites in the US. His research was specific and meticulous in an effort to *prove*, first, that the social world of the elites in the US was vastly different from the rest of the society and, second, that it was so insulated and secretive that it enabled an exercise of power that few in American society (including the 'interest group' theorists) could witness and understand.

Domhoff's power structure research was helpful in clarifying the concept of 'class' for a generation of scholars, making it a researchable subject and something more than a theoretical construct. His research on social connections, kinship patterns, and rituals that promoted 'cohesiveness' among the economic and political elites influenced graduate students in sociology, political science, economics, as well as anthropology. Domhoff expanded beyond the economic definition of class as based solely in production, and illustrated how class consciousness developed, how segments of the ruling class were often at odds with one another, and yet how the cohesiveness among families with economic power created a 'governing class' with both the economic and political means to dominate decision-making in a democratic society. When examined, the complexities of ruling-class formation, reformation and power-wielding activities began to explain a lot about economic and political power of the Vietnam era.

Domhoff's observation of what makes the governing class cohesive is remarkably relevant to descriptions of today's actors in the corporate scandals of Enron, WorldCom, and Wall Street. His methods were structural: identifying social networks woven around corporate boards, club memberships, elite school enrolment and philanthropic organizations.

Although this national upper class has its ethnic, religious and new-rich-old-rich antagonisms, is nonetheless closely knit by such institutions as stock ownership, trust funds, intermarriages, private schools, exclusive city clubs, exclusive summer resorts, debutante parties, foxhunts, charity drives, and last but not least, corporation boards. (1967: 4)

Domhoff's discussion of the distinction between 'control' and 'influence' of the ruling class is also helpful. He notes that in various spheres of public life the ruling class dominates decision-making differently: in the executive branch of the federal government, major corporations, foundations and universities, they exert control. Whereas, in Congress and most state and local governments, they exert 'influence'.

However, the interesting thing about 'control' and 'influence' in a country where the concept of a governing class calls forth notions of sinister men lurking behind the throne, is that members of the American governing class in fact serve their interests from positions of authority. Authority-based control, rather than covert influence, is their dominant mode. (1967: 11)

He was less capable of analysing the behavioural patterns and cultural practices *within* ruling-class networks – something an anthropologist would expect. Questions arise out of his research: how did these social clubs, corporate boards and elite schools operate? How did members of the ruling class – or its different factions – make sense of their place in the economy and social hierarchy? What values, different from other social groups, drove corporate and social behaviour? Today, these questions beg for an ethnographic study of ruling class life and institutions. But, 30 years ago when Domhoff asked 'Who rules America?', the fact that he could identify the broad *scope* of networks and show how individuals could *insulate* themselves in a system of invisible power was an important step.

Today, Domhoff's ruling-class networks are still viable, and their political power strong. Social norms among executives of corporations, accounting and law firms, and brokerage houses allow unethical practices that amount to fraud to masquerade as acceptable because they cleverly avoid the literal interpretation of the law or because they are not covered by regulations. 'Insider' trading of information is a very powerful tool that cements social relations among corporate officials, yet harms outsiders (stockholders, consumers, local communities) in the long run. Further, the ability of this social class to literally 'man' or staff the upper echelon of the regulatory system (i.e. the Security and Exchange Commission) or reside in the White House (Vice-President Cheney), illustrates that it is firmly in 'control' of political authority.

However, while the 'power structure' argument states that members of the ruling class occupy political office and head federal agencies, it does little to explain how this works and why it remains impervious to change by angry citizens. The work of Ralph Nader used the state as a vantage point from which to probe how corporate values penetrated and captured political institutions. Domhoff's concept of ruling-class 'control' over the executive branch of government was amply documented in the studies of regulatory agencies in the 1970s by Nader's Raiders. Ralph Nader, a young lawyer and consumer advocate in the 1970s, organized a series of investigative research projects (almost ethnographic in nature) on the structure, day-to-day practices and cultural norms of regulatory agencies such as the Federal Trade Commission (Cox et al. 1969), the Interstate Commerce Commission (Fellmeth 1970), Food and Drug Administration (Turner and Nader 1970), and the Anti-Trust Division of the Justice Department (Green et al. 1972). Reports from this research were published and distributed by major paperback publishers, putting them in the hands of a public already deeply suspicious of the comfortable relationship between the regulators and the regulated. After the success of Nader's *Unsafe at Any Speed*, a critique of the automotive industry, the American public was ready to consider the multiple means by which political decisions were quietly guided by economic interests.

Nader's rich documentary project illustrated how everyday government/business practice amounted to corruption and betrayal of the public trust. The FTC study, the first of several, detailed numerous failings of the agency through the everyday practices of its members, which effectively sealed it off from consumer complaints. Re-reading these studies, one is reminded of the types of criticism heaped upon developing nations for their problems of political corruption. Nader, in a subsequent book on anti-trust enforcement, begins with: 'This is a report on crime in the suites ... a study of corporate radicalism so deeply insinuated into the politico-economic fabric of the society that a veritable revolution against citizens has occurred' (Green et al. 1972: ix). Though not used directly, the word 'corruption' can be substituted for 'crime' because this implies that 'crime committed by persons of respectability and high social status [for whom] a violation of the legal code is not necessarily a violation of the business code' (Green et al. 1972: 147). In the anti-trust study, they note: 'many consider industrial collaboration to be the inevitable result of competitive capitalism ... The encouragement at trade-association meetings for all to raise their prices, camouflaged in speeches on poor profit margins of all the members, is legion.' In other words, unethical practices are 'a way of life' (Green et al. 1972: 148–9).

The review of the intellectual contributions from Mills, Domhoff and Nader reveal that *institutionalized* corruption is growing and that it has a lengthy history in the US. However, until recently 'corruption' has not been a widely used term to describe shady corporate behaviour – rather, the reference has been to concepts such as 'white collar crime' or 'influence'. This is not an insignificant oversight, as discussed shortly. Further, the above review suggests there is a corporate culture that sanctions a different code of behaviour among the wealthy and powerful. Definitions of morality, public interest and personal responsibility in corporate board rooms and executive offices may in fact be quite different from those of the rest of the middle, working and poorer classes.

THE DIFFERENCE BETWEEN CRIME AND CORRUPTION

Apart from the above-described documentation of a networked, somewhat cohesive ruling or elite class with economic power and political authority, there has emerged another line of inquiry into corruption. This is the criminologist's study of 'white collar crime'.

Often the two approaches – criminology and sociology of power – are assumed to be part of the same enterprise, and thus discussed interchangeably. Sometimes this is warranted, such as when Enron executives deliberately shredded documents that had been requested by the courts – a clear violation of the law. The same goes for brokerage houses which provide insider tips on stocks for favoured clients. But there are many situations in which corruption is not necessarily explicit criminal behaviour. Making a clearer distinction between corruption and crime is essential if we are to make sense of the corporate corruption in the US.

The indiscriminate blending of terms (such as 'scandal', 'crime', 'unethical' and 'corruption') hides the significance of the difference between crime and corruption in the US. Corruption implies something systematic, institutionalized and perhaps endemic to an organization or culture. It is pervasive, infused or embedded in the system. Unethical, scandalous and criminal are descriptors that are attributed to behaviour, especially individual or aberrant action. Also confusing is the fact that corruption has traditionally been applied primarily to political activity and institutions – especially today with the focus on political corruption in developing nations. Until recently, corruption has not been a term regularly applied by the media to corporate behaviour.

It is useful to understand corruption as distinct from, but sometimes including, crime. It is not only a matter of law-breaking. In fact, it is not about the individual at all. It is, instead, part of a *pattern* of behaviour that may or may not be criminal. It is an *accepted* set of relationships or actions that serve some purpose of the group as a whole. In fact, the phrase 'white collar crime' throws us off track. If crime and corruption are interchangeable, then a person identified as corrupt is really no more than an individual example of a bad apple in a bushel of good ones.

Sociology's traditional focus on social problems establishes the basic assumptions behind contemporary research on corporate crime. The last 50 years of white-collar crime research echoes the literature on deviant behaviour. Two recent textbooks – Ermann and Lundman's *Corporate and Governmental Deviance* (2002) and Friedrich's *Trusted Criminals* (1996) – represent the contemporary perspective in this field. Corporate crime is one of several types of white-collar crime: occupational crime, governmental crime, finance crime, technocrime, state-corporate crime, enterprise crime.

[W]hite-collar crime is a generic term for the whole range of illegal, prohibited, and demonstrably harmful activities involving a violation of a private or public trust, committed by institutions and individuals occupying a legitimate, respectable status, and directed toward financial advantage or the maintenance and extension of power and privilege. (Friedrichs 1996:10)

On the solution side of the deviance paradigm, government regulation and business self-regulation are the appropriate antidotes to white-collar crime (Clark 1990). Regulation, it is said, has less of a stigma associated with it than criminal law; thus it acts as a deterrent. Recently, however, sociologists have suggested that there is little evidence to show that regulation *actually* works as a deterrent (Simpson 2002). Criminologists also promote other crime-reducing strategies, such as self-regulation by industrial associations, and moral appeals through business ethics courses.

The extensive attention paid to the deviant behaviour of the corporate criminal leads down an unproductive path. Criminology is problem-oriented. But the need to *explain* corporate behaviour, and especially corruption, requires other paradigms. Corrupt or criminal *behaviour* is individual. If an alleged crime occurs, individuals are held responsible and receive their punishment through the courts. But, *corruption* is institutional, patterned – perhaps criminal and unethical from outside, but not necessarily perceived as such by insiders. Corporations are not put in jail. All of the attention to the individual criminal executive is a detour from figuring out how corruption works. An example is the coverage of the prosecution of Enron's executives, CEO Jeffery Skilling and Chief Financial Officer Andrew Fastow. All eyes are on the courtroom, on the deals made to reduce charges and expose others, on the jury's predisposition, and on possible jail sentences – thus isolating the executive as the criminal. The corporate culture that bred corruption, and the social expectations of the elite that ruled the organization, have escaped scrutiny.

AN ANTHROPOLOGY OF CORRUPTION IN THE US

In a recent issue of *Social Analysis*, British, American and Australian anthropologists discuss the Enron and WorldCom scandals in brief articles. A few important conclusions emerge, summarized by Gledhill from University of Manchester (2003). One: clearly corruption is not confined to Third World nations, but is evidenced in the US and the EU – although in different forms (Shore 2003). Two: there is a history of American capitalism linked to the globalization of capital which creates a context for corruption (Aiyer 2003). Three: there are social practices among the corporate elite not all that different from those of Sicilian mafia families (Schneider and Schneider 2003b). These short reviews suggest we re-orient the study of corruption away from long-held standard assumptions which locate it in the Third World, ignore its historical roots and trajectory, and miss the types of social behaviour that explain institutionalized corruption.

This issue of *Social Analysis* begins an anthropological contribution to an old discussion in the US.

C. Wright Mills had something right when he explained how behaviour and business practice has become institutionalized. An anthropologist would make the same point differently. He/she might identify cultural patterns in organizations, point out how values are part of widely held belief systems shared among participants in a community. Where Mills might highlight the *structure* of institutionalized corruption, anthropologists would illuminate the manner in which daily corporate life and regulatory agency bureaucracies make what looks like corruption from an outsider's perspective, appear to be normal social behaviour from the inside view. These two approaches are mutually explanatory. We need both types of study and analysis.

There are two levels of anthropological inquiry which, with the aid of fieldwork and (in cases where access is difficult) documentary and historical research, could prove fruitful: (1) examination of kinship, social networks, socialization strategies and mechanisms that maintain cohesion in corporate culture; and (2) investigation of market values and their role in institutions of American social life.

Reproducing and insulating the corporate elite

The family firm is at the foundation of early corporate organization in the US. Transfers of property, sharing of corporate management among blood and in-law members, and expansion decisions were kept within the family and near-family network of male individuals. In the early twenty-first century, the family firm is no longer the archetype – but the existence of close networks based on shared cultural meanings and built around kinship and close personal friendships has continued into the era of global capital. In the nineteenth century, codes of conduct and rules governing behaviour of family members restrained aberrant behaviour. Today, shared corporate values predicated on the rights of property and the rule of the market unites corporate and political leaders into a tight-knit network. Recent media treatment of corporate scandals and insider trading schemes articulates just this point, and evoking C. Wright Mills' *Power Elite*, makes the connection between capitalist wealth and political authority. Two striking examples are: Kevin Phillips' book on the Bush family, *American Dynasty* (2004), which paints a picture of an aristocratic kinship network that passes power and wealth from one generation to the next, and a *New Yorker* article (Mayer 2004) that documents a long-standing connection between Vice-President Cheney, his previous employer Halliburton, that company's business with the Pentagon dating back to the 1960s, and individual political figures from the Nixon/Ford era who now staff the Bush administration. Echoing the muckraking of Ida Tarbell (1904) and Upton Sinclair (1985/1906) 100 years ago, such accounts also reveal cultural and social information obtained through interviews and scores of documents – all of which might spark the anthropologist's inquiry.

Research on kinship and personal networks of the elite can be elusive for the participant-observer. Domhoff's (1967) documentation of America's interlocking board directorates, social club and elite school memberships, and family lineages was strictly based upon public sources in libraries and archives. Sociologists who study white-collar crime note that the best means to observe and document corporate social life and world-view is through case studies of regulatory agencies. Access and documentation is easier. Susan P. Shapiro's *Wayward Capitalists* (1984) is an example of this approach, although her research is primarily based upon documents rather than interviews and fieldwork. Anthropologists, however, can study government agencies using field methodologies. Interviews with regulators, lobbyists, and congressional oversight committee members and staff could reveal some of the informal (not necessarily illegal or unethical) networks, social rituals, and cultural meanings operative in a particular regulated industry. In fact, Shapiro's research on the SEC led her to reconsider the concept of white-collar crime itself in a classic article of the field (1990). The sociology of white-collar crime, she notes, should focus on the crime, not the criminal: 'I suggest that white collar criminals violate norms of trust, enabling them to rob without violence and burgle without trespass' (1990: 346). Her description of the 'social organization of trust' is suggestive for the anthropologist.

Other avenues of inquiry might derive from anthropology's attention to the social purpose of 'gift-giving', doing favours, opening doors of opportunity and sharing information in a social group as a means to maintain a collective identity and social cohesion. When do 'gifts' become bribes, unethical favouritism and fraudulent violation of public trust? Jane and Peter Schneider's research on the Sicilian mafia (2003a) has led them to suggest that there is a connection between that criminal subculture and the 'business subculture' of contemporary corporate America (2003b). They explore the similar cultural practices such as selective recruitment, fraternity, initiation rights, favour-granting and aggressive 'power projects' – to name a few – that characterize both worlds. Today there is enough material in the *Wall Street Journal* and the other business press to start an ethnography on corrupt corporate culture. Fieldwork in the traditional sense may not be possible, but that shouldn't limit 'studying up' to expose the culture of power, as Laura Nader has reminded generations of anthropologists (1972).

Market values and corporate predation

At another level, the ethnographer's inquiry into corporate corruption must also entertain questions pertaining to the market values of twenty-first century capitalist society. To what extent are corporate values mirror images of the market values that permeate social institutions in the wider society? How do the ideologies of the market influence the behaviour of the Enrons and WorldComs and the way we interpret and/or accept their behaviour as part of the cultural norm? And how have market values of competition, individualism and private property rights affected traditional non-market institutions? The point for corruption studies is that the capitalist, market-driven social values are an important context for research.

James Carrier's edited volume (1997) suggests that it is time for anthropologists to embark upon the 'study of the market' in Western culture. Such a book prompts these questions, relevant to the study of corruption: What does the market mean to corporate executives? What does it mean to citizens? To different social classes? Are corporate market ideologies replicated through multiple sectors of American life? In-depth ethnographic interviews of individuals representing different positions in economic life may reflect the commonality or differences between the corporate executive and the citizen, and perhaps help explain why corporate corruption is institutionalized but invisible. Can the predatory and aggressive schemes of Enron and WorldCom executives be extensions of consumer, business and government beliefs about the proper function of the market? Are there core market values embedded in regulatory agencies, consumer world-views and business schools that encourage and perhaps condone more muted versions of these now-familiar corrupt strategies? To what extent do alternative perspectives on the market model counter or erode the potential for corporate predation on the public interest?

CONCLUSION

Corporate corruption in the United States did not begin with Enron or WorldCom. Nor is anthropology the first academic discipline to examine its characteristics in corporate America. But we have a public that is just awakening to the pervasive nature of corruption in capitalist America, and a field of research that has historically relegated corporate crime to individual criminal behaviour and the policing of regulators. These factors have created an environment in which the predatory behaviour of America's largest and most politically influential firms appears to have caught us by surprise. We actually know very little about corruption. Anthropology's tools and perspectives on culture can shift our framework toward research that helps explain how corruption has found a home in corporate institutions, is self-reinforcing and insular, and spills out into our political institutions, challenging our democratic foundations.

REFERENCES

Aiyer, A. (2003) Lights Out, *Social Analysis*, Vol. 47, No. 3: 141–6.

Carrier, J. (ed.) (1997) *Meanings of the Market: The Free Market in Western Culture* (Oxford: Berg Publishers).

Clark, M. (1990) *Business Crime: Its Nature and Control* (New York: St Martin's Press).

Cox, E.F., R.C. Fellmeth and J.E. Schulz (1969) *Nader's Raiders Report on the Federal Trade Commission* (New York: Grove Press).

Dahl, R. (1961) *Who Governs?* (New Haven, CT: Yale University Press).

Domhoff, G.W. (1967) *Who Rules America?* (Englewood Cliffs, NJ: Prentice Hall).

—— (1971) *Higher Circles: The Governing Class in America.* (New York: Vintage Books).

—— (1975) *The Bohemian Grove and Other Retreats: A Study in Ruling-class Cohesiveness* (New York: Harper Colophon Books).

Ermann, M.D. and R.J. Lundman (eds) (2002) *Corporate and Government Deviance: Problems of Organizational Behaviour in Contemporary Society*, 6th edn (New York: Oxford University Press).

Fellmeth, R.C. (1970) *Interstate Commerce Omission, the Public Interest and the ICC: Ralph Nader Study Group Report on the Interstate Commerce Commission* (New York: Grossman).

Friedrichs, D.O. (1996) *Trusted Criminals: White Collar Crime in Contemporary Society* (Belmont, CA: Wadsworth).

Gledhill, J. (2003) Old Economy, New Economy; Old Corruption, New Corruption, *Social Analysis*, Vol. 47, No. 3: 130–5.

Green, M., B.C. Moore Jr and B. Wasserstein (1972) *The Closed Enterprise System: Ralph Nader's Study Group Report on Antitrust Enforcement* (New York: Grossman).

Kolko, G. (1977, reprint) *The Triumph of Conservatism* (New York: Free Press).

Mayer, J. (2004) Contract Sport: What Did the Vice-President Do for Halliburton?, *New Yorker*, 16–24 Feb.

Mills, C. Wright (1956) *The Power Elite* (New York: Oxford University Press).

Nader, L. (1972) Up the Anthropologist: Perspectives Gained from Studying Up, in D. Hymes (ed.) *Reinventing Anthropology* (New York: Pantheon Books).

Phillips, K. (2004) *Aristocracy, Fortune, and the Politics of Deceit in the House of Bush.* (New York: Viking).

Schneider, J. and P. Schneider (2003a) *Reversible Destiny: Mafia, Antimafia, and the Struggle for Palermo* (Berkeley and Los Angeles: University of California Press).

—— (2003b) Power Projects: Comparing Corporate Scandal and Organized Crime, *Social Analysis*, Vol. 47, No. 3: 136–40.

Simpson, S.S. (2002) *Corporate Crime, Law, and Social Control* (Cambridge: Cambridge University Press).

Shapiro, S.P. (1984) *Wayward Capitalists: Target of the Securities and Exchange Commission* (New Haven, CT: Yale University Press).

—— (1990) Collaring the Crime, Not the Criminal: Reconsidering the Concept of White-collar Crime, *American Sociological Review*, Vol. 55, No. 3: 346–65.

Shore, C. (2003) Corruption Scandals in America and Europe: Enron and EU Fraud in Comparative Perspective, *Social Analysis*, Vol. 47, No. 3: 147–53.

Sinclair, U. (1985) *The Jungle* (New York: Penguin, first published 1906).

Sutherland, E.H., G. Geis, and C. Goff (1985, reprint) *White Collar Crime: The Uncut Version* (New Haven, CT: Yale University Press).

Tarbell, I. (1904) *The History of the Standard Oil Company* (New York: McClure, Philips).

Turner, J. and R. Nader (1970) *The Chemical Feast: Ralph Nader's Study Group Report on the Food and Drug Administration* (New York: Grossman Publishers).

Weinstein, J. (1968) *The Corporate Ideal in the Liberal State, 1900–1918* (Boston, MA: Beacon Press).

PART III

Narratives and Practices of Everyday Corruption

9 NARRATING THE STATE OF CORRUPTION[1]

Akhil Gupta

Research on corruption in the social sciences is faced with an unusual dilemma: if social analysts can successfully point the way to ending corruption, then they are left without a job. A cynic might say that perhaps this is why academic prescriptions to end corruption have had so little success. But such a person would at the very least be accused of overstating his or her case: efforts to discover how to set the right incentives so that public officials are not tempted into accepting bribes, or how to police or enforce strict codes against corruption, how to make government services more efficient, or systems of regulation more transparent, etc. continue to be very important and useful, both for their academic merit and for their administrative utility. However, one must ask: is there more that one can say in the study of corruption?

It is not often that social scientists get to tackle a colourful topic like corruption and it seems rather a waste to lose the very qualities that make corruption such a fascinating subject. Yet this is precisely the fate of corruption studies. I do not mean this frivolously; what I propose is that we take seriously, that is, as a 'social fact', the hold that corruption has on the popular imagination. The comedian Jaspal Bhatti (1987) has made a career out of jokes about corruption, even creating a popular TV series around the theme.[2] Doing fieldwork in a small village in North India, for instance, I heard stories about corruption more often than almost any other genre of folklore. A scholar of contemporary India who ignored narratives of corruption would miss something tremendously important in social life. A structural functionalist might plausibly argue that similarities in the experiences of corruption, and the circulation of common narratives about it, serve as an important means of 'social cohesion' in rural India.

The implications of this for anthropological or sociological analysis are many, but let me note just one or two of the most important ones for now. If we recognize that the phenomenon of corruption cannot be grasped apart from narratives of corruption, then it has implications for not only our methods of investigation, but what we consider the object of our analysis. The experience of corruption on the part of all parties involved in such a transaction occurs in a field *overdetermined* by stories about such acts, stories whose reiterability enables the participants in that particular social drama to make sense of their actions.[3] This reflexive reiteration of actions and their narratives makes the analysis of corruption inherently complex as a social phenomenon, a complexity that, in my opinion, has been insufficiently appreciated in the scholarly literature.

Apart from making the phenomenon more complex, such an approach also reinvests the study of corruption with its rightful charisma. To say of corruption that it shows that the right bureaucratic incentives are not in place is true enough, but this insight fails to engage the sociological imagination. Such an approach does not help us explain what makes corruption such a significant social phenomenon. After all, there are other features of social life that are just as ubiquitous as corruption but that draw little comment from people who live in those social worlds. Why is it, then, that corruption is the subject of so many stories, such intense discursive production? Why are rural people in north India so fascinated with corruption? Why do they talk about it so much, and why does it occupy their imaginations to such an extent? As far as I am aware, no one has really attempted to tackle these questions, and it will perhaps take many years of scholarly work to arrive at adequate answers.

Corruption's infatuation with storytelling might be revealed by asking a simple question: where would a good analysis of corruption be without its stories? Even when these stories are not narrated in the text, as in economics papers, they often underlie the analysis: despite the fact that they are seen as 'illustrating' the theory or providing 'case studies' or 'examples,' they do much more. One can easily invert the relationship and argue that the stories are the bedrock on which the superstructure of analysis is often constructed. As a form of storytelling, corruption's narrative structures are remarkably rich and resilient, depending on some time-tested recipes. It is not entirely surprising that stories of corruption in rural India are often narrated using idioms and analogies from religious epics. After all, corruption narratives are steeped in many of the qualities of epic stories: heroism, debasement, the fall of humans from the path of virtue, resoluteness, the overcoming of impossible odds and superhuman sacrifices, and the providential actions of an unknowable deity, which could be anyone from the chief minister to the district magistrate. If one concluded from what I have already said that, as a subject of incessant public discussion and debate, and as an object of social analysis, the rich and engrossing narratives of corruption have been exhaustively studied, one would be sorely disappointed.[4]

For my purposes here, I want to ask what such stories are good for; in other words, what is the work that such narratives of corruption accomplish? One suggestion is that the discourse of corruption becomes a very important site enabling rural citizens and bureaucrats to imagine the state. One can employ the discourse of corruption to glean what people imagine the state to be, what state actions are considered legitimate, and how ideas of the rights of citizens and subjects are constituted (Gupta 1995).

'Corruption' might also be such a fecund signifier because it serves as a site for debates prompted by conflicting systems of moral and ethical behaviour. Any discussion of corruption necessarily assumes a standard of morally appropriate behaviour against which 'corrupt' actions are measured. But what single scale is to be employed to determine what is morally right? When social scientists employ such a scale, is it built on the model of the Weberian bureaucrat – the role-fulfilling, disinterested professional occupying a location in an organizational structure solely due to professional competence and merit? Such an individual, of course, is as much a figment of a modernist imagination as his or her counterpart – the role-blurring, unprofessional person who has gained his or her position through hereditary means, political connections or other morally dubious methods, like buying a public office. Although modernist imaginations sometimes appear commonsensical or uninteresting, in fact, there is an important element of fantasy and Othering present even in the most banal representations of such 'traditional' practices and societies. (For this, the Other need not be explicitly present in the discussion, but merely be an absent presence at the opposite pole of modernity.) In a social situation where there is no widespread social agreement about which scale is to be used to judge 'correct' ethical behaviour, the analysis of corruption itself becomes, so to speak, corrupted.

My own work on this question takes the larger question of the role of narrative in the constitution of states, in which corruption narratives play an essential part. My ambition is to rethink and reassess theories of the state from an anthropological perspective. Such a perspective would be concerned centrally with problems of meaning, everyday practices and representation, concerns that have been largely peripheral to more institutional and organization-theory-based approaches to the state. Attempting to think of states as cultural artifacts, whose distinctiveness is embodied not only in culturally embedded imaginaries, but in culturally marked practices, is an essential corrective to strongly institutionalist perspectives that would unproblematically compare states to one another along variables from rates of economic growth to degrees of urbanization. Once we begin to see that the state comes into being through narrative as much as it does through statistics, it opens the door to a rich analysis of ideology, hegemony and legitimacy.

This chapter is part of a larger project that deals with various facets of representation and everyday practices of state institutions, from the implementation of development programmes aimed at women and children to practices of constructing a 'file' and the spatializing strategies of states. My concern here is mainly with representations of the state created by state officials themselves. How states are understood by people who work for and within them, how officials view the multiple levels, centres, agendas and organizations that go into the making of 'the state', and how they view the beneficiaries of state programmes, are key questions that help us make sense of many of the workings of state bureaucracies. The memoirs, fiction, autobiographies and poetry produced by state officials could give us interesting insights into state institutions. Yet, as far as I am aware, they have been virtually untapped by theorists of the state, except perhaps by diplomatic historians.

Take the topic of corruption. What better source for understanding corruption, one might think, than the stories produced by those very people who have had the closest look at the phenomenon, and perhaps even been complicit in corrupt actions? State officials are essential cogs in the machine greased by corruption, and they have produced a large corpus of reflective and illuminating texts. On the other hand, bureaucrats might be shy to divulge details of their own illegal actions or those of their colleagues, or find such behaviour so routine as to not require comment. Comparing the representation of corruption in forms of life-writing by bureaucrats to that found in the work of anthropologists and other social scientists might help us better understand corruption in particular, and the state more generally.

In this chapter, I triangulate between some of my own fieldwork data, a prize-winning novel (Shukla 1992) written by an official of the Uttar Pradesh (UP) state government, where I did my fieldwork, and the work of one of the major social anthropologists of India, F.G. Bailey (1963). Such a strategy allows me to juxtapose material gathered by participant-observation with representations of the state found in realist fiction and the anthropological representations of a classic ethnography. Although my fieldwork was conducted over 40 years after the ethnography and the novel, and is therefore in no way intended to be a comparative exercise, the continuities and discontinuities that I observed are useful in thinking about the role that corruption narratives play in the constitution of states.

ENGINEERING DEVELOPMENT

One day, soon after I had started my fieldwork, I went to the Block office of Mandi *tehsil* (sub-district), one of the offices where I did participant-observation. There, I met two people who I had never seen before, both relatively young men, one of whom was assiduously poring over a register in the office. Mr Das was an engineer hired by the DRDA (District Rural Development Authority) while his friend, Mr Chowdhury, was employed as an engineer at the District Council (Zilla Parishad). Mr Das had the task of inspecting all the work that was done with funds allocated by the Jawahar Rojgaar Yojana (Jawahar Employment Scheme). He thus had the task of functioning, de facto, as an anti-corruption officer, although that was not his primary job description.

To understand the context in which I accompanied these two engineers on an inspection trip, I have to say a little more of the historical moment in early 1992. The Indian government had replaced an older programme to generate employment with the Jawahar Employment Scheme, in the process radically changing the method of allocating funds for the programme. Instead of being given to the bureaucracy, funds were now directly allocated to the village headman. In a famous statement authorizing this change, Rajiv Gandhi had complained that most of the resources for development were being lost because of bureaucratic corruption, so much so that less than 10 percent of the funds was reaching the intended recipients.[5] As one might imagine, this change dramatically reduced the unofficial incomes of district officials, and was the cause of much grumbling and expressions of dissatisfaction.

One official at the Block office, decrying the new rules, said that under the old system, when the money came to the District officials, out of Rs 100, at least Rs 90 was spent on the programme, even if they took Rs 10 for themselves. Now, he said, there is absolutely no accounting for how the money is spent. It is given to the headman, and he can do with it what he pleases. At least, under the old system, the money was not directly given to 'the public'. Similar sentiments were voiced by the head of the Block office. Even if Rajiv Gandhi was right, he told me, at least 10 percent of the funds was getting through to the intended recipients. Now, he said, not even 5 percent of the funds are used properly.

Das and Chowdhury denounced the Jawahar Employment Scheme on the grounds that the government had decided to allocate money directly to headmen without making them accountable in any way. They were astonished that there was no paperwork required in the scheme: the headman could spend the money as he pleased, without even noting what he had spent it on. If the headman (with the assent of the village council, an elected body of nine people) decided to build a cobblestone road (*kharanjaa*), nobody prepared an estimate for how much the road would cost, how much material would be needed, etc. The headmen just go ahead and start the work; when the money runs out, they stop, even if the road only reaches halfway to its intended target. Das felt that this was as good as throwing government money away.

We started toward a village where Das had to inspect one such road in a standard-issue government jeep. After a short distance of smooth riding, the road ended abruptly and was replaced by an incredibly bumpy track. It turned out that the construction of that particular road had actually been supervised by Chowdhury, who complained that he had asked for funds from the District Council, but the chairman of that body was far too busy bestowing favours on villages that had supported him in his election and villages where he had friends and relatives to pay him any heed. The dirt road, Chowdhury explained, had been unable to withstand the rainy season, hence its present condition.

The village we arrived at was inhabited primarily by scheduled castes and Muslims. When we reached the village, Das inquired after the headman, and was told that he was not in the village at that time. Nobody seemed to know where he was; his own family claimed to have no knowledge of his whereabouts. Das went looking for the new road. When asked, villagers seemed not to know but directed Das to two possible locations. The village panchayat officer, who had accompanied us on the trip, and was the secretary in charge of running the village council meetings, had no idea where the new road was supposed to be. However, he did tell us that the village had only 400 residents, and had been allocated Rs 7,000 in the first instalment of the Jawahar Employment Scheme.

Das noted the problems with the road that he identified as the new one. The bricks had been laid with their broad side up, whereas placing them on their narrow and deep side would have made the road stronger and the bricks would have been less likely to break. (Of course, laying them with their broad side facing up required less bricks, and hence made the road cheaper.) Both engineers complained about the poor construction. Then Das asked to inspect the headman's register (where he was supposed to record the costs of various items).

People in the headman's household claimed not to know where the register was kept. 'Why don't you wait a little?' they said, 'He should soon be back.' Both engineers knew this particular ruse only too well. In his most soothing voice, Das assured the headman's family that he did not want to look at the registers because he suspected something was wrong, but because he just wanted to make sure that he had looked at the right road. The headman's family again responded by saying that they did not know where he kept the register.

Since it was clear that nothing further was to be gained by waiting around, Das and Chowdhury jumped into their jeep and headed off to the second village. They asked the secretary to guide their path, but he did not seem to know where the village was. Das sarcastically inquired how he managed not to know the route to the villages where he was supposed to be recording village council minutes; the secretary replied that he usually took another route since he came by bus and he was unfamiliar with the shortcut that they were using while riding the jeep.

A big puddle greeted us at the entrance to this village. So the jeep was parked there, and the secretary was sent to find the headman. He returned a few minutes later, saying that the headman had gone to Mandi for the day. Das decided to conduct the inspection anyway. Once again, the secretary had no idea where the new road in this village had been built. Das and Chowdhury went to one road, part of which appeared to be new and part of which appeared to have been widened. Then they went to another part of the village and found what appeared to be a new road there which Das decided was the most recent one.

Once again, he asked to see the headman's register, and once again, he was stonewalled by the headman's relatives. He then asked to meet the deputy headman, and was told that he was not available. Next, he requested that one of the members of the village council be introduced to him, but nobody could be located. The secretary did not seem to personally know any of the members of the village council. What he did learn from the secretary was that Rs 8,000 had been spent on the road here, and it was much better laid and longer than the road in the previous village that we had visited. Das traced the length of the brick road by noting down the names of the people who lived in the houses at each end of the road. When we were leaving, Chowdhury asked the secretary how much of the money allocated for the project had actually been spent on it. The secretary replied, 'You have seen it with your own eyes; what can I say?' Chowdhury did not wish to let go: 'You must have received something out of all this, some money for *chai-paani* [refreshments].' The secretary said, 'All I get is Rs 50 here or Rs 100 there, nothing more than that.' 'Oh, come, come,' Das interjected, 'don't tell us that. It doesn't matter how much you make, what matters is how much you think actually gets spent on these things.' The secretary remained silent.

On our way out, Chowdhury commented that villagers had no manners these days; the situation is so bad that we have to ask people for a drink of water. 'The villagers are uneducated, they don't have good manners, and they don't know much about anything.' The contempt that state officials had for villagers appeared to be reciprocated; the villagers seemed to regard them with a great deal of distrust and definitely did not display the warmth towards them that they would have extended to almost any stranger who came there. In their indifference, they scorned these representatives of the government who were bringing the 'benefits' of development to them. None of the men sitting in groups, playing cards or talking in the middle of the village, made so much as a move to come near the officials and engage them in conversation or help them in any way.

That such an attitude was not isolated or unusual was borne out on other occasions, and was the subject of commentary by state officials. In another instance, a Block-level official told me, 'Nowadays nobody respects government officials.' Had things changed in the years that he had been a government employee, I asked? 'Absolutely! When I first joined [government service]', he said, 'people used to consider it an honour if I sat down in their house and had tea with them. Now, they will not even offer tea to you unless they feel they have something to gain.' I was curious: When did this change occur and why? It was a consequence of villagers' getting more educated, I was told, without the slightest hint of irony. 'The more educated a man becomes, the more selfish he gets [*jitnaa padh-likh laytaa hai, utna hee usmay swarth badh jata hai*]. It was due to this that villagers no longer had any respect for state officials.' As for when, my informants often traced this change to the period when subsidies first began, that is, counterintuitively, to the very time when the state began to emphasize its developmental role in the provisioning of social welfare rather than a purely infrastructural or repressive role.

Once we were back in the jeep, Das let the secretary feel the brunt of his fury. 'It is obvious that you don't come to these villages at all', he said. 'I want to see your diary where you note down all the work that's been done [in these villages]. Bring your records from these two villages to my office tomorrow.' The secretary looked quite sheepish, and explained that he lived in a village far away, on the other side of the district.

After Das had cooled down, he explained to me that there were five such pairs of engineers who were responsible for going around the district and inspecting the work done under the new employment scheme. But the other pairs never went on such trips, because they realized it was just a waste of time. 'We are the only ones who regularly conduct these inspections', he said. All they could do was a physical inspection; they couldn't actually compare the construction to a plan and check if something had been done incorrectly, since no plans for construction needed to be drawn up by village headmen. Apart from verifying that the structure was actually built, and did not just exist on paper, there was little they could do as it was impossible to determine how much it might have cost just by a visual inspection. And on those few occasions when they did manage to catch a headman because he was so blatantly corrupt, he managed to escape punishment by using his political connections. The government required them to do these inspections, but they felt it was a waste of petrol and resources, since nothing really came out of it.

State officials like Das and Chowdhury were frustrated in their efforts to check the corruption of headmen under this new scheme of disbursing development resources. Government officials across different levels of the bureaucracy displayed a remarkable unity in their view that the new method of disbursing development revenues was a mistake, because headmen had neither the education, technical competence nor managerial skills to make effective use of resources. However, this reaction was not a disinterested one. Monies that were now going to headmen had previously flowed through the bureaucracy, and had constituted a substantial portion of these very bureaucrats' unofficial earnings. Stripped of their resource base, development officials were intent on finding fault with the new employment programme. Also, once officials like Das and Chowdhury no longer had resources to distribute, but were merely instruments of surveillance and discipline, villagers and village officials had less need to act deferentially toward them. Officials higher up in the development hierarchy found themselves in the unenviable position of supervising people like headmen and secretaries of village panchayats who controlled more resources than they did.

In presenting this extended description of the actions and statements of a pair of government officials, what I have shown is how much corruption, the suspicion of corruption and stories of corruption mediate officials' own understandings of the state. Notice that I did not describe any incident of bribe-taking, or report as an eye-witness on the misuse of funds, or record someone's statements about their abuse of official privilege. The only person who admitted to any corrupt actions was the secretary, but the trifling amounts he claimed to have received as illegal payments could hardly be seized upon as evidence of a crisis of governability in rural India. Despite this lack of hard evidence of any corrupt action, or perhaps because of it, narratives of corruption were liberally deployed by all parties concerned.

What is clear is that divested of resources, development officials consistently employed a story of the misuse of development funds due to the corruption of headmen in complicity with the secretary. Such stories of corruption, incompetence and mismanagement attained their force through repetition. But, very importantly, they were instantiated through inspection trips like the one that I have described. Given this narrative of corruption, the half-built, half-baked roads that these engineers saw in the villages made sense; the inspections reinforced and substantiated a story whose plot was already given. It was clear that they interpreted the lack of cooperation shown to them by the headmen's families in not surrendering the registers as further evidence that they were trying to hide something, namely, the misuse of government monies. Even their relation to other state officials, such as the secretary, was mediated by the suspicion that he was misappropriating funds.

While narratives of corruption were *relatively* autonomous of corrupt actions, and had their own life and efficacy, they did not function independently of such actions. Any particular action could be inserted into different, and sometimes opposing, narratives of corruption. For instance, although stories about the corruption of headmen were widely shared among state officials and villagers, there were divergent assessments of whether the Jawahar Employment Scheme was a success or not. Many villagers, and even some state officials, complained that it was at least better than what it had replaced, because the previous programme merely lined the pockets of the officials, who were much more competent in siphoning off most of the funds for themselves. The headmen's lack of familiarity with bureaucratic procedure, and greater accountability to villagers on whose votes they depended for the next election, at least ensured that they spent a larger proportion of the money on their villages than officials ever did. And since the money was now allocated to each village, this ensured that funds were not taken from villages which had no political clout and given to those that were the homes of powerful politicians. Different, and competing, narratives could thus be mobilized to interpret the actions of headmen.

I heard about a headman who took advantage of the fact that a canal was being dug near the outskirts of his village to get truckloads of gravel delivered to his village for a nominal fee. This relieved the company of the responsibility of getting rid of waste, and secured a cheap source of foundation for the brick road that the headman wanted to construct. He had the road built, then showed that he had actually purchased the gravel at market rates from the nearby town, and pocketed the difference. Was this an instance of local enterprise or an example of corruption? The person who narrated this story to me was a state official who clearly intended it to be a criticism of what was wrong with the new employment programme. But would some villagers have pointed out the efficiency shown by the headman in having a good road built using an opportunity that presented itself – almost free gravel – that would certainly have gone waste if it had been left to a government department?

In the next section, I will juxtapose this account of the role played by narratives of corruption from my own fieldwork to two other sources, a work of fiction written by a former bureaucrat and a classic ethnography written by one of the most prominent political anthropologists of India.

OFFICIAL FICTIONS, REALIST ANTHROPOLOGICAL REPRESENTATIONS

The novel that I first wish to look at, *Raag Darbari* (Shukla 1992), authored by an ex-Indian Administrative Service officer, is in my opinion one of the richest works of fiction produced *by* a state official *about* the postcolonial Indian state; the other is the work of one of the foremost anthropologists of politics in India, F.G. Bailey, and is entitled *Politics and Social Change: Orissa in 1959*.

There are many similarities between these two books. Both deal with India in the late 1950s. Bailey's title is unusual in that, instead of just constructing a timeless picture of a 'traditional' society as many structural functionalists were wont to do, he is very careful to specify the exact time of his observations: he is talking about Orissa in 1959. He is acutely aware that the society he is observing is in the process of rapid change, and he is in fact providing us with an ethnography of this change, particularly of how a new form of governance – political parties and democratic elections – articulates with existing institutions of village and local politics. The exact dates for the action in *Raag Darbari* are never clearly specified, yet the author's own remarks, as well as the new state programmes that are being introduced into rural UP clearly define the setting as the late 1950s and early 1960s. Both books describe 'backward' areas: whereas *Raag Darbari* is set in eastern UP, *Politics and Social Change* describes a village, Bisipara, in that now infamous parliamentary constituency, Kalahandi, whose name is synonymous with famine deaths, the ultimate index of the failure of the development objectives of the postcolonial Indian state. Bailey's book was first published in 1963, soon after the events being described had taken place. *Raag Darbari* was first published in Hindi in 1968, won the Sahitya Akademi Award in 1970, and has been a popular book ever since.[6]

Raag Darbari is a work whose insights into politics and the state in rural India are without comparison. I do not think that there has been any novel that gives a more clearly etched picture of the large villages and small *tehsil* towns where the majority of rural Indians encounter 'the state'. Shrilal Shukla, the author, was born in 1925 in a village near Lucknow, and served in the UP state provincial service, and then the Indian Administrative Service, being posted mainly around Lucknow.

The action in the novel takes place in a largish village in eastern UP called Shivpalganj. The *raag* being sung refers to the schemes hatched at the *darbar* of the local leader, Vaidyaji, who is an ayurvedic doctor by profession, but whose real occupation is to manage the village farmers' cooperative, the local college and, during the course of the novel, to win control of the village council or panchayat. The use of the term '*darbar*' is significant because Shukla clearly wants to suggest that modern state institutions have functioned to create a new class of rulers in rural India. Vaidyaji goes about consolidating his authority through these institutions with an appearance of supreme detachment, as if he regarded with total contempt the strong-arm tactics he employs to obtain control over village institutions, and with a Gandhian phrase ready for every occasion. Although the novel is not told from the perspective of any one character, the loose plot concerns the arrival in the village of Rangnath, Vaidyaji's nephew (sister's son), who is doing a master's degree in history (it becomes clear that the subject is really Indology) in the town. Rangnath is clearly the character whose address is that of the urban, educated readers of the novel. His growing knowledge and disillusionment with village life is richly documented, but the novel does not sympathize with him, showing rather that his disgust with the events that unfold shows his lack of connection to the rural world, created in part by the irrelevance of the book knowledge to which he has devoted so much of his life. Shukla paints a picture in which government institutions are integrally involved in all aspects of village life. There is no room for romanticism in the fictional world of Shivpalganj; anyone who believes that the 'real India' lies in its villages, which were models of harmony and cooperation before the advent of big, bad modern institutions, would be quickly disabused of this view by reading this book. Shukla portrays a world where cynicism about all institutions and traditions is rampant, and he does so with a savage wit that spares none.

I will focus on representations of corruption, particularly during the course of elections, in both the novel and in Bailey's book. In the anthropology of India, the last three decades have seen a precipitous decline in the study of elections, elected bodies and the formal political sphere.[7] This, combined with a general neglect of state bureaucracies and unelected state officials, has created a situation in which I found a vast gap between the preoccupations of scholars and those of villagers. By contrast to the scholarly literature, not only are public officials ubiquitous in the countryside represented in *Raag Darbari*, state institutions are intricately woven into the everyday life of villagers, so that almost no aspect of their lives is unaffected by government bureaucracies.

Perhaps a couple of examples from the novel would help make the point. Vaidyaji is the manager of the village cooperative union, which is the site of an embezzlement. The supervisor, Ram Swarup, an extremely close underling of Vaidyaji's, brings two trucks to the godown, and loads them with the wheat that has been stored there to be sold as seed to farmers. Instead of transporting the wheat to the other godown of the cooperative five miles away, as everyone assumed he would, the wheat is taken to the grain market in town and sold for several thousand rupees. Ram Swarup subsequently disappears. Vaidyaji's reaction to the embezzlement is, oddly enough, relief. His reasoning, however, is impeccable:

There had never been a case of fraud in our union and so people began to suspect something was wrong. Now we can say we are honest people. There was an embezzlement and we didn't hide it. We admitted it as soon as it happened ... one thorn has been removed from our flesh. (p. 36)

The union then passes a resolution that the government should grant it compensation for the 8,000 rupees that it had lost. Rangnath, Vaidyaji's urban nephew, is uncomprehending: 'What's it got to do with the government? The Union Supervisor embezzled the wheat, and you want the government to make it up to you?' (p. 71). Vaidyaji replies, 'Who else will give it?' They inform the police that the supervisor is absconding: 'If the government wants our union to survive, and to continue to benefit the people, it will have to pay the compensation. Otherwise this union will collapse' (p. 71). Village cooperatives, along with democratic governance in the form of panchayats and educational institutions, were the three key institutions that were supposed to structurally transform rural India during the first two five-year plans, when the central government relied on institutional reform, rather than new investment, to spur growth in agriculture. Thus, Vaidyaji's appeal to the government was based on a shrewd calculation of the importance given to this key institution of village life.

It is elections to these institutions – the village cooperative, the panchayat, and the local college – that supply the key dramatic elements in *Raag Darbari*. Vaidyaji's role in Shivpalganj can perhaps better be appreciated by paying closer attention to Bailey's description of the emergence of a new type of political creature with the advent of 'modern' political processes in rural India.

Bailey contrasts two villages in Orissa and traces the rise of two different types of brokers that emerge. Bisipara is in a 'backward' area of Orissa. It is an 'isolated' village with a strong moral community in which 'outsiders' are clearly distrusted and treated with suspicion. Traditional leaders in Bisipara are quite far removed from the workings and logics of government officers and programmes. Hence, they have to rely on a broker, a person who knows enough about the ways of bureaucracies to effectively represent the interests of villagers, a person who can 'stand up to officials' (1963: 58) and who has the right contacts among urban-based politicians and bureaucrats. In a 'traditional' village like Bisipara, Bailey makes clear, a broker gains a lot of power but possesses little legitimacy, being distrusted both by villagers and by officials. The reason is that the broker has to mediate and translate between two moral universes that are incompatible and perhaps even incommensurable. A broker for a village like Bisipara is a full-service provider, often spending all his time in mediating between villagers and a whole range of government agencies like the administration, police, hospitals, or law courts.

Bailey also presents us with the contrasting case of Mohanpur, an urban village on the outskirts of Cuttack. In contrast to Bisipara, Mohanpur is an 'integrated' village, which has no independent political life played out on the village stage, since most people who live there are involved in the politics of Cuttack city and Orissa state. However, Bailey argues that Mohanpur is not thereby just a suburb of Cuttack, but has its own moral community. Given that dozens of Mohanpur's residents are employed in government agencies and bureaucracies, they are well-positioned to help when fellow villagers need assistance. Thus, a large number of specialized brokers exist who have specialized knowledge and contacts in particular departments of the bureaucracy; however, precisely because of this, there is no need for a full-service broker who would deal with the entire range of government offices.

Shivpalganj, the fictional eastern UP village of *Raag Darbari*, is neither an isolated village like Bisipara nor an integrated one like Mohanpur, but somewhere in between. Vaidyaji is a broker who lives in the village and yet mediates between the village and officialdom. But he does so by controlling all the major village institutions. Unfortunately, we do not get a good analysis of local politics in Bailey's book, since he is primarily concerned with the reception and impact of state-level elections on village life. In *Raag Darbari*, one finds that the articulation between state bureaucracies and village institutions animates, or re-animates, village politics. For instance, Vaidyaji had suddenly started showing an interest in the village council, work which he had so far regarded as demeaning. The reason was that he had read something in the newspaper which interested him, in which the prime minister had reportedly said that

'village uplift' was only possible on the basis of schools, co-operative committees and village panchayats ... Suddenly Vaidyaji realized that he had been working for the village's uplift through the Co-operative Union and the college, and the Village Panchayat was completely out of his hands.

'*Aho!*' he must have thought, 'That's the reason why Shivpalganj is not being properly uplifted. Why didn't I realize it earlier?' (1992: 104–5)

Being in touch with external events allows Vaidyaji to realize that perhaps a fresh new development initiative would involve the revival of village councils as a cornerstone of government initiatives to bring democracy to the grassroots.

Although Bailey's archetypical portraits of the isolated (Bisipara) and integrated (Mohanpur) village provide us with some insights into the articulation of state and national politics with village life, we don't get much of a sense of the role of ideology in this process. Bailey refers at several points to the cynicism with which people in both the villages he studied regarded state and national politics. In *Raag Darbari*, too, we get a sense that developmentalist and nationalist discourses fail to be 'owned' by the people of Shivpalganj. Vaidyaji himself has a Gandhian saying ready for every illegal act that he authorizes or practises. Similarly, leaders and bureaucrats are seen as cynically employing this discourse for their own ends. This becomes particularly obvious when public officials come to Shivpalganj in the course of tours and inspection visits. One reason why Shivpalganj was so frequently visited by politicians and officials was that it was close to a town and on the main road.

By this time of the year, a major influx of leaders and servants of the people had already begun. All of them were concerned about the progress of Shivpalganj and as a result they delivered speeches. These speeches were especially interesting for the ganjahas (villagers). From the very start the speakers set out in the belief that the audience comprised a bunch of idiots, and the audience sat firm in the opinion that the speakers were fools. (1992: 55)

With this attitude of mutual respect, the villagers listened as every speaker tried to convince them that India was a farming nation, using clever arguments to prove their point, and urging the villagers to grow more food for the progress of the nation (1992: 56).

Anything lacking in the speeches was made up for by a publicity campaign ... For example, the problem was that India was a farming nation, but farmers refused to produce more grain out of sheer perversity. The solution was to give more speeches to farmers and show them all sorts of attractive pictures. These advised them that if they didn't want to grow more grain for themselves then they should do so for the nation ... The farmers were greatly influenced by the combined effect of the speeches and posters, and even the most simple-minded cultivator began to feel that in all likelihood there was some ulterior motive behind the whole campaign. One advertisement ... showed a healthy farmer with a turban wrapped around his head, earrings and a quilted jacket, cutting a tall crop of wheat with a sickle. A woman was standing behind him, very pleased with herself; she was laughing like an official from the Department of Agriculture. Below and above the picture was written in Hindi and English – 'Grow More Grain'. (1992: 56)

However close Shivpalganj might be to the model of Bailey's 'integrated' village, a vast gulf separates village people from state officials. This is not due to villagers' lack of familiarity with government bureaucracies and officials. Rather, it is due to the fact that when officials and villagers do come into contact, they attribute radically different meanings to their exchange: it is this misunderstanding and misreading that we get very little sense of in the work of social anthropologists like Bailey.

CONCLUSION

Although it would be a mistake to attempt to make too close a connection between Shukla's biographical experiences and the characters and plot of *Raag Darbari*, it is clear that his incomparable insights into the functioning of state institutions in rural India could not have been possible without a lifetime of participant-observation in the bureaucracy. More than the work of almost any social scientist I can think of, Shukla's fiction gives us a humorous and perceptive understanding of the everyday practices of state institutions, the interests of various parties involved, the creative employment of nationalist and developmentalist discourse to quite different ends by variously positioned actors, and a wonderfully textured sense of how different subjects inhabit the state and are interpellated by it. Behind the satirical tone, one also senses an anger, seen especially in the treatment of the one sympathetic character, Langar, who represents the law-abiding layperson mistreated by all the branches of the state. Shukla's portrayal of rural India has few parallels in the ethnographies written by professional anthropologists, especially insofar as the relation between village life and state programmes are concerned.

What are the implications of this analysis for theorizing the state, particularly its relation to corruption? The most important theoretical point here is that the state needs to be understood from the standpoint of everyday practices and the circulation of representations. The puzzle is why culture has mattered so little to theories of the state. No one would dispute that the institutional forms that nation-states have taken everywhere in the world are remarkably uniform, despite the great differences of history and culture that separate different parts of the world from each other.[8] But an approach that focuses on institutional forms, capabilities and organizational structures misses something critical, namely, what states *mean* to the people who inhabit them or are interpellated by them. States, like nations, have to be imagined through representations and through signifying practices; such representations are not incidental to institutions but are *constitutive* of them. Given this, the study of everyday practices and of the circulation of representations that go into constituting particular states might tell us not just *what* they mean, but *how* they mean, to whom and under what circumstances. The materiality of files, orders, memos, statistics, reports, petitions, inspections, inaugurations and transfers, the humdrum routines of bureaucracies and bureaucrats' encounters with citizens, is the stuff out of which the meanings of states are constituted. Such routines are remarkably little studied in comparison with the machinations of state leaders, shifts in major policies, regime changes or the class basis of state officials, to name just a few themes that have loomed large in the study of states.

This chapter also has implications for the anthropological study of South Asia, from which so much of the classic literature on corruption has arisen. In the 1950s, Nehru and the Planning Commission pursued a policy of rapid industrial growth, hoping that institutional change in rural areas would unleash forces of productivity. Hence the government pinned its hope on land reform, community development and village cooperatives as mechanisms that would lead to increased yields without substantial new investments in infrastructure. It is within this context that a whole generation of anthropologists did sophisticated and systematic work on village governance and state institutions, focusing on the new types of political agents who were emerging with the routinization of democratic politics. Bailey's work is part of this movement, but there were a number of other very important anthropologists who did similar studies in different parts of India: Bernard Cohn (1987), Oscar Lewis (1954), Adrian Mayer (1967), D.F. Miller (1965), Ralph Nicholas (1963, 1968), and Morris Opler et al. (1959), to name just a few. If village panchayats were to be resurrected as instruments of democracy at the grassroots, and if cooperatives and community development schemes were to transform rural India, what was the political system already like and how would it change and respond to these new initiatives?

The failure of many of these ambitious schemes of social engineering envisioned as the key to transforming rural India in the Nehruvian vision was often laid at the door of corruption. If there was a reason for the lack of success of the development enterprise in India, it had to be the persistence of 'archaic' and traditional forms of official behaviour, in which gift-giving shaded into bribery, and was considered legitimate. Corruption was often compared to a cancer on the body politic.[9] The anthropologists who studied political processes at the grassroots complicated the pat solutions of many macro-theorists by showing how difficult it was even to define 'corruption', let alone eliminate it. Was the broker identified by Bailey who mediated between government officials and villagers, and collected a fee for his services, a part of the 'corrupt' system or was he a legitimate facilitator akin to a lawyer who guides his client through the court system?

Democratic elections, political parties and a regular system of democratic political participation have deepened their reach, so that they have slowly started affecting the lives of poorer and lower-caste people in rural India in the 1970s and 1980s. Especially since the early 1990s, with the reformulation of the idea of democratic village governance through a reinvigorated panchayati raj, and the allocation of new financial resources to village councils, the changing relation of rural citizens to the state and the deepening of the promise of democracy in changing relations between castes and classes is being played out in novel ways. The state-level success of political parties of Dalits, or lower-caste groups, like the Bahujan Samaj Party is due to slow-moving but enormously consequential shifts in lower-caste consciousness in the villages. This has led to the renewal and reinvigoration of discourses of, and about, corruption. Rural people belonging to the upper castes often interpreted the rise in corruption as the 'natural result' of the rise of Dalits, especially in the bureaucracy. In this view, 'corruption' was the consequence of investing power in people who were, by their very nature, unfit to rule.[10] On the other hand, lower-caste groups have lent strong support to politicians such as Laloo Prasad Yadav, whose government has been implicated in a massive fodder scam, and Mayavati, the charismatic former chief minister of Uttar Pradesh, who spent large sums of government money on projects that had a great symbolic significance for Dalits.

Corruption then emerges as a critically important area to study, because narratives of corruption help shape people's expectations of what states can and will do, and how bureaucrats will respond to the needs of citizens. One policy implication that follows from this is that reformers inside and outside states need to think not only about changing incentives for bureaucrats so that they are not tempted to privately appropriate resources that are targeted to the poor, but also to alter the narratives through which the state is constructed, including narratives of corruption. Calling for greater transparency from above is an insufficient response to this problem. The work that needs to be done if pressure is to be brought from below on state institutions is critically also ideological work, and not just about institutional reform.[11]

NOTES

1. I would like to thank Robert Rollings for research assistance. This chapter was written for the workshop 'Understanding Corruption: Anthropological Perspectives', held at Goldsmiths College, London, on

21 June 2002. Subsequent versions of this chapter were presented at the Anthropology Department, Harvard University, 28 April 2003; and at the Socrates workshop 'Agency, Discourses of Power, and Collective Representations' at the University of Vienna, 30 August 2003. I am grateful to colleagues at all these places for their comments and questions.

2. Bhatti's success since the late 1980s has spawned a number of television shows, including his own work that satirizes the higher education system (2001), and the popular serial, *Office Office*.

3. For these ideas on the iterability of social practices, I am drawing especially on the work of Butler (1993) and Bourdieu (1977: 78–95; 1990). The intertwining of linguistic and social iterability is central to their understanding of the (always contingent) reproduction of relations of inequality (see in particular Butler 1997 and Bourdieu 1993). Despite the very significant advances made by their work, much remains to be explored for an understanding of the imagined state and its narratives, particularly in terms of corruption.

4. Among the few scholars who have made promising interventions in this direction are Pavarala (1996), Visvanathan and Sethi (1998), and Parry (2000).

5. Rajiv Gandhi's charges were not without support in the discourse of social scientists. Robert Wade (1982, 1985), for example, recounts how the 'market' for public office combined with a systematic bureaucratic appropriation of illegal revenue has slowed India's developmental efforts. The problem for anyone who seeks to establish the exact extent of corruption is that the practices may be well known but remain for the most part unobservable. Without being able to measure the frequency of their occurrence, government policy-makers and social scientists alike become participants in the overdetermined field of narratives.

6. An English translation by Gillian Wright was published by Penguin India in 1992, and it is from this version that I will quote from in this chapter.

7. I am using 'politics' here in the narrow sense of formal political processes, such as voting, campaigning and participation in structures of governance. Anthropologists have been paying a great deal of attention to the politics of phenomena such as communal conflict, grassroots environmental or anti-globalization movements, urban movements for housing, and neoliberal governmentality. And it is not as if scholars have ignored things like peasant movements or lower-caste movements or contests for village leadership, all of which have involved the study of formal political processes. See, for example, the work of Wadley (1994), Jeffery and Jeffery (1998), Michelutti (2002), Dipankar Gupta (1997), and political scientists such as Basu and Kohli (1998), Chandra (2004) and Jaffrelot (2003), to name just a few. Despite the insights generated by such work, in terms of sheer volume, it compares poorly to the publications of previous decades.

8. Much has been made about the similarity of institutional forms of states in the work of sociologists such as Meyer (1980) and Meyer et al. (1997).

9. Incidentally, Nehru himself is often blamed for tolerating 'corruption' and not coming down harder on corrupt officials, leading to a 'soft' state

(Myrdal 1968) and the institutionalization of forms of bribery that are considered the bane of Indian bureaucracies today.

10. Of course, such statements conveniently overlooked that most politicians, and especially most bureaucrats, continue to come from the upper castes.

11. Populist leaders like Indira Gandhi understood this only too well but had neither the means nor the intention of delivering on their promises.

REFERENCES

Bailey, F.G. (1963) *Politics and Social Change: Orissa in 1959* (Berkeley: University of California Press).

Basu, A. and A. Kohli (eds) (1998) *Community Conflicts and the State in India* (New York: Oxford University Press).

Bhatti, J. (Director) (1987) *Ulta-Pulta* (Television Series) (Doordarshan).

—— (2001) *Professor Money Tree* (Television Series) (Mumbai: Alpha Punjabi).

Bourdieu, P. (1977) *Outline of a Theory of Practice* (Cambridge: Cambridge University Press).

—— (1990) *The Logic of Practice* (Palo Alto, CA: Stanford University Press).

—— (1993) *Language and Symbolic Power* (Cambridge, MA: Harvard University Press).

Butler, J. (1993) *Bodies that Matter: On the Discursive Limits of 'Sex'* (New York: Routledge).

—— (1997) *Excitable Speech: A Politics of the Performative* (New York: Routledge).

Chandra, K. (2004) *Why Ethnic Parties Succeed: Patronage and Ethnic Head Counts in India* (Cambidge: Cambridge University Press).

—— (2000b) The Transformation of Ethnic Politics in India: The Decline of Congress and the Rise of the Bahujan Samaj Party in Hoshiarpur, *Journal of Asian Studies*, Vol. 59, No. 1: 26–61.

Cohn, B. (1987) *An Anthropologist Among the Historians and Other Essays* (Delhi: Oxford University Press).

Gupta, A. (1995) Blurred Boundaries: The Discourse of Corruption, the Culture of Politics, and the Imagined State, *American Ethnologist*, Vol. 22, No. 2: 375–402.

Gupta, D. (1997) *Rivalry and Brotherhood: Politics in the Life of Farmers in Northern India* (New York: Oxford University Press).

Jaffrelot, C. (2003) *India's Silent Revolution: The Rise of the Lower Castes in North India* (New York: Columbia University Press).

Jeffery, P. and R. Jeffery (1998) Gender, Community, and the Local State in Bijnor, India, in P. Jeffery and A. Basu (eds) *Appropriating Gender: Women's Activism and Politicized Religion in South Asia*, pp. 123–42 (New York: Routledge).

Lewis, O. (1954) *Group Dynamics in a North Indian Village: A Study of Factions* (New Delhi: Programme Evaluation Organisation, Planning Commission, Government of India).

Mayer, A.C. (1967) Caste and Local Politics in India, in P. Mason (ed.) *India and Ceylon: Unity and Diversity*, pp. 121–41 (London: Oxford University Press).

Meyer, J. (1980) The World Polity and the Authority of the Nation-state, in A. Bergesen (ed.) *Studies of the Modern World-system*, pp. 109–37 (New York: Academic Press).

Meyer, J., J. Boli, G. Thomas and F. Ramirez (1997) World Society and the Nation State, *American Journal of Sociology*, Vol. 103: 144–81.

Michelutti, L. (2002) Sons of Krishna: The Politics of Yadav Community Formation in a North Indian Town (PhD Dissertation, London School of Economics and Political Science).

Miller, D.F. (1965) Factions in Indian Village Politics, *Pacific Affairs*, Vol. 38, No. 1: 17–31.

Myrdal, G. (1968) *Asian Drama* (New York: Random House).

Nicholas, R.W. (1963) Village Factions and Political Parties in Rural West Bengal, *Journal of Commonwealth Political Studies*, Vol. 2, No. 1: 17–32.

—— (1968) Structures of Politics in the Village of Southern Asia, in M. Singer and B.S. Cohn (eds) *Structure and Change in Indian Society*, pp. 243–84 (Chicago: Aldine).

Opler, M., W.L. Rowe and M.L. Stroop (1959) Indian National and State Elections in a Village Context, *Human Organization*, Vol. 18, No. 1: 30–4.

Parry, J.P. (2000) The 'Crisis of Corruption' and 'The Idea of India': A Worm's Eye View, in I. Pardo (ed.) *Morals of Legitimacy: Between Agency and System*, pp. 27–55 (New York: Berghahn Books).

Pavarala, V. (1996) *Interpreting Corruption: Elite Perspectives in India* (New Delhi: Sage Publications).

Shukla, S. (1992) *Raag Darbari*, trans. Gillian Wright (Delhi: Penguin India).

Visvanathan, S. and H. Sethi (eds) (1998) *Foul Play: Chronicles of Corruption in India 1947–1997* (New Delhi: Banyan Books).

Wade, R. (1982) The System of Administrative and Political Corruption: Canal Irrigation in South India, *Journal of Development Studies*, Vol. 18, No. 3: 287–328.

—— (1985) The Market for Public Office: Why the Indian State Is Not Better at Development. *World Development* 13(4): 467–97.

Wadley, S. (1994) *Struggling with Destiny in Karimpur, 1925–1984* (Berkeley: University of California Press).

10 WHERE THE JEEPS COME FROM: NARRATIVES OF CORRUPTION IN THE ALENTEJO (SOUTHERN PORTUGAL)

Dorle Dracklé

'They're all corrupt here!' I often heard this sentiment or similar ones expressed during my field interviews when the conversation turned to politics and the local economy. But also in quite ordinary conversations in cafés, in bars, on the main square and at political meetings, virtually everyone could agree that corruption is the worst scourge of the Alentejo. Describing corruption as omnipresent, uncontrollable and dangerous, the speaker invariably positioned himself as its victim, as himself suffering under the chicanery of politicians, bureaucrats, police and businessmen. So positioned, he is naturally above all suspicion of being himself involved in corrupt activities.

From the beginning to the middle of the 1990s, I conducted field research on politics, bureaucracy and local concepts of economy in the south of the Alentejo, in the town and district of Odemira. It was a time when, because of Portugal's entry into the EU, all these areas were marked by a forced transformation. The town of Odemira is a classical agrotown characterized by a highly developed bureaucratic apparatus; it is the regional headquarters for all important national and local administrative bodies, schools, banks and medical care, and on top of all this is the economic centre of an extensive agricultural hinterland and a slowly developing coastal tourism. Every day people travel to the district capital in order to carry out their business and shop, and not a few are thereby under way the entire day because of the bad public transportation. In Odemira everyone meets everyone else: poor, old farmers from the scattered peripheral settlements applying for EU subsidies at the branch office of the Ministry of Agriculture; day labourers looking for work; agro-industrialists who need a permit for a new annexe; cheese- and cake-sellers from the surrounding villages who display their wares in front of the school complex;

experts from the capital who are writing opinions on a EU project; and all the local employees of businesses and public administration. In this maze of administrative departments and human needs, a deeply felt insecurity unfolds itself. An insecurity that arose from a transformation seen as rapid and forced and felt as a 'crisis' (Dracklé in press), as a fundamental insecurity. It is against this backdrop that the stories about corruption which my informants tell themselves and told me are to be heard. These are stories about shady real estate deals in the Alentejo in which Portugal's Minister of Finance was involved, about the suicide of a young farmer from a neighbouring town who could not repay the instalments on his EU loans – allegedly he used the money to buy too many jeeps and other luxuries. Stories circulate about officials, farmers and businessmen enriching themselves at the public expense. Everyone accuses everyone else of having set aside portions of public monies for himself.

In this chapter, I shall treat the poetics and politics of corruption in the district of Odemira. I consider corruption as a discursive trail, a rhetorical figure, that can be used to make sense of the world, of everyday life, of human relations, and of politics and power. It will be of interest to understand where the speaker in question places himself, what position he gives himself in this picture. Thus emerges a varied landscape of fragile relations that transform themselves into greater units, the nation, the EU, into imagined communities which function according to abstract rules, rules that, for the inhabitants of the Alentejo as for the characters in Kafka's novels, are incomprehensible and yet omnipotent. But even when these Kafkaesque power structures are condemned, they may still offer one opportunity or another that the Alentejanean gladly takes advantage of. His attitude towards this varies considerably depending on his place in the system: it makes a great difference whether he is a member of the bureaucracy or whether he speaks about it from the outside.

CORRUPTION AND INSECURITY

As in all studies of corruption, it will be equally impossible in mine to adduce exact figures, for instance of the degree of corruption. It will also be impossible to document cases of corruption in such a way that they could stand up to empirical scrutiny. After all, I was not on the scene in the Alentejo as an anthropological spy whose mission it was to unmask the people there and finally prove that all Portuguese are corrupt, or if not all, then still so-and-so many percent in comparison with certain other countries – and in the end in contrast to Germany.

The problem of the reliability of data in studies of corruption is generally recognized and certainly one of the chief reasons that the social sciences have hitherto approached the subject only very hesitantly. In cases of corruption we have mainly to do with 'soft data'. In our interviews people expressed their opinions about things experienced by themselves or by relatives, colleagues and friends. Occasionally, even we became ourselves involved in smaller cases of corruption – for instance, in order to placate a traffic policeman. The majority of cases, however, are second-hand reports and would not be admissible in a court of law; that is, not even a social scientist may simply write that so-and-so did this or that, because ethical principles forbid it. At the same time, there can be no doubt that corruption has real consequences which can be terrible.

From the theoretical point of view, denunciation can hardly be the purpose of social anthropological studies of corruption. Of interest here, on the contrary, are questions pertaining to the context of action in which corruption occurs, to the people and constellations of relations involved, and in sum the question about the importance of corrupt practices in the constitution of local and translocal relations. Finally, the question should be posed about the meaning assigned to the concept of corruption in the given local circumstances – whether these be the world of the social scientist or the world of a certain regional example with supra-regional references. It is also a question whether these concepts can be reciprocally translated – and how this process of translation is reflected in anthropological studies.[1]

Thus it is interesting to know not only what my interlocutor means when he says 'They're all corrupt here', but also how our conversation proceeded. For instance, when he continues: 'Tell me, why aren't you investigating Germany?' A good question, especially because in the beginning and middle of the 1990s Germany was notorious for its wrongful use of EU subsidies to support its ship-building industry, while the strange financial transactions of the trust company appointed to wind up the East German economy were so scandalous as to draw international attention. Quite shrewdly, my interlocutor here saw that it is always a good move, when one sees oneself in the inferior position (corruption is always looked upon askance and casts the speaker and his country in a bad light), to pull the other down to at least the same level. Aren't they also all corrupt in Germany?

My interview partner had a good nose for these things. Had I not imagined myself to be a researcher studying local politics and bureaucracy, who only in passing asked about where all the subsidies silt up? In conversation with my interviewees, I had swiftly to bid farewell to this approach. I was reminded of it again only when, after having concluded my project report, I received from the sponsoring institution, the German Research Council, a commentary letter about the report – which is unusual. It urged me to make my research available to the EU bureaucracy in Brussels. After a lecture on my work to my faculty, colleagues asked me – laughing but serious – 'Why don't you investigate us here in the Department? You needn't go to Portugal to research corruption!'

The ordinariness, the normalness of corruption, whether in small things or in the grand style, is the most characteristic feature of the phenomenon. Corruption is such an everyday phenomenon that this is probably a further reason why social anthropologists have taken so little notice of it.[2] Corruption is part of everyday life, and not only of everyday life in bureaucracies but also in institutions, in groups, in human relations in general, regardless whether these are public or private. It is a phenomenon that appears whenever formal or informal networks are formed. Corruption arises independently of whether these networks are embedded in a definite organizational culture, in various administrative systems, in weak or strong state structures or in transnational organizations and businesses.[3]

Although corruption scandals in Portugal have occurred in both political and economic areas, public discourse is almost entirely shaped by stories of corruption in administration and politics. Bureaucratic units play an important role in southern Portugal and, as in every centralized state, they are historically strongly oriented beyond local institutions to the district and national capitals, and now also increasingly to Brussels as the capital of the European subsidy purse and the centres of power bound up with it. This splitting up of the bureaucratic apparatus across various, opaque levels, and vagueness about spheres of responsibility, appointments and financial and administrative resources, are everyday experiences for the inhabitants of Odemira. In addition, they are beset by a feeling of existential indeterminacy and insecurity, a feeling of living constantly in a world of crisis – for example, of being abandoned to the rapid transformation of economic conditions that has taken place under the influence of the EU, without being able to do anything about it. Instead of speaking of a 'production of indifference' (Herzfeld 1992) by bureaucracy, one may proceed in the case of corruption from a 'production of insecurity' and the corresponding wish and attempt to surmount existential insecurity. The blessings and the curse of corruption in this respect are highly ambivalent: if one person can obtain guarantees for a transaction through networks and connections, another feels himself threatened by the absence of financing, information and connections. Corruption is a nervous system (Taussig 1992). Its whole drama is revealed only in light of the existential insecurity which people feel towards it and to which they give expression. There exists no measurable index for this insecurity; it is a structural component of all human groups.

My concern as social anthropologist is to preserve the complexity of the stories that circulate, that circulate, that people tell, that people tell me. These stories retailing certain incidents are consonant with decontextualized data which confirm a relatively high index of corruption for Portugal (Transparency International 2001). These data also rest on interviews and inform us of certain correlations. In agreement with my results, a public opinion survey by Transparency International (TI), carried out with the assistance of Portuguese newspapers, showed the Portuguese assume that local administrative units are the most corrupt – outstripped only by sports organizations. But what does this mean exactly? What goes on in local administrative units? What goes on in the local administration of Odemira? What does it mean when my informants assume that here they are all corrupt? To what does this sentiment refer, what kind of discourse is this, what do the people who work in the local administration think about this estimate?

THE PHILOSOPHY OF THE TOILET KEY

The sentence that I quoted at the beginning – 'They're all corrupt here!' – underwent in the course of conversations about the local district administration (*Câmara Municipal*) a small qualification: 'They're all corrupt in the Câmara!' Even the national media complain that the district presidents behave like provincial princes. Bribery, favouritism and general venality that is rife in certain departments, the setting aside of public monies, the distribution of gifts of a financial kind to friends, relatives and colleagues – all these forms of corruption are regular topics in talk about the district administration in Odemira.

Depending upon the position of the speaker, all administrative employees are said to belong to the Communist Party, to be members of the same family, to be favourites of the district president, to put public monies in their own pockets. The citizens complain about this amongst themselves, experience one or another form of official rejection or discrimination and interpret it in their own way. In this connection the subject of officials who let some piece of business 'disappear into a drawer' (*meter na gaveta*) comes up frequently. By this is meant the common, but unprovable, method of letting files, applications, letters, etc., disappear into a desk drawer. This ensures a protraction of the business which the applicant can bring to an end by paying, or by knowing someone who knows someone who can put in a good word for him.

Letting things 'disappear into a drawer' pretty well describes a case that was heard on November 1991 before the court in Odemira. An official of the judiciary, who had served for 20 years on the local court, was tried for the offence of having let files disappear, protracted trials and done various other kinds of favours for various people. Only the arrival of a new judge (in Portugal district judges are rotated every two to four years), who energetically worked through the old, still pending cases, had set the ball rolling. He discovered cases that had been pending for 20 years. A review of these cases resulted in the conviction of the culpable official for various offences.

Such stories also circulate about officials who have long held high positions in the local administration. When a citizen went to one of these to enquire about the progress of one piece of business or another, he always received the answer that everything was *quase pronto* (almost finished) but never that it was done. This procedure is encouraged by a rule that permits officials to carry out lucrative side-work on behalf of the administration, such as notary certifications, but only a definite number of these commissions per month. If the contingent has been used up, the customer is fed with hopes of being served next month – one does not wish to lose him to the competition. Naturally the accumulation of cases thus delays the whole process, unless strings can be pulled.

Stories of corruption also gather round the official inspectors. The alleged venality of these officials is almost legendary. Everywhere one hears stories about the corruptibility of the district administration architects, of construction supervisors, of inspectors of the agricultural bureau in charge of subsidies, of the official veterinarian, of rangers in the national park – indeed of everyone active in a supervisory position. Influenced by experiences with the administration and afflicted by constant uncertainty about their legal rights, it is understandable that the citizens eye mistrustfully all bureaucratic procedures and suspect all employees of the Câmara of corruption.

Inhabitants of the Odemira district express deep disappointment about the ponderousness of the local administration. The district president, Justino Santos, has a similar feeling towards the central administration. Both, the citizens of Odemira and their district president, see themselves as victims of bureaucratic processes. They complain about false promises, about injustice, about creeping, never provable corruption. At the same time, there exists a hope, a hope that the authorities possess a competency in the management of public affairs – a hope of a nearly divine power that takes just, rational and incorruptible decisions for everyone. The constant disappointment of this hope produces finally a climate of social indifference (Herzfeld 1992). Such a climate district president Justino Santos sees represented above all in the actions of the responsible officials in the various administrations. He calls these people bureaucrats and makes known, by his choice of words and tone, his disapproving stance towards them. The bureaucracy, he says, is the worst evil in

Portugal. For a single building application he must consult 23 General Administrations. And each one wants this and that. So must everyone feel who is defeated before he opens the door, checked by those who are glad to make difficulties for others so that they need work less themselves. Or because they enjoy it when other people fail.

> Justino Santos: Look, the entire bureaucratic system is designed to hinder all progress. The real obstacle to the economic development of our district is the bureaucracy, at every level.
> Please excuse me, I am going to ... well, I call this the philosophy of the man with the toilet key.
> Yes, it may even be the man in the lowest position; one usually says that the official in charge of the toilets is at the very bottom of the ladder.
> But he is keeper of the toilet key.
> And I come to him and have to go ...
> So I say to him: I have to go.
> He shoots back: Do you have a permit to urinate?
> No, I don't – but I don't need one!
> Oh yes you do, and also this and this and this, and only when I have it all ...
> Then, he says, you may go to the toilet.
> And I don't need to go any longer, I've already wet my trousers.
> And he feels his whole authority in the moment of my greatest distress.
> This is the philosophy that today still determines our public administration. Also in the Câmara. Also at the level of local government, there are still such types.
> A solution?
> A change in the mentality of the people would be necessary, because to be a public official (*funcionário público*) is a good position on the social ladder. The fundamental problem, I believe, is the mentality.

What is this 'mentality'? The district president, in Portugal a famous leftist and member of the Communist Party of Portugal (PCP), is representative of a new generation, the generation of politicians (particularly in southern Portugal and the Alentejo) who stood for change after the revolution of 1974. For the break with arbitrary rule, which was equated with the fascist dictatorship. And against the ponderousness of officialdom, especially from the point of view of communistic 'red city halls' of the Alentejo, against the bureaucratic authority of the central government. 'That is still Salazar;[4] he is still in the Portuguese system' angrily cried a member of the oppositional Socialist Party (PS) in the course of complaining, during his campaign for the district council, that the central government simply refused to remit EU monies, with the result that Odemira was constrained to take out expensive loans. What are 'those at the top' doing with the money?

There is no explanation for the unreasonableness of a bureaucratic system that perpetuates itself in its own unreasonableness. There appears to be no way out. For a district administration with great need of financial support because of the extreme economic underdevelopment of the region and the bad social situation of many of the inhabitants, the well-being of the population depends on the official at the top, the district president. He is the figure who, because of his extensive power, is described as a provincial prince. If he can obtain something for his district from the central administration, access to resources opens; if not, much comes to grief. He needs a flair for this, says Justino Santos, and he needs a certain education – background, family connections and knowledge of the ways of the higher officials in Lisbon are an invaluable advantage. Many negotiations take place in the ministries and with the general administrators; in the long corridors of the ministries, the famous long corridors with many doors. The point is to open one or another of those doors.

Access to the levers of power in Lisbon is strongly personalized. If relations with the official in charge are good, the matter will be processed swiftly and passed on. There exists a net of acquaintances and assistants, a *piscar de olhos*, a wink of agreement between individual employees of the central and local administrations. Recourse to this informal network, to contacts with officials of the central administration, is the most important instrument in the hands of the local authorities with which to achieve their own ends.

It would be an odd bird, according to Justino Santos, who refused to go along with this political strategy of governing – to go along with the friend, the acquaintance, the mediator. 'In Portugal', he explained to me, 'this is called *amiguismo.*' The word is impossible to translate; the closest approximation might be something like 'friendshipism'. Perhaps such an arrangement should be called less 'corruption' in the strict sense than a kind of self-protection, dictated by common sense. One would be ill-advised to rely on the official channels and the legal subtleties of the administration when a speedy result is desired. It is also impossible to discover any clue proving institutionalized clientelism, for in return for these services and favours no money changes hands. The relations remain uncertain; also the results. Only in the net of reciprocal contacts and obligations is help to be found; only here are there moments of stability amidst the uncertainty, amidst the permanent crisis. The place of power remains always diffuse. Who has the power to accelerate a project? For instance, the expansion of the harbour at Vila Nova de Milfontes, for which the town has fought for 20 years, and for whose realization there finally exists some hope in the year 2003?

Thus the district authorities, and with them the elected representatives, remain dependent on the network of acquaintances at all levels: on the doors in the ministerial corridors that open or do not open; on the next higher administrative instance, which distributes grants or does not, depending on networks of friendship; on, finally, *amiguismo*. This is the toilet keeper's moment of power.

A QUARREL AMONGST ARCHITECTS

Most complaints about the corruption of the district administration have to do with building permits. In a letter appended to the Portugal Survey of Transparency International, its sender describes exactly the same kind of abuses about which the inhabitants of Odemira complain with respect to the district administration and its official architects:

> We have come to accept that architects for the local Câmaras will take on commissions for work in their municipality. They will disguise this work by doing it through an office located outside of the boundaries of their municipality. We can live with that. However, there are Câmaras where this small-time corruption is not enough for the architects involved, and they are now letting it be know that any substantial project, if it wishes to have a smooth passage through the system, is subject to a title from $10.000.000 upwards. This money is not paid directly to the architect, but to the firm which represents the architect... (Transparency International Portuguese Chapter 2001)[5]

The law forbids architects working for the local administration to perform other services in this district, such as the execution of building plans, in order to avoid a conflict of interest. Since the employees of the Câmaras earn relatively little, however (many members of the middle and lower groups have several jobs in order to provide themselves with an appropriate standard of living), many of these architects maintain offices in neighbouring districts. Although even then the carrying out of commissions in the district is prohibited, suspicions and accusations are continually voiced.

A long conflict between architects resident in the Odemira district and the Câmara and its official architects and engineers arose over accusations of corruption connected to the refusal of a building application for the construction of a fish farm in a nature reserve (Krauss 2001). The application was turned down by the Câmara on 'aesthetic' grounds, since the two-storey building was to be placed in the wildlife park and a second storey was not permissible outside the zones designated in the town development plan. After the applicant and his architect left the meeting of the district council in a rage, the still unclarified effects of the project on the environment were discussed in detail. A variety of reports had not yet been submitted; for example, it was still an open question whether the antibiotic used for fish farming would affect the spawning area in the natural environment of the Bay of Milfontes.

The discussion continued and it transpired that the district councillors felt that the sponsor had treated them inappropriately: 'The learned man from Porto treated us like stupid children, as if we were still in the fourth form, without culture, as if we were cretins, uncultivated (*inculto*), illiterates' (Justino Santos). The Câmara stuck to its decision.

Two weeks later the Câmara received a petition, signed by four architects of the district who demanded that the official identification of construction sites (name of the firms and architects) must, in future, correspond to the laws, for there had been demonstrable cases of corruption among the employees of the Câmara, who had built houses in the district although the law clearly prohibits it. This misconduct offends against the ethical principles of their profession. After all, every freelance architect must pay licensing fees to the Câmara, whereas the offending architects, as officials of the Câmara, enjoy an exemption. The head of the Câmara knew of this misconduct and had been covering it up in a preferential and abusive way (*apadrinhada, abusivo*).

A further grave accusation concerned the planning competency of the Câmara. The signatories of the petition criticized the Câmara's guidelines for town planning for their lack of clarity, for they do not follow the newest development plans. The architects therefore request the Câmara finally to apply the recently issued legislation in order to restrain irregularities and corruption (*irregularidades e corrupções*). They are no longer prepared to tolerate this situation and will, if necessary, make these abuses public and also inform the higher authorities. But to begin with, they demand that the Câmara issue a statement with respect to the charges.

The meeting of the Câmara at which the petition was read was extremely tense. The head of the technical department, the architect Duarte, was present along with the legal adviser of the Câmara. The members, independently of party affiliation, saw themselves as offended in their dignity, and had this made part of the record.

> President: Much is amiss in the Câmara, we know that. After all, we have to struggle with the problem that seven positions for technical experts, who are urgently needed, remain unfilled because nobody wishes to take a job in the provinces. But I know of not a single case of corruption in this house.
> The politician Percheiro: In order to put a stop to this talk (*parar as águas*), I propose the setting up of an investigatory committee.
> The architect Duarte: There exists no project that has been signed by any architect of the Câmara.
> The politician Guerreiro: I feel that my personal dignity has been attacked in the highest degree. I therefore demand, as representative of the PS,[6] an independent investigatory committee from outside.

The politician Percheiro: But there is no proof. We should not therefore investigate anything, but write back and demand that they first give us proof.

The legal adviser of the Câmara: They should prove the accusations with honour and dignity, and say it to our faces.

The politician Viegas: For me, this is a bomb.

President: I have spoken to the architect about it, but he is always so aggressive. So irascible.

The legal adviser of the Câmara: When he still worked here, he always authorised the projects of his wife; that was also not right, was it?

President: I said to him: In God's name, give me proof!

The architect Duarte: There is not a single project that has been carried out by any of our officials. But as you know, people in the cafés will always talk. In this case, the talk is meant to do harm (*conversas da má*).

The politician Percheiro: These are all nothing but rumours (*bocas*). In the end, we can say, write to the higher authorities, to the officials in charge, and enclose some proof.

In this exchange the participants waver among discussion of the accusations, the search for proof, and consideration of the right approach to an uncertain denunciation, a threat. Unspoken, but in everyone's mind, is the idea that the signatories of the petition know exactly who committed which offences, and that the top people in the administration also know who they are and do nothing about it. This is a classical story of elites, which originates in the central administration in Lisbon and blames the local Câmaras: the district presidents, mainly men of integrity themselves, know very well what is going on under their leadership but say nothing, so as not to frighten away technical experts (who are rare in the provinces) and disturb the peace at work. A careful weighing of the argument is necessary. A moral argument, such as that of the legal adviser who blames the accuser himself for nepotism, is not at any rate admissible in a court of law.

The members of the Câmara see themselves the object of accusations of the sort that can be heard daily in café gossip and defamations (*má lingua*). In the end, they decide to set up an internal investigatory committee including the legal adviser, an employee of the Câmara and the district politician Percheiro. The architect Duarte is to compose a reply to the petition by the next week. The administration will reject all the accusations as unfounded and express its incomprehension, especially since some of the signatories themselves once worked in the Câmara and are familiar with its internal procedures.

The excitement over the affair was considerable, and so too the irritation. A few months after receipt of the petition and the administration's reply, the investigatory committee found that there was no evidence of irregular conduct on the part of Câmara architects or other officials. Thereupon the four protesting architects submitted a petition to the administrative court in Lisbon. However, even before the court, the four were not prepared to name names or disclose their evidence – the matter remained a mystery.

Much was whispered, of course, particularly a story about a French agricultural firm that bribed officials and carried out illegal building, but this never went beyond the cafés. Since tales of corruption, bribery, *amiguismo* and *cunha*, of *irregularidades* and fraud constantly circulate in everyday life, part of the public credited also this story, as it does every other story whose subject is the rottenness of the world and which gives the narrator room for interpretation. What posture the narrator assumes, which position he represents in the course of the quarrel, is negotiated according to the situation in which he finds himself – for instance, in the café or in other circles. If a PSD representative[7] reports these incidents, it is certain that this will be built into a running discourse about the corruption of the leftist, communistic district administration. If the story is narrated by someone who is pro-Câmara or pro-Communist (PCP), events will be interpreted quite differently, probably with reference to the background and biography of the petitioning architects: they are all from Lisbon, strangers, newcomers who give themselves airs and haven't the faintest idea of the countryside and its people, who have hitherto done very well for themselves and enjoy the best connections with the Câmara. The wife of one is in any case the daughter of a rich landowner: what more does she want; hasn't she already profited enough from the poverty of others? The rich people from Lisbon, with their estates and weekend houses, should have no say here in the impoverished Alentejo. Whose hands are dirty (*mãos sujas*) in this affair should be fairly clear. Between these two opinions, which I have presented in their extreme forms, lies a broad field of negotiation and a great many different positions.

In an interview with one of the architects, I learned more about the motives for his action. To begin with, he was really very angry about the refusal of his project on 'aesthetic' grounds, for he saw this as a depreciation of himself and his designs, and moreover such decisions lose him business. But most of all he was annoyed by the enormous legal uncertainty that prevailed about building permits; decisions often took up to two years. The blame for this lies, in his opinion, with the traditional bureaucracy that hinders all development. Bureaucracy here means that officials merely push papers from one side of their desk the another, where they remain because of an incapacity for decision. He knows such dawdling from the inside; he once worked for the Câmara. The lack of creativity and competence expresses itself in negative decisions against those who can set something going.

His business is actually doing fairly well, since there is much construction work going on particularly in the coastal region.

Nevertheless, according to his information, local architects are suffering losses in the sum of millions because of the illegal activities of Câmara architects.

> Architect: This is the first time that we have had trouble with the Câmara. Communistic Câmaras in the Alentejo have the reputation for being not so corrupt as those in the hands of the PS or PSD.
> Up to now everything has always gone well, but now that there are difficulties one must do something, shake things up.
> We know quite well – everyone knows – that the architects work illegally outside the Câmara.
> They draw up building plans and have someone else sign them, and then approve their own designs in the Câmara. That is illegal and unethical ...

This architects' quarrel has a long history, and reaches back into the time before the end of the fascist regime, at the time of preferential treatment. The rash accusation of corruption touches many controversial points lying on the lines of conflict between the local population and the newcomers from the Lisbon elite. There is the complaint that the others are rich, sons and daughters of great landowners, who want to live a pleasant life in the region at the cost of the local people, and then on the top of this start mixing into their affairs; strangers who are in any case too arrogant to wish to associate themselves with anyone here. There is the complaint that these architects, who have had a very good life, now fear that the customary Portuguese dawdling will catch up with the region and that they have been chosen to put a stop to it.

Various conflicts among the social groups and networks in the Odemira district further complicate the issue. It is also complicated by the view of the central government that the provincial princes 'down there' extend their powers illegally. Everyone accuses the other of corruption, blames the other for exploiting illegal advantages. To talk about corruption is a sign of the disappearance of politics, of the work of the 'anti-politics machine' (Ferguson 1990), for corruption is non-partisan, can affect everyone, no one and nothing is safe against it. The feeling becomes widespread that political means and civic sense can do nothing against this system of partiality that favours friends and relations and one's own economic advantage. Yet occasionally one hears the wish expressed for a super-state, one that is capable of ending corruption. The hope that the EU could prove to be such an entity is certainly present.

WHERE THE JEEPS COME FROM

The European Union appears to many people in Odemira to be a sheet-anchor: 'The European Union is my hope, to be honest. I hope that everything here will become more efficient', said one local politician in an interview. It is hoped that the bureaucracy will work better and also the banks, with whom one never knows exactly where the money is for which one is waiting or which one has transferred. Some citizens eagerly await the effect of the new rules: if only the EU with its strict laws would take over the supervision! Others again fear for their room for manoeuvre. The security of rules and controls harbours the danger that the slight margin of profit for small businessmen will be additionally narrowed by the loss of non-declared revenues. Even the Communist Party is a Euro-sceptic: the laws issued by the EU are interpreted as an aggression, the fear of external determination and 'foreign masters' is much discussed. Are those 'at the top' in Brussels now also to have a say here?

The European Union also seems for many to be a gigantic money-distributing machine. This machine further aggravates existing injustices. On this point, representatives of all the non-rightist parties are one. In the opinion of the communists, the EU machine distributes its largesse only to the landowners and their children. It is mainly their sons who are in a position to participate in EU programmes for young farmers, because only they possess enough land. It is also they who sit in the director's chair at local offices of the national administration; in the branch office of the Ministry of Agriculture where one applies for EU subsidies; in the office of the waterworks which regulates access to water from the reservoir; in the offices of the nature conversation authorities. The director of the Agricultural Office is running as candidate for the position of district president, for the conservative-liberal PSD.

What do the landowners and their children do with the EU monies? They buy cars with it, says Eleugério, a bar owner, in an interview. The tax-payer – he, that is – must pay for their jeeps. Every child knows how that is done. They build fences. Currently the EU is paying subsidies for building fences. Using standard EU sizes, they fence in their land. Put cattle on it. And everything on the cheap. And then, instead of properly buying and raising cattle, as they had applied to do, they buy jeeps. They don't buy any cattle with the money but instead luxuries. And when the EU inspectors come round, then what do they do? Well, they loan out the cows to each other. The herd is simply moved from one meadow to the other. The inspectors don't even notice. They're all in it together: the veterinarian who has to approve the cattle transport, the branch office of the Ministry of Agriculture in Odemira, all of them. We talk about the case of the young farmer from a neighbouring town who recently hanged himself because he could no longer pay the instalments on his EU credit. That was the reason given in his suicide note. First nothing grows any more because of the drought, then they can't pay back their credit, and soon it's all over.

Eleugério: The young farmers (*jovens agricultures*) particularly live it up. Before, these people used to drive jalopies. And today? Jeeps and new cars. They got all the subsidies, and afterwards there was nothing left. And when the inspectors came, this is what the farmers did: simply moved the neighbour's cows to their meadows where before there were no cows at all.

This is no way to develop agriculture.

But those in the government, they're carrying on the really juicy swindles. They put the money from the EU in their pockets and there it stays. You can even read about it in the papers!

The government not only supports shady projects by big businessmen (like that of the French agro-industrialist in the nature reserve) and thereby makes itself unpopular, but it also discriminates against small businessmen and small projects. Stories of approved EU monies that never arrive or arrive much too late are ubiquitous. What is to be done? In my interviews with organizations, companies and associations that receive grants from the EU, accusations relating to delayed payment of EU monies is subject number one. What does the government do with the money in Lisbon? No one knows; the question remains unanswered. In the media, reports appear now and then about delays of money transfers; now and then fraud with EU monies is even proven against members of the government or politicians.[8] But where does the money remain for so long? One can only speculate. What does the government do with the money in Lisbon?

CONCLUSION

As I write his chapter, Portugal is going through a corruption scandal, as a result of which the Foreign Minister and the Education Minister have already had to resign. They colluded in the attempt to get round university admissions restrictions through a special regulation that would obtain a place at medical school for the Foreign Minister's daughter. Neither minister feels he has done anything wrong: 'I have a clear conscience' said the Foreign Minister António Martins da Cruz after his resignation, and the Education Minister took the same view. Conservative members of their party rushed to point out that the affair was finally a matter of helping the family. The columnist for the newspaper *O Público*, José Manuel Fernandes (2003), criticized this posture and observed of its consequences: 'The recent dwindling in Portugal of the already battered public trust is by far the worst thing about the entire scandal.'

In Odemira corruption belongs to conversations about the state of the world, about disaffection with the state, about fears of the decay of the community, about the situations of helplessness into which one falls in the course of life, about the unjust distribution of goods among people. Some cases of corruption are uncovered; others are conjectured in many circumstances of everyday life. Some stories establish themselves and are told again and again, in the form 'I know somebody who knows somebody, and this and that happened to him.' In interviews, Alentejaneans reflect together with the social anthropologist about the meaning that stories of corruption have for their lives. We speak here about nervous insecurity, the sense of constant menace, the attack on personal rights, on the safety of the body and of life.

The fear that corruption could increase and spread is the fear of arbitrariness and cruel control by one's fellow men, by one's neighbour. It is the fear of the poor that even more could be taken from them, reflected in the story of the mayor X who withholds the money for schoolchildren's milk that the authorities transfer to him. Or when a French agro-businessman, an internationally known jet-setter and playboy, sets up a poisonous vegetable factory in the middle of a nature reserve, while a normal farmer must fight for years to receive a building permit to add a small shed on to his house. Or that if one wants to pass the driver's test, one had better bring along sufficient money. Or that when a cow is stolen from the pasture, the police pay no attention to this – after all, it happens every day. Or when in the canal behind São Teotónio a dead man is found with a knife in his back, a cattle dealer, of whom everybody says he was 'one of them' ... and naturally nobody saw anything. Or when foreigners or other Portuguese from Lisbon come to the region, buy real estate, and pay for it in cash from suitcases full of money – for in Portugal there is no law that stops this sort of money-laundering. Of this, the finance official and communist representative in the district council, Cláudio Percheiro, remarked in an interview: 'In this area, Portugal is like a Third World country, only equipped with all the advantages of the First World.'

This was the view of many of the people whom I interviewed, and in the press continual accusations may also be heard as a result of corruption scandals at every level: 'Portugal is the northernmost country of Africa, completely corrupt', or 'Portugal is a banana republic.' These are helpless comparisons which express horror at the idea that the former colonial power, with its proud people, now belongs in the same category as those countries which it once colonized.

Whether and to what extent stories about corruption are true can be ascertained only seldom, and as has already been suggested, in connection with the subject of this chapter it is quite irrelevant whether cases of corruption 'really' occur. Corruption is an image, a metaphor for the Other, for the uncertainty of economic and bureaucratic processes, for the despair at everyday difficulties, for the attempt to obtain security within a maze of relations. The narration of ever new cases of corruption continually reminds the narrator of existing lines of conflict and allows a constantly new determination of his own position between them. It is a moment of security amidst insecurity, a moment of stability amidst crisis.

GLOSSARY

PCP – Communist Party
PS – Socialist Party
PSD – Social Democratic Party (conservative-liberal)

NOTES

1. Herzfeld is one of the few authors who expressly addresses this point, namely '"Western intellectuals'" tendency to contrast their own idealised political models with the "corrupt" practices of other cultures' (Herzfeld 1992: 4n).
2. One indication of this neglect may be seen in the lack of an entry on 'corruption' in the newer dictionaries, encyclopaedias and introductory works of political anthropology or of anthropology in general.
3. See Haller and Shore (Introduction to this volume), Hauschild (2000), Shore (2000), Wolf (1977).
4. António Oliveira Salazar (1889–1968) ruled Portugal under a fascist dictatorship for over 40 years, from 1926 to his death.
5. It is unclear from the original whether the sum here is given in dollars or Portuguese escudos. I assume the latter, since this appears to be within the realm of plausibility. This yields the sum of 49,880 euro, which corresponds to approximately the same sum in dollars.
6. Socialist Party.
7. Conservative-liberal party which calls itself the 'Social Democratic Party'.
8. Concerning the mediality of corruption see Gupta (1995).

REFERENCES

Dracklé, D. (in press) *Die Rhetorik der Krise* (Münster, Hamburg: LIT Verlag).
Gupta, A. (1995) Blurred Boundaries: The Discourse of Corruption, the Culture of Politics, and the Imagined State, *American Ethnologist*, Vol. 22, No. 2: 375–402.
Ferguson, J. (1990) *The Anti-Politics Machine: 'Development', Depoliticisation and Bureaucratic Power in Lesotho* (Cambridge: Cambridge University Press).
Fernandes, J.M. (2003) Opinião *O Público Online* 10 Aug. Available at: <http://www.publico.pt>. Accessed 10 Aug. 2004.
Hauschild, T. (2000) Ein müder Heller für die CDU! Ethnologen erforschen den Parteienskandal – Eine kleine Anthropologie des 'Bimbes', *Die Zeit*, Vol. 55, No. 6. Available online: <www.zeit.de/archiv/2000/6/200006.bimbo1_xml>. Accessed Nov. 2004.

Herzfeld, M. (1992) *The Production of Indifference: Exploring the Symbolic Roots of Western Bureaucracy* (Chicago and London: University of Chicago Press).

Krauss, W. (2001) *Hängt die Grünen! Umweltkonflikte, nachhaltige Entwicklung und ökologischer Diskurs* (Berlin: Dietrich Reimer Verlag).

Shore, C. (2000) *Building Europe: The Cultural Politics of European Integration* (London: Routledge).

Taussig, M. (1992) *The Nervous System* (New York and London: Routledge).

Transparency International Portuguese Chapter (2001) *Survey on the Transparency/corruption Level in Portugal*. Available at: <http//admin.corisweb.org/files/TI-P2001Survey.ppt>. Accessed 10 Feb. 2003.

Wolf, E. (1977) Kinship, Friendship, and Patron–Client Relations in Complex Societies, in S.W. Schmidt, J. Scott, C. Landé and L. Guasti (eds) *Friends, Followers and Factions – A Reader in Political Clientelism* (Berkeley: University of California Press).

11 CITIZENS DESPITE THE STATE: EVERYDAY CORRUPTION AND LOCAL POLITICS IN EL ALTO, BOLIVIA

Sian Lazar

In this chapter,[1] I explore some of the continuities and differences in perceptions of corruption at varying levels of Bolivian politics, from community organisations to local and national governments. At all levels, corruption and its necessary counterpart, public works (*obras*), are crucial discursive elements in the ways in which citizens assert their expectations of their leaders, and here I examine the extent to which they are successful. In the exercise of formal and informal mechanisms of control, which turn decisively on the interaction between perceptions of corruption and the delivery of *obras*, people imagine themselves as a collective entity, as residents of a particular neighbourhood, or 'the Bolivian people'. Through rumour and gossip, they attempt to hold their leaders to account pre-emptively. In so doing they establish a sense of the public good, and, hopefully, an obligation on the part of their leaders to serve that good.

Corruption is a problematic category for analysis because of its slipperiness: actual corruption is both everywhere and nowhere, because it is never made explicit. Telling a story about corruption often serves more to highlight the moral integrity of the teller than anything else. Corruption is always somewhere else, perpetrated by someone else. It is, furthermore, relative – the same act can be perceived by one person as corruption and by another person as legitimate recompense for services rendered. Nonetheless, corruption is impossible to ignore, because of both its discursive power and material effects. Here, I focus on the former, following Akhil Gupta's argument that 'the discourse of corruption [is] a key arena through which the state, citizens, and other organisations and aggregations come to be imagined' (Gupta 1995: 376).

Corruption is a useful analytical category for anthropologists principally because people mobilize it in various ways to constitute their understanding of the proper use of political power. Disentangling local understandings of corruption enables us to say something about local understandings of politics and the state, specifically the relationship between public and private spheres. Nye's definition of corruption is now normative: 'behaviour which deviates from the formal duties of a public role because of a private-regarding (personal, close family, private clique) pecuniary or status gain; or violates rules against the exercise of certain types of private regarding influence' (Nye 1967: 419, cited in Olivier de Sardan 1999: 27). If we accept that private and public are differently constituted in different cultures and histories (Sneath 2002), the stories told about corruption can illuminate that construction.

J.P. Olivier de Sardan writes usefully about a 'corruption complex', that is a spectrum of illicit practices beyond the strictly legal definition of corruption, and including 'nepotism, abuse of power, embezzlement and various forms of misappropriation, influence-peddling, prevarication, insider trading and abuse of the public purse' (1999: 27) as well as bribery. Others have distinguished between the market-based corruption of the bribe and the patrimonial corruption of the importance of personal networks in subverting the smooth and rational operation of a bureaucracy (e.g. Sampson 1983; Wade 1985). There has been much anthropological work on bureaucracy and the bribery of civil servants, particularly from those studying India.[2] However, I want to use Olivier de Sardan's wider notion of the 'corruption complex', because in Bolivia, the corruption that worried ordinary people the most was not the need to bribe petty bureaucrats to do their work more quickly (although that certainly happens), but the perceived propensity of those in power to steal public resources for their personal benefit. As I argue towards the end of this chapter, this is linked to the operations of personal clientelistic networks in particular ways. But, just as complaints about corrupt bureaucrats reveal the strength of acceptance of bureaucratic rationality within a society, because they do not measure up to the ideal of the disinterested public servant (Parry 2000; Taussig 1997), complaints about the rapacity of politicians reveal the importance of the idea of the proper functioning of the state in the interests of its people. The complaints are part of the way in which people assert their collective identity as citizens betrayed by venal politicians who steal public resources.

When people talked about community leaders or politicians being corrupt, they usually meant that they were seeking to use public money to serve their own interests rather than those of the neighbourhood, city or country. Other ways of describing the same thing was calling people *personalistas* or *interesados* (self-serving, or self-interested). As people accused others of corruption, they were asserting their expectations of their leaders, in two senses. First, they tended to expect that leaders would be corrupt, but second, against this they tried to assert a hope that leaders would, even if contrary to their natural inclinations, serve the public good. Articulating the expectation that leaders will serve the common good makes a distinction between public and private inherent to both local and normative understandings of corruption. Corruption talk is therefore one of the ways in which Bolivians construct a moral public sphere, and make claims to the appropriate distribution of resources, and to increased accountability.

The question is how effective is corruption talk as a way for citizens to encourage their leaders to a work for the public good? Corruption is both the means by which people stake their claim to public works, called *obras*, and the context which makes such concrete evidence of activity essential. The demand for *obras* is in turn a means of reducing the damage done by corruption, because, at the very least, some money has been invested in the community. As with community-based politics, in local and national politics, corruption and *obras* together are tropes through which citizens attempt to hold their leaders to account: so that the threat of accusation of the former leads politicians (hopefully) to build the latter. The difference between the levels of political activity lies in the relative ability to succeed in asserting those expectations. Aihwa Ong, following Charles Taylor (1995) has called this kind of ability 'citizenship capacity', meaning 'the ways citizens in different democratic countries seek to realize particular interests, including resources and citizen dignity, and the kind of political accountability they expect from their government' (Ong 1999: 54). Corruption and *obras* together are the key discursive constituents of citizenship capacity in Bolivia, at all levels of politics, and in this chapter I examine the proposition that citizenship capacity progressively diminishes as the distance between citizen and leader increases. The problem is that the generalized perception of the inevitability of corruption on the part of leaders may in fact unofficially sanction corruption, as people complain but do not expect politicians to behave otherwise. The public sphere is thereby constituted as a struggle between citizens' assertions of morality and public good and the risk of the conversion of the 'corruption complex' into a 'corruption syndrome' resulting in a spiral of low expectations of leaders.[3]

THE *JUNTAS*: AT THE INTERFACE BETWEEN STATE AND 'CIVIL SOCIETY'

Rosas Pampa is a neighbourhood of about 800 households in the southern part of the highland city of El Alto in Bolivia. Most of its residents are first- or second-generation migrants from rural areas, predominantly the Aymara-speaking regions of the Andean plateau. Adults are represented by the neighbourhood council, called the *Junta Vecinal*, and if they have children at the local school, as most of them do, by the *Junta Escolar*, or parent's association. The *Junta Vecinal* is led by an elected committee who meet roughly every two weeks, and every two to three months they hold a General Assembly for all the residents of Rosas Pampa.[4] The *Junta Vecinal's* primary responsibility throughout the year is to obtain *obras* for the neighbourhood. *Obras* can refer to public works such as the health centre or community centre, as well as infrastructure such as street-lighting, the sewage and water system, and electricity. The *Junta Escolar* consisted of three leaders (a president, vice-president and treasurer) who called a meeting of all the parents of children at the school two or three times a year, to discuss questions of, among other things, school activities and discipline, and improvement to school buildings, also called *obras*.

The day-to-day administration of El Alto relies upon the *Juntas* taking the role of brokers, nodal points for the coordination of service providers to their neighbourhoods. Legislative reforms instigated in the 1990s have meant that the community leaders stand at an interface between the state and civil society. The most important of these reforms are the Popular Participation Law and the Educational Reform Law, both of 1994. As a result of the Popular Participation Law, 20 percent of national tax income is devolved to local government, who spend it according to participatory planning processes that, in urban areas, involve the *Juntas* as community representatives. Local governments also became responsible for expenditure on local infrastructure, including education, and the Educational Reform Law provided for an expanded role for the *Juntas Escolares* in supervising the administration of schools, even, in theory, evaluating teachers.[5] Thus, the *Juntas* are part of the process through which the Bolivian government channels development money to Rosas Pampa. International NGOs also channel money through them, and are often better patrons than the local or national government. One Dutch NGO in particular has funded the building of a health centre, community centre, and toilets and classrooms in the school.[6]

The *Junta Vecinal* and the *Junta Escolar* are both state and civil society, evidence of the reach of the state throughout everyday life.[7] They existed as means of organizing residents to gain development for their neighbourhood prior to the latest attempts of the state to co-opt them, and are partially influenced by structures of leadership common in highland rural areas. However, their interactions with the state have also influenced their development: for example, some *Juntas Vecinales* are becoming increasingly party-politicized as their influence over resource allocation grows. They mediate between state and people but are not always uncontested representatives for the community, and do not always serve the interests of the collectivity, which must frequently attempt to counteract the apparent self-interest of its leaders. The *Juntas* also substitute for the state on occasions, for example when they police the neighbourhood informally, and when they implement state decisions at the local level. In many ways, they are seen as *both* continuous with politicians at the national or local governmental level *and* separate from them. The reforms of the 1990s have had important implications for corruption in Bolivia as, with greater resources going to local government, opportunities for corruption have multiplied. At least, this is what many believe, and the community organizations are increasingly coming to the heart of this debate. The legislation assumes that increased community participation through bodies such as the *Juntas* will act as a brake on institutional corruption, seemingly because they can stand in for the 'grassroots'. They are 'civil society' and therefore somehow purer than corrupt state bureaucracies.[8]

RUMOUR, 'PRE-EMPTIVE ACCOUNTABILITY' AND PROPER LEADERSHIP

In fact, in Rosas Pampa, corruption is one of the principal languages for conducting community politics. Corruption is used via rumour to articulate political allegiances or struggles, and to manoeuvre for positions of power; as well as to resist such manoeuvres. Accusations of corruption serve both to highlight the moral integrity of the accuser, as well as to throw some mud (not always undeserved) at the accused. While I was there, there were constant rumours about corruption among the community leaders. For example, it was commonly known (or thought, at any rate) that most of the leaders of the *Junta Vecinal*, in common with previous committees, had houses or land in other neighbourhoods. The belief was that successive committee members have used their positions to accumulate enough money (or building materials) to buy a plot there and build a bigger house than their property in Rosas Pampa. Even in taped interviews, women made comments about the *Junta Vecinal*'s tendency to 'extract money', as in the following quote:

The Junta, well there are times when they say 'give us a bit of time [to show how they have spent the money]', but frankly they can't say that any more; people say that they help themselves anyway. People have given quotas, but they've just redirected it to their houses. They even buy houses for themselves, and with the money make everything nice, that's what people say ... they really just take advantage of their position ... The authorities change, but they all do the same. A new one comes in, and away he goes with the money.[9]

Rumours alleged diversion of the money raised from the quotas collected by the *Junta Vecinal* for the installation of almost all of the public services. The sewage system was particularly notorious. A previous president had apparently charged quotas around twice the price of the actual cost, and people had serious doubts about the destination of the extra funds. Don Rolando,[10] the president in 1999, had charged quotas of 10 Bs (US $1.70) per house for work paving the three main streets of the zone. But he said that someone had stolen the money. One of my informants thought that Don Rolando was particularly *personalista*. She told me that when the *Junta Escolar* had obtained funds for the school toilets, he had demanded to be the builder in charge of their construction, since he was also the president of the zone at the time. However, later on the parents had discovered that stones and cement had gone missing.

Quite apart from the constant rumours and speculation, on occasion serious scandals would flare up, as the incident which put an end to Don Rolando's presidency shows.

By March 2000, the residents of the zone had had enough of him, and at a General Assembly, he and his vice-president were forced to resign, and were replaced by other members of the leadership committee. It was a case of embezzlement: Don Rolando had 'misspent'[11] US $2,000 from the money set aside for the Community Centre. Some rumours put the figure at US $25,000, and no one knew what he had spent the money on: some said he had bought a piece of land in another neighbourhood with the proceeds and taken building materials from the Community Centre in order to build a house there. Others said that he had spent the money on a mistress. Earlier in the year, he had been so stressed at creditors and builders coming and asking him for money he no longer had, that he poisoned himself, and was taken to hospital. At the time of the meeting, he was still living in Rosas Pampa, but had gone to ground. People thought that he should show his face, to say whether he had stolen the money or not, saying that he was a coward and not a real man. My neighbour, Doña Antonia, said that she thought that leaders 'shouldn't do these things' and while perhaps a woman would poison herself, a man shouldn't.

Doña Antonia was fairly resigned to his actions, saying 'we can't say anything, they won't listen to us. It's the same in [the countryside villages], they defraud just the same, it's their job.'[12] I asked, why do they do it? and she replied 'I ask myself the same thing. Perhaps because there's no money around.'[13] The sports secretary of the *Junta Vecinal*, elected after Don Rolando's resignation, was also sympathetic:

It's really bad, isn't it? I mean, I think he was in a really critical moment – I think that you only do that sort of thing when you are desperate. When there's no way out, and to do that, to get to that extreme, he must have been really desperate, to sell his reputation. Because a lot of people thought he was very able, they believed in him, but since he's done this, no, they think he must have been really desperate, he must have had debts, to get to the point where he sold his prestige, really just threw away his good name.[14]

Reactions to the embezzlement were mixed, varying from disapproval to disgust, sympathy and resignation. People were fairly unsurprised, considering it the way things are, but Don Rolando had clearly lost his status, even masculinity, in the eyes of residents of Rosas Pampa, as the comments about his weakness attest. He never recovered his reputation in the neighbourhood, and three years later was living somewhere else. The loss of reputation is no small thing for someone who has taken the trouble to become a leader. Holding a defined series of leadership positions in rural Andean communities is part of the progressive achievement of full adulthood (Abercrombie 1998; Carter and Mamani P 1989), and such perceptions hold weight in urban migrant communities such as Rosas Pampa. The sense of resignation expressed by many was, I suspect, because by the time the story got out, the processes of accountability had failed, and everyone knew that the money had been spent and was unrecoverable. Ideally, accountability in Rosas Pampa works preventively, with the sanction of rumour, so that the gossip and scandals about one set of leaders act as examples and serve to keep other leaders in check. As the sports secretary put it, one does not want to lose one's status. Here the micropolitics of reputation are informed by the struggle in the public sphere between the expectation of corrupt behaviour and the attempt to assert a different, more moral, kind of politics.

The stories above show a tension between a strong conception of communality and the perception that personal material gains are the most important motivation for leaders. On the one hand, there are direct and personal material incentives for becoming a leader, as gaining control over the distribution of state resources enables individuals and their families to benefit personally. On the other, leaders are supposed to work for the benefit of the community rather than for personal interest. People have a clear sense of what public service is, and construct that sense in part by telling stories about corruption. As argued by Johnathan Parry (2000), a notion of what corruption is requires a notion of what it is not, and indeed perceived 'crises of corruption' perhaps indicate less the prevalence of corruption and more the prevalence of a commitment to properly functioning bureaucratic rationality (see also Taussig 1997). In Rosas Pampa, there was a general consensus that *Junta Vecinal* and *Junta Escolar* leaders had stood for election because they wanted to work for the 'good of the neighbourhood', a frequent theme in conversations, meetings and interviews. Far from corruption indicating a lack of a sense of the public and public service, as argued by Olivier de

Sardan (1999) for the case of Africa, in Rosas Pampa, the notion of the public is actually constructed in part by the rumours and realities of corruption. Corruption scandals express and impose the residents' expectations of their leaders, holding future leaders to account pre-emptively with the threat that they will be removed from their position and discussed in the same demeaning way as Don Rolando was if they succumb to the temptation to divert the zone's money for their personal interests. Future leaders know that in order to be successful they should hold to their commitment to be active in favour of the zone.

This is not always easy. Andean ethnographies tend to view community leadership in rural areas as an obligation that is usually very expensive, and where prestige and duty prevail over material interest (Abercrombie 1998; Carter and Mamani P 1989; Klemola 1997). The committee members of Rosas Pampa themselves were often vocal about the fact that they were spending their own money on all the work they did. However, in practice, people in Rosas Pampa are understanding up to a point, accepting that nobody works for nothing. Leadership of a community is hard work, an obligation but also a job, and people cannot be expected to work entirely for free, particularly in the context of a serious economic recession. People are prepared to recognize that leaders of the *Junta Escolar* or *Junta Vecinal* should be recompensed, at least for their transport and lunches, when they have to go to the municipal government to ask for things on behalf of the neighbourhood. Rather pointedly, one woman said to me 'They don't get paid anything either. Who's going to work for free? They get hungry.'[15] Nonetheless, leaders tread a fine line between being fairly recompensed for their work and the expenses that they incur, and spending the neighbourhood's money on themselves. What to one person is corruption is another person's way of being paid for the work they do.

Comments from two aspiring politicians illustrate the operation of such logics in other political spheres. Rubén was weighing up the possibility of standing for future election in his natal village, and Jose Luis 'Tren' Martínez was an unsuccessful candidate for mayor of El Alto in December 1999. Both spoke of corruption in politics as a result of the investment required to be elected. When asked in 2000 for his assessment of the new government, Martínez said:

I at least think that they have made a big investment in order to enter local government, and the symptoms you can see straight away are the returns on that investment.[16]

He was referring to the considerable expense incurred over the preceding years by the new mayor in building up a network of grateful clients who then voted for him in the elections.[17] Rubén thought that in Bolivia there is 'too much corruption', as politicians go into positions of power purely to 'extract benefits'. But as far as he was concerned, he wanted 'to work more for people, get something out of it, but not much'.[18] Notable here is his view that there can be 'too much' corruption, implying that there are degrees of corruption, some of which are appropriate. He was probably being realistic about politics: as Martínez indicated, being a candidate for any position is an investment, and one usually expects returns on investments. Rubén estimated that he had spent US $700–800 on taking a dance group to his natal village, an act partly designed to increase his profile there, as he said:

My aim is to get myself known by the people there; because they look at your character, they have respect for what you do. You have to help people, and then they vote for the person that helped them. If you give them support, invest a little bit for them, they'll vote for you.[19]

He knew that if he decided to continue in politics, he would have to find the money for something more concrete, and more expensive. For him, it was therefore only reasonable to expect some return. It is the *level* of return that is contestable, along with the amount of work you do to benefit your 'people' (usually clients) or your village. This is reflected in the common assessment of one of the most successful mayors in Bolivia, Manfred Reyes Villa. He was mayor of Cochabamba for three successive terms in the 1990s, and people often said of him that 'He steals, but at least he does something.' Managing the balance between the investment of personal and state resources in favour of clients/the public, and the accusations of self-interest and corruption makes political leadership a complex proposition. It may indeed be the case that serving the public good will only induce most people to become leaders if it is combined with the prospect of personal reward.

OBRAS

People will probably always assume their leaders are corrupt, even if they are as clean as a whistle (cf. Parry 2000). As a community leader, the only way to avoid excessive criticism and overt accusations of corruption was through working 'for the good of the neighbourhood', which is proved by success in obtaining *obras*. From the residents' point of view, the achievement of *obras* was both a necessity and evidence that the leaders were making an effort and achieving results. There are good reasons for this: Rosas Pampa, which was founded in 1975, had to struggle for a considerable time to gain electricity in the late 1980s, a sewage and water system in 1994, and in 1999 the streets were not paved, causing frequent complaints about the dirt and inconvenience. Both *Juntas* had to produce *obras*, but the *Junta Escolar* had had more success than the 1999 *Junta Vecinal*: when asked their opinion about the *Junta Escolar*, many of the women I interviewed made comments about how the school had progressed, how ugly and small it was before, when children had to have classes outside in the playground, and how pretty it had become since the latest set of leaders had been in charge. Overall, the assessment of the *Junta Escolar* was favourable, because they had quite clearly improved the school. You could see where they were spending the money they charged in quotas and fines.[20] The problem was that with the *Junta Vecinal* the results were not so obvious, so the women made comments such as the following:

> [The leaders] have forgotten about the zone. They've totally forgotten. Now, recently, there seems to me to be a little bit of interest in the zone [because of the contract for paving the central street] ... But they've never had any interest in the zone.[21]

When I asked what good things the Junta had done, this particular woman replied 'No, they haven't done anything, there aren't any *obras*.'[22]

Obras constitute the acknowledged legitimate expectations of the residents of Rosas Pampa. One result of this was a series of highly ritualized inauguration ceremonies for the *obras* that had been completed during the year I lived there. The *Junta Vecinal* ceremoniously poured alcoholic libations for the new Community Centre, with the relevant NGO people in attendance. The same people came to the ceremonial opening of the four new school classrooms which they had part-funded. Both ceremonies consisted of long speeches, and poetry readings and dances from school children, followed by an official *ch'alla* (libation)[23] and toast of 'champagne' (cider) and biscuits, followed by food and, if those present were lucky, beer. Such rituals of accountability marked the triumphs of the authorities in a far more powerful and important way than rendering well-kept financial accounts could ever do.

The combination of corruption and *obras* as discursive constituents of citizenship capacity at different levels of political activity in Bolivia is also demonstrated by an examination of the 1999 local elections. By 1999, the El Alto municipality had been run by the same political party for the previous decade: *Conciencia de Patria*, or Condepa. The Condepa administrations had been notoriously corrupt and inefficient, and the party had fragmented since the death of its founder in 1997 and its subsequent electoral success and entry into national government as a coalition partner. In 1999, the situation looked ripe for an upset in its final stronghold, El Alto. Sure enough, the *Movimiento Izquierdista Revolucionario* (Leftist

Revolutionary Movement, or MIR) put an end to Condepa's reign. Their candidate, Jose Luis Paredes, gained around 45 percent of the overall vote, and the MIR won an unprecedented 7 of the 11 council places on offer. Paredes' success was down to a number of factors, principally the collapse of Condepa and his long-term work in developing an effective clientelistic network throughout El Alto. But central to the campaign was the stress that the MIR placed on the fact that they were the only party with a real plan of government for El Alto, emphasizing their fit with a technocratic politics characteristic of many Bolivian regimes, including the less democratic ones.[24]

This document, entitled the *Plan Progreso*, is extremely detailed, replete with targets and pledges which seem impossible to achieve. However, it meant that the MIR were able to present themselves as moderniszers who would fund *obras* for El Alto, more through proclaiming the existence of the government plan than actually distributing it effectively. Local party offices, especially in outlying neighbourhoods like Rosas Pampa, did not hold copies of the *Plan Progreso* for interested people to look at: they were distributed only among active party members. The *Plan Progreso* helped the MIR to put clear blue water between themselves and Condepa, stressing that they would be more efficient and less corrupt than the previous administration. The MIR media campaigns also focused on this theme: Jose Luis Paredes frequently appeared on TV with his 'whip against corruption' in his hand.[25] In the electoral campaigns, corruption was indelibly linked with the ability to produce *obras*.

Although many people talked so often and so negatively about politicians being corrupt, I suspect that residents of El Alto who almost longingly described the mayor of Cochabamba as someone 'who steals but at least does something' would rather have a corrupt mayor who provided *obras* than a completely honest one who did nothing visible. The focus on *obras* is unsurprising given the needs that actually exist in residential zones of El Alto, and anyway, at high levels of power, complete honesty is often thought impossible (cf. Parry 2000). Since most people felt all politicians to be equally corrupt, the issue of corruption did not enable electors to choose between the political parties. Ultimately, they assessed the value of a politician despite and beyond their presumed corruption. One informant's comment about the MIR reflects this: 'They're corrupt, but at least they keep their promises.'[26] By early 2003, the *obras* in El Alto were certainly visible, as the MIR had asphalted some roads, built a stadium and finished pedestrian bridges that Condepa had left uncompleted. This increased activity was in part because the MIR wished to improve its election prospects in El Alto for the national elections of 2002. Accusations of corruption at campaign time are part of politicians' weaponry, and a component of the cyclical nature of politics, as one party gives way to another, but they also constitute a pressure to perform, at least to some extent. At the neighbourhood level, the president who took over from Don Rolando has also proved to be more visibly effective than his predecessor, and in a meeting in May 2003 was re-elected for another year's term of office. Of course, these are not simple stories of effective citizenship capacity. There is still considerable suspicion of the MIR administration, particularly with regard to the durability of their *obras*, given a perceived tendency to divert money through the purchase of lower-quality materials than those in the budget. The *obras* have also been concentrated in the neighbourhoods which are known to support the MIR. Community and municipal politics are linked, as Don Rolando was a well-known Condepista, and therefore unlikely to achieve very much from a MIR administration. However, the *Junta Escolar* of 1999 also remains in place, largely because they are known to be effective and thus have been able to withstand the accusations of corruption levelled at them. They have also been careful to keep good records, because, as the treasurer told me, 'people talk'.

CORRUPTION TALK, POWER AND RESOURCE ALLOCATION

Corruption talk enables people to make evaluations of those in power, according to how *personalista* or *interesado* they are. What is at issue is the *extent* to which public money is diverted for personal gain, or, more importantly, redistributed to the people, either through *obras* or through jobs. These are linked to the clientelistic structures that pervade politics, as the party 'militants' are the ones who can hope to get the jobs planning, supervising or building the *obras* once their candidate has won. This is an indication of what Bayart (1993) calls a 'politics of the belly' (see also Olivier de Sardan 1999). Bayart argues that, in Cameroon, politics is about the accumulation of wealth and its subsequent redistribution, in order to satisfy and increase a politician's clientele. Politicians are entitled, and expected, to accumulate wealth personally, and use it to benefit their social networks, including above all their family. How acceptable this is in Bolivia varies according to the context, but what is similar is that Bolivian patrons are expected to redistribute their wealth, and the wealth of the state, through the provision of jobs to their clients (Gamarra and Malloy 1995). Each time a new political party takes over the administration of a municipality, ministry, etc., the previous set of civil servants is fired and the new party's activists take their place. Despite the rhetorical emphasis on *obras*, the largest part of a municipality's budget goes on wages for its functionaries (Blanco Cazas and Sandoval 1993). While Condepa was in power in El Alto, half of the budget went on wages, a third on debt servicing, and less than a fifth on new *obras*.[27] It is here that local administrations are caught between two imperatives: the need to give wages to their militants and the need to fund *obras*. They are lucky if they are able to combine the two.

Of course, the evaluations that people make of politicians do slip, and vary according to context and person, but their mobilization illuminates the kinds of expectations people have. And in the Bolivian case, corruption, and political life in general, cannot be understood apart from the expectations and needs people have for tangible evidence of political activity. Hence the frequent repetition of increasingly unrealistic promises of *obras* for El Alto during election campaigns. *Obras* are concrete (often literally) evidence that politicians have been working in the people's interests, however much money they might have siphoned off for their own benefit. Condepa held the allegiance of many of people because they 'helped poor people' through clientelistic party mechanisms, that is giving jobs and wages, even if they did not pay back the zones with many actual *obras*. However, that tolerance was only extended up to a point, because given the presence of a promising alternative, enough residents of El Alto were fed up of having an inactive municipal administration to vote Condepa out.

The 1999 elections *may* be an example of a successful assertion of citizens' expectations at the municipal level, although its extent should by no means be overstated, and it was at any rate exceptional. On the whole, citizenship capacity is perhaps rather more effective at the community level than with regard to local or national politics. The actions of the present leaders of the *Junta Vecinal* and *Junta Escolar* show the extent to which pre-emptive accountability can work at community level. At municipal and national levels, a pervasive disillusionment with politics expresses itself in narratives of politicians' corruption, which articulate the powerlessness people feel with regard to political (and economic) elites, expressed well by the following comment I overheard: 'We queue up in order to pay taxes, they queue up in order to steal.'[28] As the effectiveness of citizenship capacity reduces, citizens progressively feel distanced from their leaders, and corruption talk becomes a way to express feelings of powerlessness and explain the failure of politics to respond to the needs of ordinary people. The lack of felt representativity in the political system is thus made apparent.[29] Through narratives of politicians' corruption, Bolivians assert their expectations of the state and attempt to hold politicians to account. In doing so, they represent the nature of the state and the reality of their citizenship back to themselves, not in a favourable light. I often heard from friends, of all classes, that although Bolivia has everything in terms of natural riches, the politicians steal everything, so Bolivia has not been able to 'advance'. Here, the subalterns blame the elites: Bolivia is not underdeveloped because of its citizens being backward, or because of an inauspicious environment, or because of its place in the global economy. Rather, a country that could be wealthy is betrayed by elite leaders, who are *personalistas* and *interesados* – the 'people of Bolivia' are citizens betrayed by venal politicians. Thus self-esteem and pride in the country, land, environment and the masses of the people, can be maintained. The people telling these stories are collectively imagining themselves as 'citizens despite the state' rather than citizens who are constituted through a positive relationship with the state.

Discourses of corruption reveal some of the values underlying political life, as well as perhaps discursively constituting political life in Bolivia. This is true for all of the levels at which the state operates, from community to national politics. Political leaders, including community leaders, do not always serve the interests of the collectivity. However, their failure to do so does enable the construction of a notion of what those interests might be. Occasionally, the collectivity defines itself against, or despite, the actions of its leaders, through accusations of corruption which in turn reinforce a notion of a common or public good that can be violated through corrupt practices. Here, rumour and gossip are means of constructing public opinion, conducting local politics and articulating values about the use of political power. These rumours, and the occasional real successes in getting rid of leaders perceived as especially corrupt, are a way of asserting the morality of the public sphere. That morality is under threat from corruption, but also put into stark relief by corruption. Thus ordinary citizens assert their own collective morality in the face of their expectations of the immorality of their leaders.

NOTES

1. My thanks to Olivia Harris and Cris Shore for comments on earlier versions of this chapter.
2. For example Wade (1982, 1985), Gupta (1995, and this volume), Visvanathan and Sethi (1998) and Parry (2000); but also see Shore (2000) and Sampson (1983) for the European Union and Romania respectively.
3. I am grateful to Cris Shore for this observation.
4. General Assemblies are usually attended by about 100–150 people, who represent their households, or their streets, and feed back information to those who are unable to attend. In a survey I conducted, a remarkable 77 percent of respondents said that they regularly attended some form of civic activity, and most of them went to the General Assemblies. When discussing the *Junta Vecinal* committee, people often called them 'the authorities/leaders of the neighbourhood', rather than its representatives. The most active member of the committee is the president.

5. For more detailed comment on popular participation, see McNeish (2002), Booth et al. (1997), Gray Molina (2003); on the education reforms, see Hornberger (2000) and Comboni Salinas and Juàrez Nunez (2000).

6. The *Juntas* are also increasingly finding themselves representing the community to private enterprises, such as the electricity or waste disposal companies.

7. Much of the work on corruption in India has similarly argued for an interpenetration of the state in ordinary life, but has tended to focus principally on the reach of a bureaucratic system controlled more or less from the top down (Gupta 1995, and this volume; Visvanathan and Sethi 1998; Wade 1982, 1985).

8. Support for 'civil society' is often seen as the appropriate response to corruption in development 'good governance' policies. See, for example, 'Civil Society Participation and the Anti-corruption Strategy of the World Bank', at <http://www1.worldbank.org/publicsector/anticorrupt/civilsociety.htm>.

9. 'Yo diría de la Junta, deben – hay veces, si pues, "un ratito ya" dicen, pues, pero ya no es eso; dicen que ellos ya se sacan. Les han ayudado [con dinero, cuotas], entonces ellos nomás a sus casas se lo hacen llegar. Si ellos nomás hasta casas se compran, con eso se hacen arreglar, dice. ... Ellos nomás dice que se aprovechan ... Otro cambia, lo mismo se hace. Otro cambia, con la plata se va.'

10. I use pseudonyms throughout this chapter. Don and Doña are polite Spanish terms for Mr and Mrs.

11. The Spanish word is *'malgastar'*, which can also mean 'to waste'.

12. 'No podemos decir nada, no nos van a hacer caso. Igual es en [mi *pueblo*], igual engañan, es su trabajo.'

13. 'Eso mismo digo yo. Tal vez porque no hay plata.'

14. 'Da mucha bronca, no? Es decir, yo creo que estaba en un momento bien crítico, no, en un momento – ya, yo creo que solo uno puede hacer algo así cuando uno está desesperado, no? No tiene una salida, y a hacer, a llegar hasta este extremo, yo creo que ha debido estar bien desesperado para hacer eso, no, para vender su prestigio. Porque mucha gente más o menos pensaban en su capacidad, creían en su capacidad, pero como que ha hecho, no, se piensan que ha debido estar realmente desesperado, ha debido tener deudas, hasta vender su prestigio, todo su persona echarlo al tacho realmente.'

15. 'Tampoco no les pagan nada. ¿Quién va a caminar gratis? Tienen hambre, pues.'

16. 'Yo por lo menos tengo la idea de que ellos han hecho una inversión fuerte para ingresar a la Alcaldía y el síntoma inmediato que se nota es la recuperación de esa misma inversión.'

17. The mayor himself, in an interview with the weekly newspaper *Pulso* (19–25 Nov. 1999: 12–13), estimated that he had spent around US $30,000 of his own money investing in community projects such as building basketball courts, buying TVs for schools, being 'godfather' to graduating classes.

18. 'Yo quiero trabajar más para la gente, sacar algo pero no mucho.'

19. 'Mi fin es hacerme conocer con la gente de allá; porque se fijan en tu persona, tienen respeto por lo que haces. Hay que ayudar a la gente, y después vota por quien te ayuda. Si tu les das un apoyo, invertir un poco para ellos, votan para ti.'

20. Fines are charged when parents do not attend demonstrations organized by the central Federation of *Juntas Escolares*.
21. '[Los dirigentes] se han olvidado de la zona. Se han olvidado totalmente. Ahora recién me parece que hay un poco de interés en la zona ... Nunca han tenido interés de la zona.'
22. 'No, no han hecho nada, no hay obras.'
23. A *ch'alla* is a libation, which consists of dropping some alcohol onto the floor, to feed Pachamama, and for good luck. See Abercrombie (1998) for a detailed discussion.
24. Gamarra argues that the technocratic element of Bolivian government, particularly noticeable in the administration of 1993–97, is evidence of the authoritarian legacy of the dictatorship era (Gamarra 2003).
25. He called it his 'chicote contra la corrupción'. The *chicote* is a small whip that parents use to discipline their children.
26. 'Son corruptos, pero por lo menos cumplen.'
27. *Pulso*, 19–25 November 1999.
28. 'Nosotros hacemos fila para pagar impuestos, ellos hacen fila para robar.'
29. Representativity is a key problem for Bolivian party politics. See Gamarra and Malloy (1995), Domingo (2001) and Gamarra (2003).

REFERENCES

Abercrombie, T.A. (1998) *Pathways of Memory and Power: Ethnography and History Among an Andean People* (Madison: University of Wisconsin Press).

Bayart, J.-F. (1993) *The State in Africa: The Politics of the Belly* (London: Longman).

Blanco Cazas, C. and G. Sandoval (1993) *La Alcaldia de La Paz. Entre populistas, modernistas y culturalistas 1985–1993* (La Paz: ILDIS – IDIS).

Booth, D., S.M. Clisby and C. Widmark (1997) Popular Participation: Democratising the State in Rural Bolivia – Report to Sida (Swansea, unpublished manuscript).

Carter, W.E. and M. Mamani P (1989) *Irpa Chico. Individuo y Comunidad en la Cultural Aymara* (La Paz: Libreria – Editorial 'Juventud').

Comboni Salinas, S. and J.M. Juàrez Nunez (2000) Education, Cultural and Indigenous Rights: The Case of Educational Reform in Bolivia, *Prospects*, Vol. 30, No. 1: 105–24.

Domingo, P. (2001) Party Politics, Intermediation and Representation, in J. Crabtree and L. Whitehead (eds) *Towards Democratic Viability: the Bolivian Experience*, pp. 141–59 (Basingstoke: Palgrave).

Gamarra, E. (2003) Political Parties since 1964: The Construction of Bolivia's Multiparty System, in M. Grindle and P. Domingo (eds) *Proclaiming Revolution: Bolivia in Comparative Perspective*, pp. 289–316 (London and Cambridge, MA: ILAS and David Rockerfeller Center for Latin American Studies, Harvard University).

Gamarra, E. and J. Malloy (1995) The Patrimonial Dynamics of Party Politics in Bolivia, in S. Mainwaring and T. Scully (eds) *Building Democratic Institutions: Party Systems in Latin America* (Stanford, CA: Stanford University Press).

Gray Molina, G. (2003). The Offspring of 1952: Poverty, Exclusion and the Promise of Popular Participation, in M. Grindle and P. Domingo (eds)

Proclaiming Revolution: Bolivia in Comparative Perspective, pp. 345–62 (London: ILAS).

Gupta, A. (1995) Blurred Boundaries: the Discourse of Corruption, the Culture of Politics, and the Imagined State, *American Ethnologist*, Vol. 22, No. 2: 375–402.

Hornberger, N. H. (2000) Bilingual Education Policy and Practice in the Andes: Ideological Paradox and Intercultural Possibility, *Anthropology and Education Quarterly*, Vol. 31, No. 2: 173–201.

Klemola, A. (1997) *The Reproduction of Community through Communal Practices in Kila Kila, Bolivia* (Liverpool: University of Liverpool Press).

McNeish, J.-A. (2002) Globalisation and the Reinvention of Andean Tradition: The Politics of Community and Ethnicity in Highland Bolivia, *Journal of Peasant Studies*, Vol. 29, No. 3/4: 228–69.

Nye, J. (1967) Corruption and Political Development: A Cost–benefit Analysis, *American Political Science Review*, Vol. 56.

Olivier de Sardan, J. P. (1999) A Moral Economy of Corruption in Africa? *Journal of Modern African Studies*, Vol. 37, No. 1: 25–52.

Ong, A. (1999) Clash of Civilizations or Asian Liberalism? An Anthropology of the State and Citizenship, in H. Moore (ed.) *Anthropological Theory Today*, pp. 48–72 (Cambridge: Polity Press).

Parry, J. (2000) The 'Crises of Corruption' and 'The Idea of India': A Worm's-eye View, in I. Pardo (ed.) *Morals of Legitimacy: Between Agency and System*, pp. 27–56 (Oxford: Berghahn Books).

Sampson, S. (1983) Bureaucracy and Corruption as Anthropological Problems: A Case Study from Romania, *Folk*, Vol. 25: 63–96.

Shore, C. (2000) *Building Europe: The Cultural Politics of European Integration* (London: Routledge).   .

Sneath, D. (2002) *Reciprocity, Corruption and the State in Contemporary Mongolia. Understanding Corruption: Anthropological Perspectives* (London: Goldsmiths College).

Taussig, M. (1997) *The Magic of the State* (London: Routledge).

Taylor, C. (1995) *Philosophical Arguments* (Cambridge, MA and London: Harvard University Press).

Visvanathan, S. and H. Sethi (eds) (1998) *Foul Play: Chronicles of Corruption, 1947–97* (New Delhi: Banyan Books).

Wade, R. (1982) The System of Administrative and Political Corruption: Canal Irrigantion in South India, *Journal of Development Studies*, Vol. 18, No. 3: 287–328.

—— (1985) The Market for Public Office: Why the Indian State is Not Better at Development, *World Development*, Vol. 13, No. 4: 467–97.

12 AFTERWORD – ANTHROPOLOGY AND CORRUPTION: THE STATE OF THE ART

Dorothy Louise Zinn

Without doubt the social universes within which disinterestedness is the official norm are not necessarily governed throughout by disinterestedness: behind the appearance of piety, virtue, disinterestedness, there are subtle, camouflaged interests ... [I]t is also among the tasks of a politics of morality to work incessantly toward unveiling hidden difference between official theory and actual practice, between the limelight and the backrooms of political life. (Bourdieu 1998: 87, 144)

Like any scholarly discipline, anthropology is nothing if not a product of the *Zeitgeist* in which it takes its shape and is cultivated. As such, this volume assumes as its timely focus the anthropology of corruption, certainly in part because there is currently a felicitous 'conjuncture', as Steven Sampson puts it, of corruption and anti-corruption discourses within a wider context of globalization, global ethics and neoliberalism. By this, I do not mean to imply that corruption merits our attention simply because of its trendiness as a topic – although such vogue might well be of use for gaining institutional and funding clout. Rather, what emerges from this volume is a picture in which corruption appears – as the editors put it – to somehow be quite fundamentally 'good to think' in our contemporary world. Indeed, on the ethnographic ground, corruption persistently crops up as one of those uncomfortable issues which can upset the well-defined agenda with which the anthropologist has stridden into the field, a weed in the English gardens of research proposals: in case after case, sensitive ethnographers have bracketed their initial research questions in order to pay heed to more insistent concerns regarding corruption amongst the people they work with. Hence, we tend to arrive at corruption through the backdoor (an appropriate metaphor when we recognize the issues of intimacy and secrecy surrounding it). The editors of this volume, Crispin Shore and Dieter Haller, have effectively managed to connect several of these ethnographic dots: by moving corruption to the centre of analysis, they draw together contributions from several different settings and perspectives in order to stimulate thought and theorizing on a broader level.

It is not that anthropology has completely ignored corruption up to now; rather, it received sporadic treatment, mostly under the umbrella of the prodigious anthropology of patronage and clientelism, which historically concentrated on the Mediterranean region and on peasant societies of Latin America and Asia, often in connection with development studies. Spanning from the 1950s to the 1970s, with peaks in the 1960s and late 1970s, the work on patronage focused on many of the issues which have now resurfaced under the heading of 'corruption': these include personalism, informal networks, moral codes (such as honour, familism and reciprocity), friendship, nepotism and mafia. Anthropological research of this sort was generally conducted in unindustrialized rural villages which featured a great social and economic disparity between the landowning elites and the peasant masses. Patron–client relations were described as multi-stranded, dyadic relations between individuals of unequal social standing: in Pitt-Rivers' famous expression, a 'lop-sided friendship' which benefited both parties (Pitt-Rivers 1961); this schema was also complemented by the analytical categories of 'mediators' and 'brokers'. Even so, the emphasis on the rural village generally downplayed patronage on wider, supralocal levels, especially within government, and the characterization of the unequal patron–client dyad hid from view other significant forms, such as cronyism among equals or elite nepotism. At the same time, an academic division of labour was consolidated whereby political scientists focused on the 'political' side of corruption as a problem of the implementation and functioning of democratic institutions in 'complex' societies – especially phenomena of cronyism, bossism and electoral machines – devoting little if any attention to the issues which traditionally attracted the interest of anthropologists of patronage (though Scott's contribution [Scott 1972] was an early attempt to straddle the divide).

As I have suggested elsewhere (Zinn 2001), after the last heyday of patronage studies in the late 1970s, settings once most closely identified with patronage in the literature seemed to have lost interest for such analysis. And yet, despite the fact that many of the societies which were once the object of ethnographic study have now joined the ranks of the 'developed' (however 'imperfectly developed' they might appear to some observers), many of the features of social interaction which in the past were marked as 'patronage' have, in fact, persisted in the present. In effect, a discursive transformation has taken place, in which the most negative features of these social interactions are now described as 'corruption', which has itself become an important heuristic device for the analysis of 'problematic' development or persistent underdevelopment. On the other hand, in recent years numerous corruption scandals in governments and corporations throughout the West have brought home the point that corruption is by no means limited to 'the Rest'. Thus, with regard to some areas corruption would seem to have substituted or updated older patronage practices, while in other areas where it was previously ignored, its existence is now recognized, at least to the point of constituting an object of study: for these reasons, in my view, a fresh anthropological perspective on corruption has long been overdue.

The contributions in this volume bear the influence of a number of trends in anthropology which have emerged in recent decades following the ebbing of interest in prior patronage studies, changes in the discipline which clearly affect the approach to corruption, both epistemologically and methodologically. Earlier in the history of the discipline, the anthropologist represented a privileged world within the most privileged societies, bringing a 'top-down' focus to bear on the study of colonized or dominated groups. Now, instead, we finally acting on Laura Nader's call to 'study up' (Nader 1972), especially in the wake of important works like Marcus (1999): in MacLennan's and Shore's chapters, we see an attention to elites which would have been nearly unthinkable some 20 years ago. If, in the eyes of many, anthropology once distinguished itself from sociology for studying 'primitive' or 'simple' societies, through the issue of corruption the chapters in this volume offer a critical anthropology of bureaucracy (pioneered by the work of Michael Herzfeld [1992]), and similarly, an attention to the construction, both institutional and rhetorical, of the modern nation-state and citizenship (for example, the European Union in Shore; the chapters by Dracklé, Gupta and Lazar). The authors have also sought to apply anthropological analysis to ongoing developments in the ethnographic present, related to processes and effects of post-Cold War transitions (Lovell, Zerilli, Rivkin-Fish, the Schneiders); the comprehension of globalization, and together with it, massive new corruption scandals (MacLennan), but also the new anti-corruption and anti-mafia movements which have emerged (Sampson; Schneider and Schneider). In this context, corruption poses a particular methodological challenge for its very nature, adverse to being registered, and for its striking discursive presence. For an anthropological investigation of corruption, then, it is necessary to employ not only the standard items in ethnography's tool-kit – ritual, symbolism, performance, values and social structure – but also more recently honed instruments for the analysis of daily life, representation, discourse, narrativity and social poetics.

Having said all this, it remains for me to clarify what might be the actual contributions of this anthropology of corruption, and how they could differ from those of other disciplines. As Scott has pointed out, each discipline approaching corruption will see it in its own terms, positing research questions and answers according to its own perspective and interests (Scott 1972: 2). Just as the literature on patronage has devoted an great deal of attention to definitional debates regarding 'What is patronage?' (cf. Gellner and Waterbury 1977, and a more recent review in Lenclud 2001), the academic discourse on corruption has treated at length the definitional problem of what may or may not be considered corruption (see the Introduction by Shore and Haller). Many non-anthropologist scholars have noted the problem of creating a definition which has cross-cultural validity, and they have argued in favour of a sensitivity to the differing cultural contexts in which corruption is studied (Lovell, in this volume; Rose-Ackerman 1999). Still, it would clearly be politically undesirable to delimit moral relativism to the point that it becomes an excuse or justification for corruption. Moreover, an excessive deference to 'cultural difference' runs the risk of essentialism and reification, for 'they' and 'their culture' would appear inevitably, incorrigibly corrupt (cf. Zerilli, this volume). Instead, having left behind a former era of anthropology in which 'cultures' were often portrayed as rather static, organic, homogeneous wholes, ethnographic works such as those featured in this volume have been devoted to creating a dynamic, nuanced rendering of cultural meaning and ambiguities, including the disagreements and contradictions within a culture. As several of the chapters here show, cultural meanings can be shared, but they are not totalizing, nor are they without contestation.

In an earlier, groundbreaking work in the ethnography of corruption, Akhil Gupta (1995) noted that precisely such cultural consensus and contestation are closely linked to issues of subjectivity, positionality and situatedness. The heterogeneity of people's evaluations of corruption and their often complex attitudes towards it are related to their subject position(s). In this sense, corruption can be examined on multiple levels in its close connection with issues of identity, one of the key concerns of anthropology in the last two decades: identity as both a process and sentiment of belonging and of 'othering'. By recuperating these aspects, anthropology tells us things that a *Homo economicus* perspective on corruption, alone, cannot. For example, in terms of personhood, corruption can create distinction and exclusion, as Dracklé's example of the 'toilet key man' demonstrates, drawing attention to a symbolic capital which might not figure in other readings of corruption. In Rivkin-Fish's chapter, too, a sense of personal identity, more than economic gain, is central to understanding physicians' informal exchanges with their patients. Corruption can be a way of emerging from 'anonymity', whether as a citizen in Soviet Russia or as a citizen in a state whose functioning is closer to the rational-universal Weberian ideal, or even in the impersonal marketplace. All over the globe, as ethnographic work has vividly depicted, 'having relations' (as Zerilli's informants put it) can guarantee privileged treatment even without resorting to an overt bribe or other illegal acts. The symbolic capital of connections, like economic capital, can be used to create status hierarchies of personhood, but these are not always strictly functional in terms of material gain or instrumental ends. Of course, we again come up against the definitional problem as to what extent we should consider 'influence' and connections as constituting 'corruption' proper, but the fact is, we cannot extricate such social practice and connectedness from a poetics of self and society. This re-presentation of self – which refuses an identical identity, the anonymity of universal citizenship and the impersonality of the ideal liberal marketplace – can be voiced through existing relations, obtained by virtue of family status or class privilege, or by entering into cronyist networks. Where such relations are lacking, however, they may be created and consolidated through the use of gifts and bribes. If social sanctions are muted, it may be the case that corrupt practices, with the illicit gain and wielding of power they accrue, also enhance personal symbolic capital in the status hierarchy.

Together with this re-presentation of self, corruption is bound up with a sense of identity on other levels; indeed, Herzfeld (1997) cites corruption as an important site of what he has termed the 'cultural intimacy' which is a part of group identity, be it on a local or national level. As several authors in this volume demonstrate, corruption requires not only complicity and trust, but also shared knowledge, a shared language; even those who choose not to 'play the game', as Bourdieu would put it, nonetheless know its rules and its stakes. Here, the ethnographic material helps us to tease out meanings of 'gift' and 'bribe' – whose definitions, like that of corruption itself, are problematic. Both the gift and the bribe are used to cement ambivalent relations (cf. Herzfeld 1992), yet as Rivkin-Fish demonstrates, their moral connotations can shift from one context to another even within the same ethnographic setting. In MacLennan's chapter on corporate corruption in America, corrupt behaviour is not defined emically as such by the actors, but rather is normalized by their shared practices and culture as members of the corporate social group. While, in many contexts, corruption can take on the connotations of a shared 'dirty secret', drawing together the group in its complicity, corruption discourse – and in particular corruption accusations – emerges as a boundary marker for identity, where the accusers position themselves as morally righteous, and the accused are variously branded as 'outsiders' (Shore's and Drackléʼs examples) or, in an orientalist fashion (Said 1978), as 'chaotic' others in need of the paternalistic intervention of those who presumably behave better (Sampson). Where the state itself is the object of corruption critique, the citizens define themselves in their collective identity as a moral group (Gupta 1995, and in this volume; Lazar, Rivkin-Fish).

Corruption, then, is not simply a matter of forming and setting into motion 'interpersonal networks' (Rose-Ackerman 1999: 106), but instead it enters into a complex construction of identity on multiple supralocal levels. This is cogently exemplified in Shore's description of the European Commission: created with the aim of fostering a European identity which would supersede previous, 'anachronistic' national identities, the European Commission has, on the contrary, given rise to new forms of particularism and privilege not unlike ethnic identity, and within this particularism, nesting dolls of various 'mafias' (as one informant put it) based, once again, on common belonging. In other cases, we see how corruption figures into local and national identity through processes of 'ethno-orientalism' (Carrier 1992): if Western societies have often described non-Westerners in 'orientalist', essentialized terms counterposed to supposedly Western characteristics, ethno-orientalism instead refers to the 'essentialist renderings of alien societies by the members of those societies themselves' (1992: 198). For instance, Zerilli discusses how corruption figures in a discourse of Romanian national identity, which embraces elements of 'othering' related to Communist and Ottoman pasts and the Gypsy minority of the present, while simultaneously making reference to an essential 'Romanian' identity. Likewise, we may consider how the Portuguese link corruption to their self-description as the northernmost country of 'Africa' or as a First World/Third World hybrid (Dracklé's chapter); or, in my own work on Southern Italy, discourses of patronage, corruption and mafia in the Northern/ Southern question are replicated on the national level as a difference between 'Mediterranean' or 'Southern European' Italy and Northern Europe/North America (Zinn 2001).

What is at stake for those who are included or excluded and for those who are doing the including and excluding? Issues of identity in corruption have very much to do with relations of power – another central concern of contemporary anthropological inquiry. Here again, Gupta's earlier work (Gupta 1995) drew attention to just such questions of power with specific regard to corruption. As with identity, these relations of power must be considered on multiple levels: be it in the local political arena (the chapters by Lazar and the Schneiders), in relations between local and central government (as in Dracklé's case), a national level (MacLennan) or in the international arena (Shore, Sampson); and as Zerilli's work indicates, there is a ongoing slippage between these various levels. Crucially, too, we must consider how social science itself is implicated in this web of power relations: since the earlier period of anthropological studies of patronage, critical reflection on our analytical categories, our relation to the subjects of our study, and the potential power effects of social science discourse has become a necessary feature of the discipline. Thus, with regard to corruption, it is not enough to take note of cultural differences which might have explanatory purchase: it is necessary to question the very bases, often ethnocentric, from which cultural difference is adjudicated. This can be seen, for example, in the notions of 'state', 'civil society' and 'citizenship', not to mention the 'public/private' distinction, variously problematized by the interpretations we find on the ethnographic ground presented in this volume. As MacLennan observes, the very term 'democracy' cannot be used unreflexively as a cipher for the uncorrupt, for in the most established, mature democracies we are still faced with problems of campaign financing, lobbies and conflicts of interest. Indeed, the very concept of representation in democracy risks pitting the 'particular' interests of one represented group against another group or the wider collectivity: one may consider pork-barrel projects which satisfy local interests as one example, or – and most poignantly for present-day concerns with the environment and militarism – the single interest of one or a few nations as pitted against the interest of the global community. Indeed, Herzfeld (1992) points out how family and local particularisms are reproduced on a national level, employing kinship and domesticity metaphors at the heart of the state; though it may seem paradoxical, nationalism and patronage are, in effect, 'cut from the same cloth' (1992: 78), and I would argue that the same applies for nationalism and corruption as particularist, anti-universalist phenomena. By probing the particular, ethnocentric categories through which corruption is analysed, we should recall Bourdieu's 'interest in disinterestedness' (Bourdieu 1998: 60), a question Sampson so rightly raises for the world of anti-corruption and its 'projectization'. Nor should we forget our own stakes in the lofty world of academics, as Dracklé recounts his German colleagues' suggestion that he study corruption in their own departmental setting.

By levelling the moral playing field with this *mea culpa*, then, is it possible or heuristically useful to say that we are all equally corrupt? Or should we retain Lovell's distinction between settings of 'endemic' and 'incidental' corruption, despite the critique of it as set forth by Zerilli? While Lovell clearly recognizes that corruption takes place in established liberal democracies, he argues that their citizens continue to perceive the public sector as predominantly uncorrupt, whereas inhabitants of 'endemically' corrupt societies suffer no such illusion. Yet in the heart of the United States, as the Schneiders show, decades of corruption and organized crime have produced deep frustration and mistrust among members of the Youngstown Citizens' Group, sentiments which seem anything but an unshaken faith in an 'incidentally corrupt' state. Does this mean that places like Youngstown could be enclaves of 'endemic' corruption within 'incidentally' corrupt settings?

Perhaps the discussion over the endemic/incidental division in corruption analyses is actually a red herring. As several of the chapters argue, the division may certainly be questionable from an etic point of view. The real distinction, as Lovell seems to imply, is in the perception of legitimacy and trust in the state on an *emic* level, precisely the level which is particularly amenable to anthropological investigation. It is not enough for us, then, to simply reveal the existence of corruption in the West, so as to dismount Western observers from an ethnocentric high horse; rather, the very epistemological bases of the entire universalist discourse must be examined for their own ethnocentricity. Once a reflexive self-awareness of this has been achieved, we need to ask, together with Bourdieu, how successfully this universalizing ideology, itself duly historicized and deconstructed, has universalized itself (cf. Bourdieu 1998: 90, 120). This can be measured to some degree in the globalization of anti-corruption discourse (Sampson), but especially by looking at how, on the ground, these universalizing discourses are taken on, never *in toto*, but hybridized and re-articulated. On this point, I find the works of Shore, MacLennan and Rivkin-Fish particularly exciting, for they document the transformation of previously existing strategies, values and meanings with new practices and institutions, which may or may not be read as corruption. Some of the other chapters in the volume may have benefited from a more extensive historical contextualization in order to help us understand the current corruption discourse vis-à-vis its other face: the unmarked, taken-for-granted universalist discourse which has inevitably – but not invariantly – emerged in each setting. We get tantalizing hints of this, for example, if we consider how in some ethnographic settings, 'civil society' is held to be purer than the 'really corrupt' state bureaucracies– a problem which Rivkin-Fish treats skilfully. Or, in Lazar's Bolivian case, there is a level of corruption which is somehow thought to be reasonable or even appropriate; if we were to perform a cross-cultural survey, I suspect that her informant's comment that a politician 'steals, but at least he does something' would turn out to be more widely held than we might think. Relatedly, in Gupta's chapter, actors deploy differing narratives to argue that corruption in development programmes is 'better' under government officials or under village headmen. In the Schneider's piece, the Republican Party county chair who described Tony Cafaro as 'very public-minded, public-spirited' is performing an interesting reconfiguration of the Weberian ideal: here, cronyistic interpersonal relations as institutionalized in the 'Cafaro roundtable' are constructed as a true site of ethical, universalist behaviour.

The sphere of market rationality, too, can be another site which points to a hybrid appropriation of the universalist discourse. In some instances, such as in the Romanian case cited in Zerilli, the use of a bribe can be a way of rationalizing the system, perceived as a way of increasing its efficiency, paradoxically, to obtain justice. Similarly, in my own work in the Southern Italian context (Zinn 2001), the use of money has increasingly complemented and transformed, even commodified, pre-existing forms like *raccomandazioni* (recommendations) based on interpersonal relations. Money is often used where there is not a particular social relationship between the actors, and it is thought to be more effective and efficient than a mere 'good word' put in, thereby yielding the hybrid category of the 'purchased *raccomandazione*', not always held to be synonymous with *tangente* (bribe). Nor should we ignore how mafia, in its various forms, has effectively combined personalism and acute market rationality, even while it subverts formal rational-legal operations in the state sphere.

The reflexive attention to our own categories and the study of power and identity are by no means the only ways in which an anthropology of corruption can benefit from wider developments in contemporary anthropology; among such developments, however, it must be noted that few analyses have availed themselves of the category of gender. I have argued elsewhere with regard to patronage (Zinn 2001, 2003) that gender analyses have much to say about many of the key points raised in the new corruption literature, and not just because we are often talking about 'good ole' boy' networks (or, perhaps nowadays, even 'good ole' girls', if we can cite the example of Edith Cresson from Shore's chapter). In effect, by examining early on the cultural construction of gender, feminist theorists were among the first to critically interrogate the public/private-domestic distinction (Rosaldo 1974), which happens to be quite central to the anthropological indictment of ethnocentricity in scholarly discourse on corruption and anti-corruption. Indeed, feminist philosophers and political scientists have dialogued with concepts such as Habermas's notion of the public sphere in ways that might be quite suggestive for the analysis of corruption (for example, the contributions in Meehan 1995); and feminist scholars have pointed out how the very consolidation of universalistic ideologies of rights and the new bourgeois subjectivity which accompanied them were premised upon the gendered exclusion of women (cf. Landes 1995). And, too, the debate over Carol Gilligan's influential work on the development of moral reasoning (Gilligan 1982) is relevant: whether or not one agrees with or reinterprets Gilligan's feminine-associated 'ethic of care' – as opposed to a strict, masculine-associated, context-free, rule-bound morality – we cannot ignore it by merely pointing to 'alternative cultural codes' or 'conflicting moral imperatives'.

Having treated above the question of identity, moreover, we must consider the *gendered* dimension of this identity. Lazar's example of the corrupt Bolivian mayor who 'lost his masculinity' is an intriguing case in point which cries out for further analysis: is corruption used, as patronage was in the past in many so-called 'honour-and-shame' societies, in a game of masculine posturing and identity enhancement? If so, what are the effects of this on local power dynamics? In Lazar's example, does the mayor's loss of masculine reputation imply another dimension of local accountability, and what is its relationship to local 'gender hegemonies' (cf. Ortner 1990)? And what could it mean, as the Schneiders have written elsewhere (Schneider and Schneider 2001), that the anti-mafia movement in Palermo can be characterized as 'feminist' and 'green' (and thus close to 'female' nature), as opposed to the corruption-ridden 'hyper-masculine' construction industry? As for the corporate world of the US described by MacLennan, famously a bastion of male privilege, it might be worth examining a possible gendered dimension to the recent conviction of homemaking icon Martha Stewart on charges of obstructing justice and lying to investigators.

The potential interest of gender is all the more apparent if we consider corruption discourse's 'othering' function: as many of the contributions here have pointed out, corruption discourse has often been deployed in an 'orientalist' fashion, but gender theory could be brought to bear in understanding the full import of the fact that, as Herzfeld puts it, 'orientalist discourses feminize the populations they purport to describe' (Herzfeld 1997: 97). The masculine/feminine dichotomy has clear implications for several recurring homologies in corruption discourse: rational/irrational, public/private, culture/nature, universal/particular. And if rational impersonality and rule-following are contrasted with 'feminine' personalism and unruly dis-order, we easily pass to dissolute, feminine corruptness, with Eve as its archetype, a female pollution of the public body, which also violates the nostalgic view of a pristine, uncorrupt past cited in many of the chapters (for example, in Zerilli).

Alongside gender, I think it is essential that we recuperate class as an analytical category in the anthropology of corruption. Indeed, as James C. Scott noted, 'Much of what we consider as corruption is simply the "uninstitutionalized" influence of wealth in a political system', and its effects with regard to a society's class structure are highly conservative (Scott 1972: ix, 33). While MacLennan's chapter explicitly treats the issue of corruption in terms of class privilege, this thread remains more muted in most of the other pieces, although provocative hints emerge throughout. True, as the Schneiders point out, those who are in subaltern class positions more often bear the stigma of labels associated to corruption; whereas business and political elites can make use of connection capital (as in cronyism or *blat* in the new Russia; see Lovell's chapter), ordinary citizens may feel compelled to resort to overt forms of bribery which are more visible and often punished more consistently. In the Schneiders' comparative analysis, the histories of organized crime in both Youngstown and Palermo are closely related to marked class inequalities and the development of class relations in their respective capitalist societies; in an earlier article (Schneider and Schneider 2001), they describe how the working class can actually be penalized by the anti-mafia movement. More work needs to be done on class, but it might very well be that striking class differentials and the status hierarchies associated with them actually play a role as both causes and effects of corruption in given settings. For this reason – although this is just an unsubstantiated hunch – I suspect that it is no coincidence that Canada and the Scandinavian countries, which consistently seem to feature the least corruption on various indices, are nations which stress egalitarian social policies.

CONCLUSION

In the final part of his chapter, Sampson states that just as with issues like human rights, researchers of corruption tend to become involved in anti-corruption activity. As engaged as we are as anthropologists, our contribution to the study of corruption certainly cannot offer pat solutions valid for every setting. The authors in this volume show us how the reception and re-elaboration of (not to mention resistance to) Western models varies greatly from one setting to another, even within the West itself. The locally grounded information provided through ethnography provides an understanding of how anti-corruption measures are received, and what might be the most effective mechanisms of accountability and institutional reform to curb corruption's excesses. Though following and enforcing 'the rules' is undoubtedly of importance, nonetheless, in light of Rivkin-Fish's material, for example – where official channels themselves are viewed as ethically problematic and unjust – it would be naïve to rely wholly on such an approach. A nuanced, critical anthropology of corruption shows us that though there may be different cultural codes and meanings, people on the ground are indeed critical and, however subaltern they may be, hold corruption to account. For example, the notion of 'preemptive accountability', in the Bolivian context studied by Lazar, points to one local anti-corruption mechanism for which institutional reinforcements might be studied.

Bribery and corruption are certainly widespread and difficult to quantify, but the anthropological contribution goes beyond registering the actual presence of these phenomena: the discourse on corruption, as Dracklé notes, may even exaggerate 'the facts'. Thus we have an ideological dimension on the *emic* level of the perception of corruption, which may or may not correspond to the objective data of the situation, but for this reason we should not imagine that it does not bear its own real effects. Indeed, Gupta's ambitious call for intervention on the narratives of corruption recognizes the far-reaching extent of this ideological dimension. In some contexts, where the state appears delegitimized by a widespread perception of corruption, the phenomenon may be further encouraged or justified in citizens' eyes as a 'necessary' form of self-defence. This perception, coupled with the weakened state monopoly on violence that we see where mafia is present, can pose a great challenge for the democratic ideal.

Finally, the liberal bourgeois 'public/private' distinction, which allows for public equality and private inequality, works to mask implicit forms of privilege, be they of class, gender or ethnicity. This privilege may constitute more or less visible cronyism, as revealed in MacLennan's chapter, which in effect is not so different from traditionalist, particularistic loyalties of a neo-patrimonialist or 'endemically corrupt' setting. And hence we return to the question of the wider dynamics of power, on various levels – locally, nationally, transnationally, globally – but always mindful of the 'interest of disinterestedness'.

REFERENCES

Bourdieu, P. (1998) *Practical Reason* (Stanford, CA: Stanford University Press [orig. ed. *Raisons Pratiques*, Éditions du Seuil, 1994]).

Carrier, J.G. (1992) Occidentalism: The World Turned Upside-Down, *American Ethnologist*, Vol. 19, No. 2: 195–212.

Gellner, E. and J. Waterbury (eds) (1977) *Patrons and Clients in Mediterranean Societies* (London: Duckworth).

Gilligan, C. (1982) *In a Different Voice* (Cambridge, MA: Harvard University Press).

Gupta, A. (1995) Blurred Boundaries: The Discourse of Corruption, the Culture of Politics, and the Imagined State, *American Ethnologist*, Vol. 22, No. 2: 375–402.

Herzfeld M. (1992) *The Social Production of Indifference: Exploring the Symbolic Roots of Western Bureaucracy* (Chicago: University of Chicago Press).

—— (1997) *Cultural Intimacy: Social Poetics in the Nation-state* (New York: Routledge).

Landes, J.B. (1995) The Public and the Private Sphere: A Feminist Reconsideration, in J. Meehan (ed.) *Feminists Read Habermas: Gendering the Subject of Discourse*, pp. 91–116 (New York: Routledge).

Lenclud, G. (2001) Le Patronage politique: Du contexte au raisons, in D. Albera, A. Blok and C. Bromberger (eds) *Anthropologie de la Méditerranée/ Anthropology of the Mediterranean*, pp. 277–306 (Paris: Maissoneuve et Larose).

Marcus, G. (ed.) (1999) *Critical Anthropology Now: Unexpected Contexts, Shifting Constituencies, Changing Agendas* (Santa Fe: School of American Research).

Meehan, J. (ed.) (1995) *Feminists Read Habermas: Gendering the Subject of Discourse* (New York: Routledge).

Nader, L. (1972) Up the Anthropologist – Perspectives Gained from Studying Up, in D. Hymes (ed.) *Reinventing Anthropology*, pp. 284–311 (New York: Pantheon).

Ortner, S.B. (1990) Gender Hegemonies, *Cultural Critique*, Vol. 14 (Winter): 35–80.

Pitt-Rivers, J.A. (1961) *The People of the Sierra* (Chicago: University of Chicago Press).

Rosaldo, M.Z. (1974) Women, Culture and Society: A Theoretical Overview, in M. Rosaldo and L. Lamphere (eds) *Women, Culture and Society* (Stanford, CA: Stanford University Press).

Rose-Ackerman, S. (1999) *Corruption and Government: Causes, Consequences, and Reform* (New York: Cambridge University Press).

Said, E. (1978) *Orientalism* (New York: Vintage Books).

Schneider, J. and P. Schneider (2001) Rethinking *Clientelismo*: A Challenge from Antimafia Palermo, in D. Albera, A. Blok and C. Bromberger (eds) *Anthropologie de la Méditerranée/Anthropology of the Mediterranean*, pp. 307–29 (Paris: Maissoneuve et Larose).

Scott, J.C. (1972) *Comparative Political Corruption* (Englewood Cliffs, NJ: Prentice Hall).

Zinn, D.L. (2001) *La Raccomandazione* (Rome: Donzelli Editore).

—— (2003) Engendering Patronage: Economies of the Masculine and the Feminine and (Southern) Italy as 'Other', *Europaea* 9 (1–2): 151–71.

CONTRIBUTORS

Dorle Dracklé is Professor of Social Anthropology and Intercultural Studies at the University of Bremen, Germany. Her current fieldwork in Portugal focuses on elites, corruption, economy and the European Union. She is also interested in media, science and technology studies, economy, politics and policy, and the teaching and learning of anthropology. Recent publications include: *The Rhetorics of Crisis: On the Cultural Poetics of Politics, Bureaucracy and Virtual Economy in Southern Portugal* (in German, 2004), *Current Policies and Practices in European Social Anthropology Education* (ed. with Iain Edgar, 2004), *Educational Histories of European Social Anthropology* (ed. with Iain Edgar and Thomas Schippers, 2003), *Images of Death* (in German, ed., 2001); and various articles, among others on media anthropology, multicultural media, life course, and suicide.

Akhil Gupta is associate professor of anthropology at Stanford University, California. His research interests are currently focused on a project on the ethnography of the state in India and environmental history. He is the author of *Postcolonial Developments: Agriculture in the Making of Modern India* (1998) and co-editor of several books including *Caste and Outcast* (with Gordon Chang and Purnima Mankekar, 2002), *Anthropological Locations: Boundaries and Grounds of a Field Science* (1997) and *Culture, Power, Place: Explorations in Critical Anthropology* (1997) (both with James Ferguson).

Dieter Haller (PhD 1991 Heidelberg, Habil. 1999 Frankfurt/Oder), cultural and social anthropologist, is Adjunct Associate Professor at the Department of Germanic Studies at the University of Texas/ Austin. He has worked as Guest Professor in Frankfurt/Main (2000), Hamburg (2001), Granada (2002) and as Theodor-Heuss Lecturer at New School University/New York (2003). His main fields of interest are port cities, borderlands, diaspora, ethnicity, Gibraltar, Spain and the Mediterranean. His latest publications are a monograph on Gibraltar (*Gelebte Grenze Gibraltar*, Wiesbaden: Deutscher Universitätsverlag, 2000), a special issue of *Ethnologia Europaea* on 'Border Anthropology' (co-edited with Hastings Donnan, 2000), an introduction to cultural anthropology (*DTV-Atlas zur Ethnologie*, München, forthcoming 2004/05)

Sian Lazar is currently Research Officer at the Centre for Latin American Studies, University of Cambridge. She completed her PhD at Goldsmiths College, London University, with a thesis on citizenship, personhood and political agency among rural–urban migrants in El Alto, Bolivia. She is co-author, with Maxine Molyneux, of *Doing the Rights Thing: Rights-based Development and Latin American NGOs* (ITDG Publishing, London, 2003).

David W. Lovell is an Associate Professor in Politics and currently Acting Rector of the University of New South Wales at the Australian Defence Force Academy. During the early 1990s, he edited the *Political Theory Newsletter*, and was managing editor of the *Australian Journal of Political Science*. In 1992, he was the Australian Parliamentary Political Science Fellow, and since 1993 he has been a member of the Executive Committee of the International Society for the Study of European Ideas, and is on the editorial board of its journal, *The European Legacy*. In 2001, he was part of the Australian government's delegation to The Hague for the Second Global Forum on Fighting Corruption and Safeguarding Integrity. His books include *From Marx to Lenin* (1984); *Marx's Proletariat* (1988); *The Theory of Politics* (co-authored, 1991); *The Transition from Socialism* (co-edited, 1992); *Marxism and Australian Socialism* (1997); *The Australian Political System* (co-authored, 1998); *The Transition: Evaluating the Postcommunist Experience* (ed., 2002); and *Asia-Pacific Security: Policy Challenges* (ed., 2003).

Carol MacLennan is an anthropologist at Michigan Tech University. Previously she worked in the US Department of Transportation on automotive regulation. She has published articles on government regulation, corporate influence in democratic decision-making, and industrial communities, and is a co-author of *The State and Democracy: Revitalizing America's Government* (with Mark Levine, Charles Noble and John Kushma, Routledge & Kegan Paul, 1988). She is currently completing writing projects on the history of corporate control over the landscapes of sugar and mining communities.

Michele Rivkin-Fish is Assistant Professor of Anthropology at the University of Kentucky. Her work examines gender, health and health care, reproductive politics, and international development in Russia. Her research has been published in the journals *American Anthropologist, Social Science and Medicine*, and *Culture, Medicine, and Psychiatry*.

Steven Sampson is a social anthropologist at the University of Lund, with research and consulting experience in Romania, Albania, Bosnia and Kosovo. His work focuses on the role of NGOs and civil society, on 'project life' in developmental contexts, and on democracy export. His current project concerns the anti-corruption movement in the Balkans.

Jane Schneider teaches anthropology at the City University of New York Graduate Center. She is the co-editor, with Annette B. Weiner, of *Cloth and Human Experience* (1987), and the author of several essays on cloth and clothing. Her anthropological field research has been in Sicily and has led to three books, co-authored with Peter Schneider: *Culture and Political Economy in Western Sicily* (1976); *Festival of the Poor: Fertility Decline and the Ideology of Class in Sicily* (1996); and *Reversible Destiny: Mafia, Antimafia and the Struggle for Palermo* (forthcoming). In 1998, she edited *Italy's Southern Question; Orientalism in One Country*.

Peter Schneider teaches sociology at Fordham University. He is co-author, with Jane Schneider, of *Culture and Political Economy in Western Sicily* (1976); *Festival of the Poor: Fertility Decline and the Ideology of Class in Sicily* (1996); and *Reversible Destiny: Mafia, Antimafia and the Struggle for Palermo* (forthcoming). He is pursuing his interests in organized crime and criminalization through research on Youngstown, Ohio, and as a founding member of a new section on these issues at the New York Academy of Sciences.

Cris Shore is professor of anthropology at the University of Auckland, New Zealand. He is co-editor, with Stephen Nugent, of *Anthropology of Elites* (2002) and *Anthropology and Cultural Studies* (1997), with Susan Wright, of *Anthropology of Policy* (1997) and with Akbar Ahmed of *The Future of Anthropology* (1995). His work focuses on issues in political anthropology, policy and governance. He has carried out anthropological fieldwork in Italy, from which he wrote *Italian Communism: The Escape from Lenin* (1990), and more recently among EU civil servants in Brussels, which led to the book *Building Europe: The Cultural Politics of European Integration* (2000). His current interest is in the politics of accountability and the rise of 'audit culture'.

Filippo M. Zerilli is currently researcher and lecturer at the University of Cagliari where he teaches cultural anthropology. He also teaches ethnographic research methods at the University of Perugia. Since 1996 he has been conducting extensive fieldwork in Romania exploring privatization and property issues. His main research interests include the history of anthropology, postsocialism, ethnography of law and human rights, changing property relations, the emotional and moral dimension of ownership claims. Among his publications are: *Il lato oscuro dell'etnologia* (CISU: Rome, 1998), and the edited collection *Dalle 'Regole' al 'Suicidio': Percorsi durkheimiani* (Argo: Lecce, 2001). He is the co-editor of *Incontri di etnologia europea. European Ethnology Meetings* (Edizioni Scientifiche Italiane: Naples,

1998), and of *La ricerca antropologica in Romania: Prospettive storiche ed etnografiche* (Edizioni Scientifiche Italiane: Naples, 2003). He is presently preparing a book focusing on the property restitution debates in postsocialist Romania.

Dorothy Louise Zinn (PhD in Social-Cultural Anthropology at the University of Texas at Austin) is an independent scholar and adjunct instructor at the Università degli Studi della Basilicata. Her areas of interest include political economy, patronage, immigration and multiculturalism. Along with numerous academic articles, she has published the volume *La Raccomandazione* (Rome: Donzelli, 2001), which was awarded the Pitré Prize for anthropological works. Dr Zinn's other professional activities include anthropological translation and collaboration with the award-winning Associazione Tolbà (<www.associazionetolba.org>) to assist immigrants and promote intercultural dialogue.

INDEX

Compiled by Sue Carlton

Abramovici, P. 66
accountability 19, 103–4, 105, 108,
    123, 129, 133
    EU and 132, 139, 142–3, 146,
    147–8
    'pre-emptive' 212, 219
aid organizations
    and aid conditionality 116
    at Prague conference 114
    fight against corruption 105, 108,
    112, 120
Alentejo, corruption narratives
    194–210
amiguismo 201–2, 205
Amnesty International 119
Anderson, Benedict 134
Andreasen, Marta 147–8, 149
anti-corruption community 105,
    107
anti-corruption discourse 10, 18–19,
    83, 111–12, 132
anti-corruption movement 103–29,
    231
    as 'a world' 110–13, 127
    anthropology of 103–6, 126–9
    and donors 129
    global civil society 103, 105–6,
    113, 117–23, 127
    globalization of 103–4, 106–7,
    127, 236
    and grants 109–10, 122
    and innocence 127, 128–9
    international conferences 113–17
    Romanian example 123–6
    studying 107–9, 127–8
    see also Transparency
    International (TI)
Anti-Corruption Summit 2000
    (Arlington) 117
anti-mafia movement 29, 40, 45,
    231, 238
Anti-Saloon League 32–3

Antitrust Division, Justice
    Department 162
Argentina 10
Arlacchi, P. 8
arms manufacturers, and 'offsets' 19
Arthur Andersen 1–2, 3, 10, 104,
    114, 157, 159
Australia, corruption investigations
    65–6

bacsis (tip) 94–5
Badawai, Abdullah Ahmad 66
Bahujan Samaj Party 190
Bailey, F.G. 176, 183, 185–6, 187,
    188, 189
Balkans
    anti-corruptionism 108, 121, 122,
    123, 126
    see also Romania
Banfield, Edward 3
Bank of Commerce and Credit
    International (BCCI) 10
Bayart, J.-F. 223
Bayley, D.H. 4
Beck, U. 133
Belgium 10
Belice Valley 36
Bellier, I. 136
Berlusconi, Silvio 4
Berthelot, René 143
Bertsch, G.K. 72
Bhatti, Jaspal 173
'Bimbes and Bimbos' scandal 11
Bisipara 183, 185–6, 187
Blanc, Jacques 138
blat 53, 59, 62, 71, 73, 76
Bolivia 212–28
    and corruption talk/rumour 6,
    212, 216–19, 223–5
    and *Juntas* 214–19, 221, 223, 224
    and *obras* (public works) 212,
    214, 215, 220–3

Bolivia *continued*
  perceptions of corruption 212,
    216–18
  and political corruption 213–14,
    216–20, 221, 222–3, 224–5
  wages to civil servants 223–4
Borsellino, Paolo 40
Bossano, Joe 12–13
Bourdieu, Pierre 110, 229, 233, 235,
    236
Bribe-Payers Index (BPI) 119
bribery 7, 48–9, 53, 68, 78
  bribe-giving/bribe-taking
    distinction 86–8, 95–6
  and gift-giving 8, 16–17, 58–60
  repairing injustice 89, 92, 237
Buitenen, Paul Van 146, 147, 148–9
bureaucracy 3, 4, 131, 176, 205, 213
  EU and 137–8, 146
  in postcommunist states 74–5
  Romania 123, 124
  Soviet 72–3, 74
bureaucrats 175, 213
  and corruption narratives 176,
    183–8, 195
Burnham, James 73
Buzau 124

Cafaro, Anthony 43, 44, 236
Cafaro family 42–3
Cafaro, J.J. 44
Cafaro Roundtable 43, 45, 237
Câmaras 198, 199, 202–4, 205–6
Cameroon 223
Campbell Works, Youngstown 33,
    34
Canada 69
capacity-building 119, 122
Carrier, James 168
Catholic Church 75
  scandals in 2–3
Cayman Islands 14
Cheney, Dick 166
China 17, 106, 114
Chirac, Jacques 65
Chowdhury, Mr 177–81
Christian Democratic (CDU) party
    (Germany) 6, 11, 150
Christian Democratic Party (Italy)
    31–2, 37
citizenship capacity 214, 221, 224

civil society 79, 125, 129, 236
  role of Bolivian *Juntas* 214–16
  see also global civil society
Clark, W.A. 71–2
clientelism 5, 7, 12, 17, 37, 76, 143,
    146, 201, 224, 230
coalition-building 113, 115, 116,
    120, 123, 127
Cohen, A. 66
Committee of Independent Experts
    (CIE) 132, 142, 146, 147
Committee of the Regions (CoR)
    138
Communist Party (Italy) 32
Communist Party (PCP) (Portugal)
    200, 205, 207
Conciencia de Patria (Condepa)
    221–2, 223–4
construction sector, and organized
    crime 37–8, 39, 40–1, 42
CORIS (anti-corruption database)
    117, 118
Corleonesi 40
corporate corruption 1–2, 5, 10,
    121, 156–70
  anthropological perspective 159,
    165–9
  and corporate elite 166–8, 233
  institutional 158–63, 165–6
  and market values 168
  and regulation 157–8, 162–3, 165
  white collar crime 159, 163–5,
    167
corruption
  anthropological perspective 2,
    6–10, 16–19, 165–9, 229–39
  and class 238–9
  and crime 30–1, 163–5
  cultural differences 9–10, 70, 132,
    149–50, 232, 235
  definitions of 2–3, 4, 8, 16, 18,
    30, 67–8, 84–5, 106, 121, 232
  degrees of 9–10, 13, 66–7
  as deviation from norm 68, 71–2,
    77, 175
  endemic 67, 75, 77, 78–9, 80, 83,
    131, 132, 235–6
  as form of exchange 77–8
  and gender 237–8
  and identity 232–4, 238
  incidental 67, 69, 70, 79, 235–6

increase in 10, 15, 105, 133
and insecurity 195–8
institutional 2–3, 9–10, 158–63,
  165–6
interactional model 4–5
joking about 85–8, 173
local understanding of 83–4, 127,
  144–5, 196, 212–13
measuring 2, 3, 4, 111, 133, 175,
  240
positive function of 3–4, 7, 11,
  71, 237
in postcommunist states 66, 67,
  74–7, 79
and power relationships 17–18,
  86, 159–63, 234–5
productivity of 17–18
and public/private distinction
  5–6, 18, 67–70, 77, 87, 213,
  214, 240
remedies 78–9, 80, 83
research 11–16, 128–9, 166,
  167–8, 173–5, 196
social science perspectives 3–6,
  12
and socio-political context 18,
  79, 84, 85
structural models 3–4, 5, 76
threat to democracy 7, 10, 75
in transitional countries 66–7, 70,
  71–2, 74–7, 78, 79–80, 83
translocal 14–15
corruption complex 213, 214
Corruption Fighters' Toolkit 118
corruption narratives 15, 18, 173–6,
  213, 236, 240
  Alentejo 194–210
  corruption talk/rumour 216–19,
    223, 224
  India 6, 173–5, 181–8, 190, 236
  role in constitution of states
    175–6, 190
Corruption Perceptions Index (CPI)
  2, 4, 111, 119, 120
Cotta's Law 134
Cox, Pat 147
Cresson, Edith 143, 144, 145, 237
crime
  and corruption 30–1, 163–5
  see also mafia; organized crime;
    white collar crime

Cuttack 186
Czech Republic 76

Dahl, Robert 160
Dalits 190
Das, Mr 177–81
Davos 103
De Bartolo family 42
Della Porta, D. 17
Delors, Jacques 139, 142
democracy 7, 10, 75, 235
Denmark 2, 69
deregulation 9, 18
developing countries 3–4, 83, 230–1
  see also transitional countries
Dilema 93
Direzione Italian Antimafia (DIR) 40
disinterestedness 229, 235, 240
Djuvara, Neagu 93
Domhoff, William 159, 160–2, 163,
  167
Dougherty, E. 17

Educational Reform Law 1994
  (Bolivia) 215
Eichel, Hans 6
Eigen, Peter 69–70, 111, 115–16,
  117, 120
Eisenhower, Dwight D. 159
El Alto 214–15, 219, 221, 222, 223,
  224
Elf-Aquitaine 3, 150
Eliade, Mircea 91
engrenage 134, 137, 150
Enron scandal 1–2, 5, 104, 114, 133,
  156–7, 158, 165
  and criminal behaviour 164
  and institutional corruption 3,
    10, 159, 161
  and market competition 168
Ermann, M.D. 164
ethical globalization 103–4, 107,
  127, 229
European Association of Social
  Anthropologists 2
European Commission (EU civil
  service)
  administrative culture 132, 134,
    135–42, 149
  corruption scandals 10, 131–2,
    142–5, 148–9

European Commission (EU civil service) *continued*
and cronyism 138, 139, 142, 143–4, 145–6
financial accountability 139, 142–3, 146, 147–8
Humanitarian Aid Office (ECHO) 142
interpretations of corruption 145–51
lack of career management 140, 141
'mafias' within 141–2, 234
models for 136, 139
personal networks 11, 139–40, 141
and reform 132, 140, 144–5, 147–9
and rules 139, 141–2
Security Office 143
Staff Regulations 135, 146, 148
European Court of Auditors 139, 147, 148
European Union
and accountability 132
anti-fraud unit (OLAF) (formerly UCLAF) 142, 143, 146, 148
and European integration (European construction) 133–4, 137
and Europeanization of elites 134–5, 137, 149–50, 234
informal administration system 137–42, 150
subsidies 207–8
and supranationalism 132, 134, 135, 137, 149, 150
Eurostat 148–9
extortion 5, 39

Falcone, Giovanni 40
Fastow, Andrew 165
FBI 42
Federal Communications Commission (FCC) 158
Federal Trade Commission (FTC) 157, 158, 162, 163
feminism 237, 238
Fernandes, José Manuel 208
Finland 69
'flex organizations' 5

Fog Olwig, K. 15
Food and Drug Administration (FDA) 157, 162
Foreign Corrupt Practices Act 1977 (US) 66, 106
Foucault, M. 17
Fox, Vincente 114, 115
France 3, 10, 133
Franchet, Yves 148
Friedrich, Carl 68
Friedrichs, D.O. 164

Gains, Paul 43, 45
Galtung, Frederik 120
gambling 39, 42
Gandhi, Rajiv 177
Gaulle, Charles de 3
Gazprom 15
Gellner, Ernest 8
German Research Council 197
Germany 10, 11, 133
Gibraltar 12–13, 14–15, 16
Giddens, A. 12
gift-giving 11
and bribery 16–17, 58–60, 70, 167, 233
hatâr 94, 95
and obligation 50, 56, 58
and reciprocity 16, 56, 70
Giglioli, P.P. 18
Gilligan, Carol 237–8
Gledhill, J. 165
global citizenship 105–6, 108
global civil society 103, 105–6, 113, 117–23, 127
Global Compact 113
Global Corruption Report 118
Global Forum on Fighting Corruption 65, 113, 116, 117
Global Witness 115
globalization 9, 231
of anti-corruption movement 103–4, 106–7, 127, 236
ethical 103–4, 107, 127, 229
good governance 2, 10, 12, 18, 122
Gorbachev, Mikhail 74
Gramsci, A. 84
Great Britain 10
Green Party 146
guanxi 17

Gupta, A. 5, 14, 15, 17–18, 212, 232, 234
Gusinski, Vladimir 15

Habermas, Jürgen 237
Haller, D. 16
Halliburton 104, 159, 166
Hallstein, Walter 136–7
Hastrup, K. 15
hatâr 94, 95
Hauschild, Thomas 11
Havel, Vaclav 114
Heidenheimer, A.J. 9
Henderson, Keith 70
Herzfeld, Michael 95, 233
Heywood, P. 70
historic buildings, destruction of 35, 44–5
Hobson, Richmond Pearson 33
human rights 104, 112
Human Rights Watch 119
Huntington, Samuel 71, 72

India 5
    bribery 7, 18
    corruption narratives 6, 173–5, 181–8, 190, 236
    engineering development 177–83
    village governance and state institutions 177–88, 189–90
insider trading 162, 164
Integrity Pacts 118–19
integrity warriors 105, 107
interest group theory 160, 161
International Anti-Corruption Conference (IACC) 114–17
    Prague (2001) 114–15
    Seoul (2003) 108, 116–17, 120
International Cricket Council 68
International Monetary Fund (IMF)
    definition of corruption 16
    and good governance 10, 18
International Olympic Committee (IOC) 10, 68, 133
international organizations
    and anti-corruption movement 103
    corruption in 10, 132, 133
Interstate Commerce Commission 157, 162
irony 85–8

Italy 7, 10, 69, 133, 237
    mafia 8, 29, 31–2, 39–40, 167, 234, 237
    see also Palermo

Japan 10
Jawahar Rojgaar Yojana (Jawahar Employment Scheme) 177–82
Jefferson, Thomas 160
Johansen, B. 30
John Paul II, Pope 75
Jolie, Eva 111, 114
Juntas 214–17
    Junta Escolar 215, 217, 218, 219, 221, 223, 224
    Junta Vecinal 215–18, 219, 221, 224

Kalahandi 183
Kautilya 77
Kazakhs 16–17
Kazakhstan 14
Kenya 117
Kinnock, Neil 144, 147–9
kleptocracy 72, 78
Klitgaard, Robert 69, 70
Koelner, Elisa 90–2, 93
Kohl, Helmut 3, 6, 11, 65, 150
Kung, Hans 117

Labour European Safeguards Committee (LESC) 145
laws, and ambiguity 4–5, 8
Lay, Cardinal, of Boston 2–3
leaders
    citizens' expectations of 218–19, 223–4
    and recompense 219–20
Leavitt 38
Ledeneva, A.V. 76
legal-rationality 71–4, 78, 79, 131, 237
    and communist system 72–4
Lenin, V.I. 72, 128
Lévi-Strauss, C. 9
lichnyi vrach (personal doctor) 49, 62
Linkon, S.L. 44
Lomnitz, C. 13
Lucknow 183
Lundman, R.J. 164

McCarthy, Joseph 38
MacMullen, A. 143
mafia
    American 32–4, 34, 41–2, 43, 234
    anti-mafia movement 29, 40, 45,
        231, 238
    formation of 31–4
    Italian 8, 29, 31–2, 39–40, 167,
        234, 237
    and political corruption 31–2,
        41–2, 43–4
Malaysia 66
Malta 6
Marcus, G. 15, 231
Marín, Manuel 143
Martínez, Jose Luis 'Tren' 219–20
Martins da Cruz, António 208
Mauss, Marcel 16, 70
Maxwell Communications 10
Mayavati 190
media 125
Media-Most 15
Mény, Y. 17
Merck 3
Mexico 106, 133
Miller, W.L. 76
Mills, C. Wright 159–60, 163, 166
'Miorita' 91, 95
mita 87
Mitchell, John 6
Mitterrand, François 3, 150
Mohanpur 186, 187
Monnet, Jean 134, 135, 149–50
Morauta, Sir Mekere 66
*Movimiento Izquierdista
    Revolucionario* (MIR) (Bolivia)
    221–3
Muis, Jules 148, 149
'multi-sited' ethnography 15
Mussolini, Benito 31
Myrdal, Gunnar 72, 110

Nader, Laura 168, 231
Nader, Ralph 159, 162–3
National Alcohol Prohibition
    (Volstead) Act 1919 32–4
    repeal of 39
National Association of Real Estate
    Boards 38
National Integrity System 118, 120

National Strategy Information
    Center 29
Nehru, Jawaharlal 189
neoliberalism 10, 12, 18, 19, 123,
    229
Netherlands 69
New Deal 157
NGOs (non-governmental
    organizations) 65, 103, 122,
    125
    see also civil society; global civil
    society
Nicolau, Irina 93
Noel, Emile 141
Nye, J. 213

obras (public works) 212, 214, 215,
    220–4
Odemira 194–5, 197, 198–201,
    208–9
    and building permits 200, 202–6
OECD Convention on Combating
    the Bribery of Foreign Public
    Officials in International
    Business Transactions 18–19
Olivier de Sardan, J.P. 213, 218–19
O'Nesti, Charles 42, 45
Ong, Aihwa 214
organized crime 5
    and construction sector 37–8, 39,
        40-1, 44–5
    and political corruption 30, 41–2,
        45
    see also mafia
Orissa 183, 185, 186

Pakistan 133
Palermo 29
    earthquake 36
    and formation of mafia 31–2
    and heroin trade 39–40, 43
    and 'long 1980s' 39–41
    and organized crime 37–8, 39–40,
        239
    and political corruption 36–7
    'sack' (*scempio*) 34–6
    and Second World War 35
Papua New Guinea 66
parachutage 142
Paredes, Jose Luis 222
Parkin, David 132

Parry, Jonathan 218
participant-observation 7, 13–14,
    95, 176, 177
patronage 8, 9, 11, 12, 17, 146, 230,
    231, 232
Patterson, Frank 138
Pepys, Samuel 77
Percheiro, Cláudio 209
personal networks 11, 14, 16,
    166–7, 233, 234, 237
Peru 133
pesches 94
PHARE programme 139
Phillips, Kevin 166
piston (clientelism) 139, 142
Pitt-Rivers, J.A. 230
Plan Progreso 222
political parties, funding 9, 10
*Politics and Social Change: Orissa
    1959* (Bailey) 183
Pope, Jeremy 118, 120
Popescu, Ion 88–90
Popular Participation Law 1994
    (Bolivia) 215
Portugal 197, 198, 209, 234
    corruption scandal 208
    and EU membership 194, 206–8
    local government 198–206
    personal networks 201–2
    see also Alentejo; Odemira
postcommunist states, and
    corruption 66, 67, 74–7, 79
Postero, N. 4, 7, 15, 18
privatization 9, 18, 75, 123
Prodi, Romano 144
Prohibition 32–4, 39
project society 121–3
projectization 109–10, 121–3, 129
Pujas, V. 146

Raag Darbari (Shukla) 183–5, 186–8
raccomandazione 7, 237
Reyes Villa, Manfred (mayor of
    Cochambamba) 220, 222
Rhodes, M. 146
Ries, Nancy 13
Rigby, Harry 73
Rio Tinto mining company 115
Rizzi, Bruno 79
Robinson, Mary 103
Romania 66, 84–99
    anti-corruptionism 108, 123–6

and communism 93–4, 95, 234
and irony 84, 85–8, 96
Ottoman rule 94, 95, 123, 234
and property restitution law-cases
    88–92
Romanian stereotype 93–5, 96,
    234
Rosas Pampa 214–15, 216, 217, 218,
    219, 220–1, 222
Rose-Ackerman, Susan 5, 9, 77–8,
    150
Royal Dutch Shell 115
Russia (post-Soviet)
    blat 53, 59, 62, 71, 73, 76
    flex organizations 5
    healthcare 47–64
        accessed through
            acquaintances 50, 51, 52, 53,
            54, 55–6, 59, 60, 62
        and bribery 53, 58–60
        and gift-giving 50, 53–4, 54,
            55, 56, 57–60
        official payment 51, 52, 61
        state system 49–50
        unofficial payment 48–9, 50–2,
            52, 59, 61–3
    and organized crime 66
Russian Orthodox Church 75
Russo, J. 44

Sajo, Andras 76
Sampson, Stephen 3–4
Sanders, T. 12
Santer Commission 132, 142–4
Santer, Jacques 140, 143, 144
Santos, Justino 199–200, 201, 203
Sassu, Stefana 90–2
Schneider, J. and P. 5, 167, 238, 239
Schuman, Robert 135
Schwartz, C.A. 73
Scott, J.C. 4, 230, 232, 238
Securities and Exchange
    Commission (SEC) 157, 158,
    167
Sethni, H. 6–7
Shapiro, Susan P. 167
Shelley, L.I. 76
Shore, C. 11
Shukla, S. 176, 183–5, 186–8
Sicily 31, 35
    see also Palermo

Siino, Angelo 40–1
Simis, K.M. 74
Sinclair, Upton 167
Singapore 66
Skilling, Jeffrey 165
Smith, Hedrick 73
Social Democratic Party (PSD)
  (Portugal) 206, 207
Socialist Party (PS) (Portugal) 200,
  206
Sokolov, V. 75
Soros, George 114, 115
Source Book (TI) 118
Soviet Union
  and corruption 71–2, 74
  and informal networks 73–4
  and legal-rationality 72–4
spaga (bribe) 94–5
Spain 10
Spence, David 149
state capture 114
states
  representations of 176, 184, 188–9
  and role of narratives 175–6, 190
Stewart, Martha 238
Strollo, Lenine 'Lenny' 42
Sudan 10
Sutherland, Edwin 159
Sweden 69

TACIS programme 139
tangentopoli scandals 10
Tanzi, V. 70
Tappin, Michael 144
Tarbell, Ida 167
Taylor, Charles 214
temperance movement 32–3
TIRI 120
toilet key philosophy 198–202, 232
tolkachi 71, 74
Traficant, James A. 42, 44
transitional countries 66–7, 70,
  71–2, 74–7, 78, 79–80, 83
  see also developing countries
transparency 2, 10, 12, 103–4, 122,
  123, 131
Transparency International (TI) 5,
  10, 65, 105, 111, 112, 117–23
  anti-corruption programmes
  69–70
  at Prague conference 108, 114–15

at Seoul conference 117
and coalition building 113, 115,
  116, 120, 123
Corruption Perceptions Index
  (CPI) 2, 4, 111, 119, 120
and definition of corruption 16,
  121
internal conflicts 120, 128
national chapters (NCs) 117, 119,
  120
and Portugal 198, 202
and projectization 121–3
role of TI-Berlin 117, 119, 121,
  123
and Romania 125
Trotsky, Leon 72

UCLAF 142, 143, 146
UEFA 10, 133
Ukraine 76
underdevelopment, and corruption
  3, 230–1
UNDP (United Nations
  Development Programme) 113,
  114
UNESCO 10, 133
Union Syndicale 138
United Nations
  Convention against
  Transnational Organized Crime
  29, 45
  corruption scandals 10, 133
  Declaration against Corruption
  and Bribery in International
  Commercial Transactions 65
United States 66, 69
  corporate corruption 1–2, 156–70
  economic regulation 157–8,
  162–3, 165
  institutionalized corruption
  158–63, 165–6, 235–6
  land reform 38
  mafia 32–4, 34, 41–2, 43, 234
  power structure 159–63, 166–8
  Prohibition 32–4
USAID (United States Agency for
  International Development) 70
Uttar Pradesh (UP) 176, 183–4, 190
Uzbekistan 74

Valery, Paul 135

Verdery, K. 89
Vidal, Gore 12
Vila Nova de Milfontes 201, 202
Visvanathan, S. 6–7

Warner, C. 150
Watt, Robert Dougal 148
Webb, C. 134
Weber, Max 71, 73, 77, 78, 131,
    138, 175
Wedel, J. 5
Welz, G. 15
Werner, C. 14, 17
West, H.G. 12
Westlake, M. 134
whistle-blowers 114, 146, 148
white collar crime 159, 163–5, 167
Williamson, David 135
Wolf, Eric 11
Wolfensohn, James 115
Women's Christian Temperance
    Union (WCTU) 32–3
World Bank 103, 113, 114
    campaign against corruption 18,
        65, 105, 120
    definition of corruption 2, 3, 8,
        18, 67, 68

and good governance 10
relations with TI 120
and Romania 125
structural adjustment programme
    116
WorldCom 1–2, 104, 133, 156–7,
    158, 159, 161, 165, 168

Xerox 3, 133

Yadav, Laloo Prasad 190
Yaroslavl 13
Youngstown Citizens' League 42,
    43–4, 45, 236
Youngstown, Ohio 29–30, 33–4
    arson attacks 44–5
    and 'long 1980s' 41–3
    and organized crime 34, 39, 41–3,
        239
    and Prohibition 33–4
    steel mill closings 41, 42, 45
    suburbanization 38–9
Youngstown Vindicator 44
Yugoslavia 66

Zafiu, R. 87
Zinn, Dorothy 7